Hand-
Knitting
Techniques

Hand-Knitting Techniques

from

Threads
MAGAZINE

The Taunton Press

Cover photo by Susan Kahn

Taunton
BOOKS & VIDEOS
for fellow enthusiasts

First printing: July 1991
Second printing: July 1993
Third printing: January 1996
Fourth printing: February 1998
Printed in the United States of America

A THREADS Book

THREADS magazine® is a trademark of The Taunton Press, Inc.
registered in the U.S. Patent and Trademark Office.

The Taunton Press
63 South Main Street
Box 5506
Newtown, CT 06470-5506

Library of Congress Cataloging-in-Publication Data

Hand-knitting techniques from Threads.
      p.   cm.
   "A Threads book."
   ISBN 1-56158-012-0
   1. Knitting.   I. Threads magazine
TT820.H26   1991   91-13243
746.9'2—dc20   CIP

Contents

7
Introduction

8
Knitting a Perfect Rib
Much depends on the cast-on and the cast-off

14
The Edges of Knitting
A catalog of one- and two-stitch selvages

16
A Knitting Odyssey
The making of a handknit Chanel-style suit

24
*Knitting Round on
Straight Needles*
In which the slip stitch comes between the
knits, and the fabric splits asunder for a
splendid finish

28
The Knitted Yarn Over
This simple stitch creates a hole in the fabric

30
*Textured Knitting on
Circular Needles*
Convert wrong-side rows to their right-side
equivalents and knit around

33
Knitting a Seamless Sweater
It's easy with circular needles

36
Knitting for Kids
Versatile designs

40
The Magic Raglan
A sweater that almost knits itself

42
Designer Raglans
The difference between the back and sleeve
widths determines the sweater's proportions

47
No-Sew Set-in Sleeves
Shaping the drop-shoulder sweater

50
Dazzling with Sequins
Whether you knit or crochet, you can add
sparkle to clothing

53
Knitting with Cotton
Stitch maneuvers help sweaters stay in shape

56
Bead-Knitting Madness
Treat yourself to a dazzling purse

62
Knitting with Fur and Feathers
How to enliven commercial yarns with
handspun exotic fibers

66
Handknitting Gloves
An impressive tribute to the creative hand

72
The Shape of Socks
When you can turn a heel, you can knit
any shape you want

77
The Oddball Sweater
Flattening chevron stripes knit in the round

82
Easy Striped Knits
Bias stripes in a basic garter stitch

84
Knit Landscapes from Leftovers
A basic drop-shoulder sweater uses up odd
bits of yarn

86
Designing with Cables
Chart textured designs drawn from nature on
your own proportional graph paper

90
Knitting from Sewing Patterns
Both hand- and machine-knitters can find
inspiration at the sewing shop

94
Knit One, Sew One
Combine wovens and knits in a single garment

98
Knit to Fit
Accurate measurements and common sense
make an attractive handknit sweater

102
Fashion Doesn't Stop at 40 Inches
The key is fit, and the hand-knitter's secret is a
fabric mock-up

108
Putting Knitted Pieces Together
Three stitches that go a long way toward
finishing sweaters

111
Crocheted Buttonholes
Decorative and functional closures that work
for knitters and sewers as well

114
Two Styles of Buttonholes

114
Tips from the Knitting Guild

116
*A Sampler of Knit Edgings
and Applied Trims*
Putting a professional and creative finish on
handknit fabrics

121
Knitted-Lace Edgings
Add an old-fashioned touch of elegance to
household linens and garments

126
Index

Introduction

ow many unfinished handknit sweaters have you got in your closet? If you've ever wondered why your knit edges aren't firm, the seams aren't flawless, and the fit is unpredictable, this collection of articles from *Threads* magazine should help.

With the help of expert knitters, we take a close look at how to form stitches for texture, pattern, and shape; how to plan and design garments, in the round or from flat pieces; how to knit complex shapes, like gloves and socks; and how to work with tricky or unusual yarns.

— Betsy Levine, editor

Knitting a Perfect Rib

Much depends on the cast-on and the cast-off

by Montse Stanley

hand knitting often looks more homemade than handmade. The subtle difference hinges on an equally subtle choice of techniques that distinguish the outstanding from the mediocre. For example, how ribbings are cast on, worked, and cast off has a decisive effect on the success of the project.

Planning a rib—Before casting on, you need to know the exact number of stitches that are required for the type of rib you want. The number of stitches for the rib will not necessarily be the same number of stitches that are needed for the main pattern. In general, single rib (k1, p1) conforms to the following rules:
• If worked at the start or end of a piece of stocking stitch, on the same number of stitches, single rib will slightly gather the body fabric—exactly what is required for the waistband of a straight sweater.
• For more noticeable gathering, the rib should have at least 10% fewer stitches than the main stocking-stitch fabric.

• If the stocking-stitch fabric has occasional cables, the rib should have fewer stitches in the cable areas. Otherwise, the rib will be gathered by the cable.
• If the main fabric is all in cables, cross-stitches, slip stitches, or other stitches that make it much narrower than stocking-stitch fabric, the rib will need fewer stitches than the main fabric.
• If the main fabric is in some kind of open-work or other stitch that makes it wider than stocking-stitch fabric, the rib will create noticeable gathers, even if the rib and body have the same number of stitches. For a straight effect, the rib may need many more stitches than the main fabric.

Double rib (k2, p2) follows similar rules, but the fabric draws in more (i.e., it's narrower) than single-rib fabric, even when worked on the same number of stitches. After deciding how many stitches your rib needs, make sure the total number fits in with the rib pattern. If you're working a circular project, you obviously need an even number of stitches for single rib and a multiple of four for double rib. However,

other projects are less obvious, and knitters, in their eagerness to get started, often forget the finer points until it's too late. Time spent calculating and checking the number of stitches may delay casting on, but you won't regret it. If your calculations give you a couple of stitches more or fewer than expected, increase or decrease when you change to or from the main pattern.

The following advice for figuring the number of stitches for a rib applies when you're looking at the ribs from the right side. If the first rib row that you work is a wrong-side row, substitute *knit* for *purl* and *purl* for *knit* in the instructions.

For a ***flat project without seams,*** whose edges you want to look alike, such as a scarf or blanket, single rib needs an odd number of stitches, and double rib needs a multiple of four stitches plus two. In general, on the right side, knit stitches look better than purl stitches at the ends of the rows, but to give a finish and some firmness to the edge, a knit-in border or selvage should follow. It need not be more than a slipped-garter selvage, shown on

From *Threads* magazine (February 1988) 15:46-51

the left side of the drawing below: Slip the 1st st of each row knitwise; knit the last st. This will make it look better and help it keep its shape. (For more on knit selvages, see the article on pages 14-15.)

If you're working a **flat project with seams,** such as a pullover, plan to have the edge stitch on each side be taken in by the seams. Edge stitches never look exactly like other stitches and are best hidden. In single rib, sew an edge with a knit stitch to an edge with a purl stitch. In double rib, each edge should end in three knit or purl stitches instead of the usual two. Sew an edge with three knit stitches to an edge with three purl stitches, taking up the extra stitch on each edge in the seam.

Joining the two sides with a ladder-stitch seam, also called mattress stitch, will make the rib look unbroken. To work it, with the right side facing you, simple catch the horizontal bar between the first and second edge stitches, first from one side and then from the other. Pull firmly on the stitches to close the seam. Usually, this seam is barely noticeable on the right side of many patterns, and it is also positioned on one of the rib's natural hiding lines.

When you're knitting a sweater with double rib, the back rib should have a multiple of 4 sts, starting and ending with 3 purl sts. The front should also have a multiple of 4 sts, but the rows should start and end with 3 knit sts. The cuffs should have a multiple of 4 sts plus 2 sts; start with 3 knit sts and end with 3 purl sts.

If you're working **strips with one free edge and one seam edge,** such as those used for jacket fronts, the free edge should end in knit plus a selvage. End the seam edge with knit plus 1 st extra on all rows if you plan to sew the strip without taking in any stitches. But if the edge stitch will be taken in by the seam, the row should end in purl, or, for an even neater join, in knit plus a chain selvage. For a chain selvage on the left edge, purl the last st of the row on that edge; then slip knitwise the 1st st of the following row. For the right edge, slip purlwise the 1st st of the row; then knit the last st of the following row. This leaves a chain spanning 2 rows, as shown on the right side of the drawing.

If stitches are to be picked up along one side of the rib, end that side in knit plus the chain selvage. Knit up the new stitches either from under the two strands of the chain or from the tight spots between two chains, as required.

Choosing needle size—Ribs are usually worked on needles one or two sizes smaller than those required for stocking-stitch fabric, and sometimes on even smaller needles. The rib must be firm. You can get

away with a fairly loose main fabric, but if the edging ribs are also loose, your project will lose its shape in no time.

Alternating knit and purl stitches gives a longer strand between stitches than knitting consecutive knit or purl stitches. Not only does the yarn travel horizontally out of one stitch and into the next, but it also has to cross the fabric from one side to the other. Because the rib stitches overlap somewhat and are actually closer together, the extra yarn goes into the stitches themselves, which become larger as a result. By working with fine needles, you compensate for this inevitable growth and obtain stitches of the appropriate size for the yarn.

Rib borders worked at the side edge of a fabric pose a problem. Unless the fabric is another loose structure that also needs to be worked on finer needles than stocking stitch requires, a rib worked along with the body fabric, on the same needles, will be too loose. There are a number of solutions, but none is ideal. You can knit the border separately, on finer needles, and sew it to the edge as explained above—a rather tedious job. Or, you can work the rib border at the same time you are knitting the body fabric, using short, fine, double-pointed needles for the rib. This saves sewing but is somewhat awkward; if you're a loose knitter, you have to put stops on the short needle to prevent it from dropping, and you must take care not to leave gaps where you change needles to knit the body.

You can also work the body and the rib on the same needles, tightening the yarn when you reach the rib. Although this option is not of much use if you're already a tight knitter, it can be easy and successful if you knit loosely.

Finally, you can work a different type of border, or, when the body is complete, you can pick up the stitches from the edge and work the rib across. This is very effective if you finish the rib with a tubular cast-off (explained on page 13).

When you're working the rib border and main fabric together, you may find that the border needs more rows. Keep an eye on the border; it must be firm but must not pull. If either the body or the rib starts drawing in, add a few extra rows; then continue to work all the way across as usual. At first there may be a little hole where the two pieces meet, but it will disappear after a few more rows.

Casting on—Some techniques are easy, others less so. Choose your method according to your project and how much trouble you're willing to go through. Work a 10-st to 12-st sample. If the cast-on is too loose or too tight, try again with finer or thicker needles. Change to the size needle the rib requires as soon as you finish casting on.

Use the popular **two-strand cast-on** when you want a plain and simple edge for either single or double rib. You can work it with one needle in the right hand and two strands

Ribbing edges

Slipped garter selvage gives some firmness. A chain selvage is good for seamed edges.

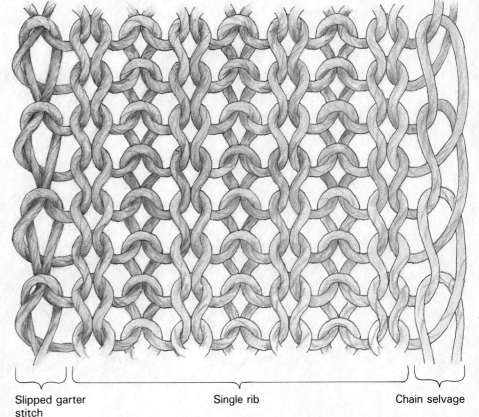

Slipped garter stitch   Single rib   Chain selvage

of yarn in the left hand, as shown below in the drawing and the photo at left. You can also work it with one strand in each hand, the left strand wound over the thumb or the index finger, which moves clockwise to catch the yarn. Either way, start with a slip knot, leaving an end about four times the length to be cast on. As long as you don't work it tightly, the edge will be strong and elastic. Be aware, however, of which side will be the right side: One side has an unobtrusive line (see left photo below), while the other presents scallops topped by bumps and doesn't blend well with ribbing. The good side will naturally be left showing with circular knitting. In flat knitting, the first row after you cast on should be a wrong-side row.

The **Channel Islands cast-on,** for single rib only, is a variation of the two-strand cast-on, but the results are stronger and more sophisticated. Instead of rotating the thumb clockwise to catch the yarn, rotate it counterclockwise, and repeat the motion to get a double wrap around the thumb. For a bold edge, wrap two strands twice around the thumb, and the usual one on the index finger, as in the center drawing below; or, for a more delicate edge, wrap the usual single strand around the thumb. After casting on 1 st through the double wrap, make a yo for the 2nd st: Bring the yarn on the index finger under and around the right needle. Repeat these two actions.

The two sides of the fabric created by this method are different. The side shown in the center photo below should be the right side of the work. As with the two-strand cast-on, this will naturally be so in circular knitting: On the 1st round, purl the yos and knit the sts. In flat knitting, start with a wrong-side row, knitting the yos and purling the sts.

The **alternate cable cast-on** is a variation of the ordinary cable cast-on, whose cordlike edge is often too emphatic. It is for single rib only. The ordinary cable cast-on is worked with two needles and one strand of yarn: Insert the right needle between the last 2 sts on the left needle, knit 1 new st, and place it on the left needle, as in the top drawing at right, below.

For the alternate cable cast-on, knit 1 st, as in the sequence above, and purl the next st, as in the bottom drawing at right, below. Continue alternating 1 knit st with 1 purl st until you have cast on all the sts. (If you forget what comes next, see which side the yarn is coming from. If it comes from the front, knit the next st; if it comes from the back, purl the next st.)

In flat knitting, the first row after the cast-on row should start with a knit stitch if the last cast-on stitch was a knit, and with a purl stitch if the last cast-on stitch was a purl. In circular knitting, knit the stitches that come forward, and purl the stitches that stay back. In either case, on the first row or round, all knit stitches must be worked through the back of the loop; otherwise they will be twisted. The method can be used on either the right or wrong side and blends in well with rib.

The **provisional cast-on,** for single rib only, is worked with a contrasting (preferably slippery) yarn that is later unraveled. Nearly all patterns, including double rib, will ladder once the provisional cast-on has been removed—some or all of the stitches will unravel, and the work will be ruined. Single rib is an exception. Some people do what they call "invisible cast-on," using a technique similar to the two-strand cast-on with two different yarns. You can get more uniform results if you cast on with any method and later unravel the cast-on row by snipping the yarn between the stitches and pulling them out one by one. This may seem slow, but the first row is easier to work, and the stitches are less likely to drop than those produced by the invisible cast-on.

If you want to use provisional cast-ons often, you should learn the Japanese crochet method instead of the invisible. It may take slightly longer, but you'll pro-

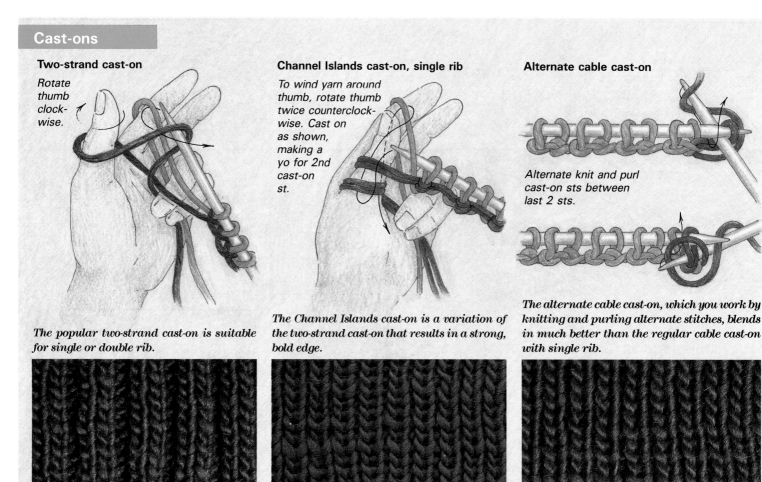

Cast-ons

Two-strand cast-on

Rotate thumb clockwise.

The popular two-strand cast-on is suitable for single or double rib.

Channel Islands cast-on, single rib

To wind yarn around thumb, rotate thumb twice counterclockwise. Cast on as shown, making a yo for 2nd cast-on st.

The Channel Islands cast-on is a variation of the two-strand cast-on that results in a strong, bold edge.

Alternate cable cast-on

Alternate knit and purl cast-on sts between last 2 sts.

The alternate cable cast-on, which you work by knitting and purling alternate stitches, blends in much better than the regular cable cast-on with single rib.

duce an even first row with ease, you'll get a firmer base to start knitting, and you'll find unraveling great fun and very easy.

Crochet a loose chain with a contrasting color of slippery yarn. Make one link more than the number of sts required. Then, to fasten the chain, cut the yarn and pull the end through the last loop. For your 1st row, using the main yarn, knit up 1 st from the loop at the back of each link, starting with the 2nd-to-last link and working from right to left, as in the left-hand drawing below. After you have knit several rows, you can unravel the chain to free the lower loops of the 1st row. Pull the loop at the back of the last link to draw the yarn end through. As you pull the free end of the yarn, the chain will unravel link by link.

After unraveling the provisional cast-on, you'll have a soft, spreading but stable edge. For a more controlled edge, like the one shown in the left-hand photo below, cast on and work the 1st row with very fine needles; work the 2nd row with somewhat thicker needles and, finally, change to the ordinary needle size on the 3rd row.

The *tubular cast-on*, shown in the photo on page 8 and in the center and right-hand photos below, for single and double rib, gives a beautifully rounded edge that makes it looks as if the rib is turning over to continue on the other side. It can easily

be adapted to encase a drawstring or an elastic. The tubular cast-on perfectly matches the tubular cast-off, and both are ideal for projects that start and end with ribs, such as sweaters knit from cuff to cuff.

Although tubular cast-ons and cast-offs are rarely seen in Great Britain or the U.S., in many other countries no self-respecting knitter will use anything other than tubular edges, particularly cast-off edges. In my home town of Barcelona, for example, casting off a rib by the tubular method is considered part of the service of wool shops.

The tubular cast-on is also sometimes called "invisible," perhaps because two of the three ways of working it use a provisional cast-on as the first step. The third version starts directly with the main yarn. It involves holding two strands in the left hand and flicking the needle with the right hand. Like the "invisible" version of the provisional cast-on, the action is reminiscent of the two-strand cast-on, although the results are again different. I'll give full details of my own favorite method, the yarn-over tubular cast-on.

The tubular cast-on is very strong but has a tendency to loosen and wave, especially in edges that need to stretch and recover, such as cuffs and waistbands. Always work it with needles two or three sizes finer than those you're using for the

rest of the rib. First try one or two samples to select the correct needle size.

The following instructions are for an odd number of sts. For an even number, inc 1 st at the end of the 1st row of step 3.

1. With a contrasting, slippery yarn and fine needles, cast on half the sts. If the total is an odd number (e.g., 101), cast on 1 st more than half (51). Since this provisional cast-on will be unraveled, you have a choice of methods: 2-strand cast-on, ordinary cable cast-on, or Japanese crochet method of provisional cast-on, in which case combine its knitting-up step with step 2 below.

2. With the main yarn, knit 1 row, increasing after each st (except the last st) by making a yo, as in the center drawing below.

3. Work 2 or 4 rows in tubular stocking stitch: Knit the knit sts, slip the purl sts purlwise with yarn in front. The 1st row starts with knit, and the yos are the purl sts and should be slipped. For a drawstring casing, work an even number of extra rows. In circular knitting, work every alternate round as follows: Purl the purl sts, slip the knit sts purlwise with yarn at back.

4. Continue in single rib, changing to the size needles you need for the rib. For double rib, after step 3, knit 1 knit st, drop the next purl st, knit the next knit st, and then purl the dropped st and the next st, as in the two right-hand drawings below. ⟹

Provisional cast-on, single rib
Japanese crochet method

Crochet a loose chain with one link more than sts needed. From loop at back, knit up 1 st from each link. Unravel crocheted chain after knitting several rows.

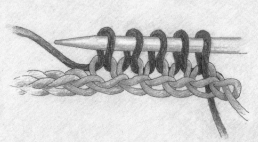

Tubular cast-on, single rib

On row after cast-on, knit all sts, making a yo after each st, except last one.

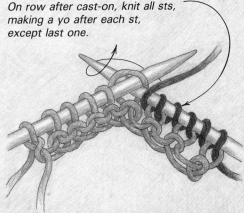

Tubular cast-on, double rib

After even number of rows in tubular stocking stitch, change to double rib by dropping every other purl st and picking it up after working knit st next to it.

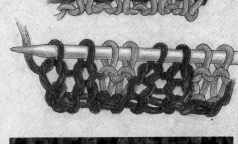

The Japanese crochet method of provisional cast-on results in a soft, stretchy edge that blends in well with single rib.

The tubular cast-on, suitable for single rib (below) and double rib (right), results in a neat, rounded edge.

The two-row cast-off. This method leaves a large, flat chain at the edge.

Decrease cast-off

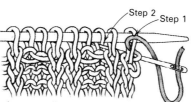

K2tog by inserting needle first into 2nd st, then into 1st st.

The decrease cast-off, for single rib only, results in a crochetlike edge.

Tubular cast-off, single rib

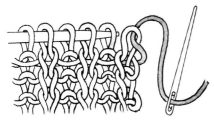

Insert needle knitwise into first (knit) stitch, and drop it. The first time around you go into this stitch only once.

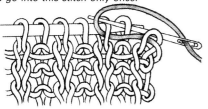

Insert needle purlwise into third (knit) stitch, then purlwise into second (purl) stitch. Drop second stitch. The first time around, you go into it only once.

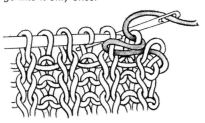

Insert needle knitwise into fourth (purl) stitch, from back. Repeat from beginning.

Tubular cast-off, double rib

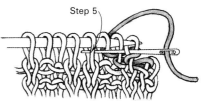

Insert needle purlwise into first knit stitch (step 1). Then, working from back and under knitting needle, insert needle knitwise into first purl stitch (step 2).

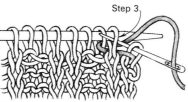

Insert needle knitwise into first knit stitch, looping yarn over top of stitch, and drop it. Then insert needle purlwise into second knit stitch (step 3).

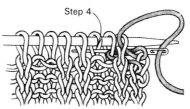

Loop yarn up, and working in back from right to left, insert needle purlwise into first purl stitch, then knitwise into second purl stitch (step 4).

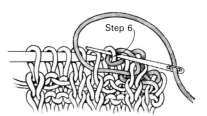

Insert needle knitwise into second knit stitch, and drop it. Insert needle purlwise into third knit stitch (step 5), and drop first purl stitch.

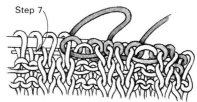

Insert needle purlwise into second purl stitch, and drop it (step 6).

Working around from back, insert needle knitwise into third purl stitch (step 7). Repeat from step 3.

The tubular cast-off (single rib above, double rib at right), which you work by grafting, results in a rounded edge that perfectly matches the tubular cast-on.

Casting off—Good methods for casting off ribs are few and far between. The ordinary cast-off, whereby you work stitches one by one and pass each stitch over the next, gives a very poor edge, even when you work the cast-off row in pattern, knitting the knits and purling the purls. This poor edge is probably the main reason for the widespread use of folded rib bands in necklines and in other instances where the rib is worked from stitches picked up from an edge. Although a folded band can sometimes be effective, more often it looks out of place because of its bulkiness. Fortunately, there are alternatives.

The *two-row cast-off,* for single and double rib (top-left photo, facing page), leaves a large, flat chain at the cast-off edge. When it is worked at the same tension as the rest of the rib, it is significantly tighter. To achieve a more elastic edge, work both the final cast-off row and the row before it with thicker needles.

Work 1 row in pattern, casting off every other st in the usual way: For single rib, pull the knits over the purls, but not the purls over the knits; for double rib, pull the 1st knit or purl st over the 2nd st. Half the sts will be left. Cut the yarn.

Turn the work and cast off the remaining sts without working them: Slip the sts purlwise onto the right needle, one at a time, and pull the previous st over. Secure the last st with the yarn end if you're working in rounds, or into a seam if you're working flat. If necessary, temporarily secure the st with a safety pin.

The *decrease cast-off* (top-right photo, facing page) gives a complex-looking edge, reminiscent of a crocheted edge, but it isn't difficult to work. It is for single rib only. Assuming that the 1st st is a knit, p2tog and slip the new st back onto the left needle without twisting it.

K2tog, first inserting the needle into the 2nd st, and then into the 1st st (see drawing at top center, facing page). Slip the new st back onto the left needle. Repeat these steps. If the 1st st is a purl, reverse the order.

The *tubular cast-off* (photos and drawings, facing page) is by far the best method of casting off a rib. For single or double rib, it has all the advantages of the tubular cast-on (page 11) and matches it perfectly. It is also ideal for avoiding folded rib bands, often seen in necklines. Casting off by the tubular method involves sewing and therefore may seem more difficult than it really is. It is essential, though, to work loosely on edges that are expected to stretch and recover, such as necklines.

When you're working a *tubular cast-off in single rib* (steps 1-4, facing page), in flat knitting, first work 2 or 4 rows of tubular stocking stitch: Knit the knit sts, slip the purl sts purlwise with yarn in front. In circular knitting, work the 1st and 3rd rounds this way; but on the 2nd and 4th rounds, purl the purl sts and slip the knit sts purlwise with yarn at back. In either

case, work an even number of extra rows or rounds if you want a drawstring casing.

You now have two independent layers of stocking stitch, one at the front and one at the back of the fabric, both on the same needle. Join these layers by grafting (also called weaving or Kitchener stitch). If you already know how to graft, practice the tubular cast-off by slipping the front layer (knit stitches) onto one double-pointed needle, and the back layer (purl stitches) onto another. You can later graduate to the one-needle method. If you don't know how to graft, learn the one-needle cast-off method, shown at far left on the facing page.

For the practice grafting yarn, cut a length of contrasting yarn about four times the width to be cast off and thread it onto a large, blunt sewing needle. The contrast yarn will let you see the series of V's that forms at the edge. (When you graft on a real project, use the attached knitting yarn.) If the V's are distorted, you're catching a wrong stitch, catching the right stitch in the wrong way, or pulling the yarn unevenly. If the V's are very flat, you're pulling too tight; each V should be the same size as the stitches you're joining.

Step 1. Starting with a knit st, insert the sewing needle knitwise into the 1st st. Drop the st.
Step 2. Insert the sewing needle purlwise into the 3rd (knit) st. Don't drop the st. Pull the yarn through, but not too tightly.
Step 3. Insert the sewing needle purlwise into the 2nd (purl) st. Drop the st.
Step 4. Insert the sewing needle knitwise into the 4th (purl) st. Don't drop the st until you pull the yarn through.

Repeat steps 1 through 4. If the 1st st is a purl st, start with step 3, substituting *1st st* where it says *2nd st, 3rd st* where it says *4th st,* etc. With practice, you can drop all 4 sts as soon as the sewing needle has gone through them, and you can cut the process down to two movements: 1 and 2, 3 and 4.

For a *tubular cast-off in double rib* (steps 1-7, facing page), work the last 2 to 4 rows as for the tubular cast-on in double rib: Knit the 1st knit st and slip the 2nd purlwise with yarn in back; purl the 1st purl st and slip the 2nd purlwise with yarn in front. For grafting, you'll need a length of yarn about four times the width to be cast off.
Step 1. If the 1st 2 sts are knit, insert the sewing needle purlwise into the 1st st. Pull the yarn through.
Step 2. Working around the back of the knit sts, insert the needle knitwise into the 1st purl st. Pull the yarn through.
Step 3. Insert the needle knitwise into the 1st knit st. Drop the st and insert the needle purlwise into the 2nd knit st. Pull the yarn through.
Step 4. Working around the back of the knit sts, insert the needle purlwise into the 1st purl st, then knitwise into the 2nd purl st. Pull the yarn through.
Step 5. Insert the needle knitwise into the 2nd knit st. Drop the st and insert the nee-

dle purlwise into the 3rd knit st. Drop the 1st purl st. Pull the yarn through.
Step 6. Insert the needle purlwise into the 2nd purl st. Drop it. Pull the yarn through.
Step 7. Working around the back of the 3rd and 4th knit sts, insert the needle knitwise into the 3rd purl st. Pull the yarn through.

Repeat steps 3 through 7, substituting *3rd st* where it says *1st, 4th* where it says *2nd,* etc. Straighten the loops as they come off the needle. The cast-off will start to one side, but the grafting should make a clear line of V's. If the 1st 2 sts are purl sts, omit steps 1 and 3 and the first part of step 5. Substitute *1st knit st* where it says *3rd, 2nd* where it says *4th.*

Putting it all together—To sum up, think before you cast on. Check to make sure that you have the correct number of stitches and that the rows start and end with the proper sequence. Use smaller needles than you would for stocking stitch.

If you don't want to spend time perfecting new cast-on techniques, use either a two-strand cast-on, showing the good side, or a cable cast-on, alternating knits and purls. If you feel more adventurous, try a provisional cast-on for a very soft edge on single rib; a Channel Islands cast-on for a strong, well-integrated edge; or a tubular cast-on for a perfectly rounded edge. To cast off, try the two-row cast-off if you want a decorative edge and the tubular cast-off for a rounded edge, matching the tubular cast-on.

Combining the tubular cast-on with the tubular cast-off is the perfect answer for sweaters worked from cuff to cuff. But you can also use one without the other. For example, you can cast on the waistband and the cuffs with the two-strand cast-on or a provisional method and cast off the neckband with the tubular method. If you prefer a cast-on that doesn't blend so well with the tubular cast-off, such as the Channel Islands cast-on, knit the neckband separately and graft it to the neck edge. The cast-on will now be the outer edge. If you like the two-row or decrease cast-off, use a Japanese provisional cast-on and start at the top of the waistband and cuffs.

When you've finished the body and sleeves, unravel the cast-on, and work the ribs in the opposite direction. Because the rib is easy to redo if you use this method, it is also good on sweaters for growing children or when you expect the cuffs to wear out earlier than the rest of the sweater.

There are many other possibilities that you can now have great fun discovering. Whatever your choice, your ribs need never again be dreary.   □

Montse Stanley, a Catalan living in Cambridge, England, was originally an architect. She has written Creating and Knitting Your Own Designs for a Perfect Fit *(Harper & Row, 1982) and* The Handknitter's Handbook *(David & Charles, 1986).*

The Edges of Knitting

A catalog of one- and two-stitch selvages

by Theresa Gaffey

the success of a knitted garment depends in part on the way you work the selvages, the first and last stitches of each row. You can achieve neat seams and edge borders only through careful knitting and careful choice of selvage stitch, based on the particulars of your project, yarn, and stitch pattern. Personal preference has a lot to do with it too. If you knit swatches of the various selvages I describe, you'll find that some come more naturally to your fingers than others.

There are two main types of selvages: one-stitch and two-stitch. The one-stitch selvage is more common and is generally appropriate for edges that will later become parts of seams or will be picked up for a ribbing or other finish. The two-stitch selvage is more decorative and better for edges that require no further finishing, such as those on a scarf or shawl. It also helps prevent edges from rolling, thereby ensuring a flat fabric. Many one-stitch selvages are similar in the way they are worked, and they result in similar edges. Two-stitch selvages are also similar in appearance, though they are each worked differently. Some methods produce a firmer stitch than others, and this might be the basis for choosing among them.

When designing a seamed project, be sure to add your selvage stitches to the total number of stitches needed. The selvage stitches are used up in the seam; they do not contribute to the width of the knitting or to the pattern stitch. Different selvages require different methods of joining seams. Garter selvages, for example, are best joined with a backstitch or an overcast stitch, whereas chain selvages are more easily joined with a woven seam.

You might want to use different selvages in the same project. For a vest, for instance, you might want a garter selvage at the side seams of the body to make seam matching easy, and a slipped-stitch selvage at the armhole to make it easier to pick up ribbing stitches.

One-stitch knit selvages

To American knitters, knit edges are probably the most familiar selvages. Knit edges involve either knitting or purling the first and last stitches of each row instead of slipping any of these stitches.

Garter selvage—Knit the first and last stitches of every row. This method produces a firm edge appropriate for stockinette stitch or for any pattern stitch where the edges may tend to be loose. The knobs created along both edges help you match sides for row-to-row seams. (See drawing.)

Stockinette selvage—Knit the first and last stitches of every right-side row; purl the first and last stitches of every wrong-side row. Stockinette selvages are smooth, with each stitch corresponding to one row, so it's easy to pick up stitches later when you're weaving the seam. (See drawing.) You can weave the stitches one for one, or, in lighter yarns, every other one. If your knitting is loose and airy, a stockinette selvage will tighten up your seams. This is the selvage I use most.

One-stitch slipped selvages

Slipped-stitch selvages form a chain along each fabric edge and are often used when the stitches will be picked up later or when the seams are to be joined edge to edge. Always tighten the slip stitches firmly before continuing the row, or they'll become oversized. Note that on this type of selvage, each stitch equals two rows.

Slipped-garter selvage—With yarn in back, slip the first stitch of each row knitwise (as if to knit); knit the last stitch. This method creates knobs along both edges. It makes a tighter edge than a plain garter selvage. (See drawing.)

Chain selvage—On each right-side row, slip the first stitch knitwise; knit the last stitch. On each wrong-side row, slip the first stitch purlwise (as if to purl); purl the last stitch.

This means you slip the first stitch of every row as established in the row below. That is, if the stitch below is a knit stitch facing you, slip the stitch knitwise; if a purl stitch, slip the stitch purlwise. Then complete the row according to your pattern stitch. For stockinette stitch, slip knitwise on knit rows and purlwise on purl rows.

(See drawing.) For garter stitch, slip the first stitch of every row purlwise to ensure the chain selvage. Pull the slipped stitch firmly. If it's still too loose, try pulling both the first and second stitches.

There are a number of variations of the chain selvage. They differ according to exactly how the stitch is slipped or how the last stitch is worked. Some of these variations are simply regional habits and take the names of the European countries where they originated. There's no reason to recommend one over another; it's merely a matter of personal preference. The English and German selvages may seem awkward, but they're worth a try if you have trouble maintaining an even edge.

Slipped-stitch selvage—On each right-side row, slip the first stitch purlwise, without twisting the yarn around the first stitch; knit the last stitch. On each wrong-side row, slip the first stitch knitwise; purl the last stitch.

French selvage—On each right-side row, slip the first stitch knitwise; knit the last stitch. On each wrong-side row, slip the first stitch purlwise, being careful not to twist the yarn around the first stitch (see drawing); knit the last stitch.

English selvage—On the right side, slip the first and last stitches knitwise. Note that the yarn will be in front, between the first and second stitches, after the work is turned. On the wrong side, purl the first and last stitches of each row. (See drawing.)

German selvage—On each right-side row, knit the first stitch; slip the last stitch purlwise. On each wrong-side row, purl the first stitch, and slip the last purlwise.

Slip-and-knit-stitch selvage I—On the right side, slip the first stitch purlwise; knit the last stitch. On the wrong side, slip the first stitch knitwise; knit the last stitch.

Slip-and-knit-stitch selvage II—On every row, slip the first stitch knitwise, holding the yarn in front of the work; knit the last stitch. Do not twist the yarn around the

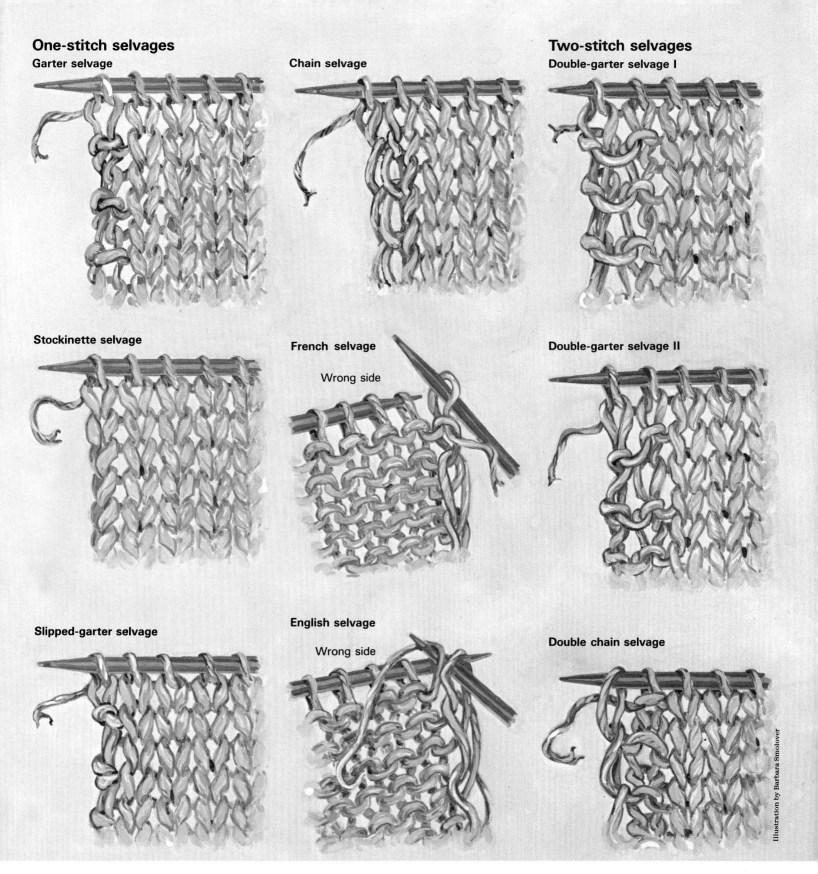

One-stitch selvages
Garter selvage

Stockinette selvage

Slipped-garter selvage

Chain selvage

French selvage
Wrong side

English selvage
Wrong side

Two-stitch selvages
Double-garter selvage I

Double-garter selvage II

Double chain selvage

Illustration by Barbara Smolover

first stitch. Each edge should be smooth. This is probably the easiest selvage to knit.

Two-stitch selvages
Two-stitch selvages are more attractive than one-stitch varieties and are often used when no other finish will be added to the project, such as for the edge of a scarf. These selvages are rarely used for seams because the extra stitch usually adds too much bulk.

Double-garter selvage I—On every row, slip the first stitch knitwise through the back

loop (with yarn in back). Knit the next stitch. Work to within the last two stitches of the row; knit these stitches. (See drawing.)

Double-garter selvage II—On every row, slip the first stitch knitwise (with yarn in back) and knit the next stitch. Knit the last two stitches. (See drawing.)

Both double-garter selvages produce firm, flat edges. These edges will still curl under somewhat, making double-garter selvages suitable for lapels or cap sleeves, where you want a little bit of curl.

Double chain selvage—On the right slip the first stitch knitwise. Purl the second stitch. At the end of the row, purl one stitch, and slip the last stitch knitwise. (See drawing.) On the wrong side, purl the first two stitches and the last two stitches. The double chain selvage is the firmest and flattest of the collection. Use it wherever you want a flat, smooth edge, such as at the top of a summer shell.   □

———————
Theresa Gaffey designs knitwear and teaches knitting in Atlanta, GA.

A Knitting Odyssey

The making of a handknit Chanel-style suit

by Linda Dyett

Linda Dyett's Chanel-style suit was handknit at 8 sts to the inch. The custom-charting, fitting, and lining reveal the secrets of skilled Old World couturiers. (Photo by Bob Frame)

In December of 1985, I unsheathed my 14-in. size 3 needles, cast on 178 sts in a thin French wool bouclé, and embarked on a knitting odyssey: creating a Chanel-style suit. At the outset, I gamely anticipated a few months of part-time knitting, spliced into a hectic and erratic free-lance writing schedule. Wrong. I bound off my last stitch 14 months later, in January 1987.

Spectators on buses, subways, and wherever else I could snatch a moment gasped at the size of the task. And I occasionally had misgivings that the project was unnecessarily time-consuming, idiosyncratic, and quixotic in this age of the user-friendly home knitting machine. But the completed suit is exquisite, the more so for being handknit. What makes it superb isn't just the beautiful materials or the even stitchery (which any patient, competent knitter can achieve). Far more vital is the streamlined late '80's Chanel style in a slightly rustic stockinette fabric, and the finishing and lining that took two experts a couple of weeks to accomplish.

Selecting a Chanel style

When Gabrielle Chanel was born in Auvergne, France, in 1883, the mode in women's dress was an ankle-length bouffant skirt over a corseted bodice. During World War I, however, when women of all classes joined the work force, they needed practical clothes. Quentin Bell, in *On Human Finery,* notes that the war slackened "the demands of those social forces which tend to provide conspicuous waste and conspicuous leisure. The ethos of a nation in arms demands that class shall be forgotten. . . ." These anticlass dictates of the early 1900s became a manifesto for Chanel (who adopted the informal first name of Coco).

From the start, Chanel had a unique sensibility that simple, even paltry, materials and commonplace designs could be chic. In 1913, she set up business in Biarritz, making and selling boater hats. Her severe and efficient styles were a raging success. An astute businesswoman, she realized that

From *Threads* magazine (October 1987) 13:48-55

her hats needed the accompaniment of simple, comfortable clothes, and that *she* ought to produce them.

After the war, Chanel set up a dressmaking shop in Paris. Unlike brilliant contemporaries, such as Vionnet, she was not a creator of original lines. Her particular genius is that she borrowed unlikely prototypes from outside the fashion arena. Her famous little black dress evolved from the maid's uniform. Her daytime separates were based on practical sportswear and military wear. In particular, Chanel was inspired by British men's clothes (an affair with the Duke of Westminster undoubtedly familiarized her with basic styles).

Chanel's pivotal role in fashion history was to make women's clothes as practical and unfettered as possible. "Are there frills in the lines of an aircraft?" she once remarked. "No. I thought of aircraft when I created my collection." Her peasant origin, claims Edmonde Charles-Roux, author of *Chanel and Her World* (Vendome, 1981), discloses the most about the bold and indomitable couturier. She aimed to make poverty—or the look of poverty—chic.

In 1916, Chanel developed a passionate interest in wool jersey, in her search for a machine-made fabric that would replicate both the stretch and homey charms of knitting. Prior to this time, jersey had been used strictly for underwear, and no doubt Chanel admired the fabric as much for its unconventionality and lack of pretension as for its give. By 1920, she had adapted wool jersey for her suits and had it woven to her specific designs and colors by the manufacturer Rodier. She used it as though it were a luxury commodity, adding fine buttons, carefully made buttonholes, perfect cut and finish, and superb silk linings. (Chanel often used precious fabrics in the interiors of her garments—a form, perhaps, of reverse snobbery.)

The suit—in black or navy during the '20s and '30s, in pastel tweeds with braided trim during the '50s and '60s—became a Chanel staple. Its short, straight, sexy skirt allowed for easy maneuverability; its boxy jacket had large outside pockets and high-cut armholes to provide freedom of movement. Her typical round, collarless neckline is based on that of the straight jersey marine jacket, or cardigan, first worn by the Earl of Cardigan, a British general in the freezing Crimean War.

As Cecil Beaton put it, Chanel's "trick, or...genius was to convert the drab look to a model of brilliant simplicity.... Ruthlessly women were stripped of their finery, fitted with a tricot or skirt or a plain dress; and when they looked like Western Union messenger boys, when they had been reduced to chic poverty, then and only then did she drape them with costume jewelry, with great lumps of emeralds and rubies, and cascades of huge pearls."

Her suits are true classics, and I, for one, given the opportunity, could be tempted to ransom several of my close relatives to own any of the originals. So I decided to knit a suit in the early Chanel style, updated for the '80s and '90s.

Fortunately, some marvelous prototypes were at hand. Karl Lagerfeld had taken over the couture helm at the House of Chanel in 1983. (Lagerfeld also designs Chanel's ready-to-wear.) The half-Swedish, half-German Lagerfeld, born in Hamburg in 1939, is, like Chanel, a unique product of his time—a time of mimicking styles, rehashing fashion's recent past. By updating her proportions, adding '80's flair and a sexy wit, he has revivified Chanel's image. He has integrated her signature trademarks, and sometimes spoofs of them, into clothes with otherwise space-age lines.

After poring over pictures of Chanel suits from the '20s onward, I came across an unusually sleek Lagerfeld rendition on the cover of *Women's Wear Daily*. It had the familiar oversize pockets, buttons on the cuffs, and a cardigan neckline. But its jacket was tunic length, and its skirt was well above the knee. This suit was out of sync with the late-1985 passion for calf-length skirts and peplum jackets. It had a hypermodernistic quality I thought I hated. But the suit haunted me, and within a few days I decided that its long-short proportions were sublime and that its somewhat abstracted Chanel details constituted the wave of the millenium. This suit, I decided, would stand me in good stead for the next 20 or so years.

Choosing the yarn and the knit pattern
I presented the photo of the suit to Otilia Ruz, a pivotal figure in this story. Ruz, a handknit designer and an instructor at Wallis Mayers Needlework (33 E. 68th St., NY, NY 10021), is a Chanel specialist. For 30 years before she emigrated from her native Cuba in 1967, she was co-owner of a salon specializing in custom-knit Chanel suits. Ruz is one of a precious, small, and dwindling breed of skilled handknit couturiers, with an instinctive sense of elegance not unlike Chanel's.

Born in 1910, Ruz recalls that as a girl, "I always had knitting needles in my hands." To suit Cuba's tropical climate, she learned to design, chart, and knit her own fine-gauge dresses. Acquaintances asked her to knit for them, and Ruz formed a partnership with her friend, Nena Roca, who handled the business end. By the mid-'30s, Chanel suits with crocheted finishing braid were the most popular commodities of the couture-knit salon Ruz-Roca and were wholesaled to Bergdorf Goodman, I. Magnin, and Hattie Carnegie. Designed and custom-fitted by Ruz, they were knit by up to 80 local women. Usually it took six weeks of full-time work to produce a suit.

In 1967, Ruz and Roca moved to New York, where, at first, they continued their business. But local labor proved too expensive, and Ruz wouldn't switch to machine-knitting production. So she provided her custom service to handknitters at Alice Maynard, one of the oldest yarn shops in America, and in 1985 started at Wallis Mayers, where she still offers designs and hands-on instruction.

I asked Ruz if the 1985 Lagerfeld-Chanel suit could translate into a handknit. "Absolutely," she replied, provided I knit it in a thin yarn—to allow for gradations of shape and delicate details.

I wanted a slightly crunchy texture, as in rich tweed menswear suiting, so I decided on bouclé (meaning "curl"), a three-ply yarn with two foundation threads twisted with a third delivered in the reverse direction and at a quicker rate to produce a bulky effect. Ruz had sometimes used thin wool-rayon bouclé, but I wanted a luxury yarn—all wool, or maybe a wool-silk blend—in a two-tone tweed color combination. I tried various patterns in two hues of Frivolous, from Joseph Galler Inc. (27 W. 20th St., NY, NY 10011), but the result was too nubby. Finally, I decided on basic-black Frivolous with a thin, ecru 8-Ply Silk Cord, which is milled in Italy and distributed by Crystal Palace Yarns (3006 San Pablo Ave., Berkeley, CA 94702).

Ruz and I then swatched stitch patterns. She knit a long sampler strip, which I carried around and studied in various moods. The houndstooth pattern, a Scottish-tweed weave, was traditional but just raffish enough for my purposes. I went with it. Though I've not been able to discover if Chanel ever used it, the houndstooth check is certainly within the range of Scottish woolen twills she favored, and Rodier in the '30s had produced an oversize version of the check.

Houndstooth is a pattern of broken or jagged checks, each check usually measuring ½ in. to 2 in. The design you see in woven houndstooth-check fabric is neither

Otilia Ruz designed the knit patterns, measured Dyett, and charted instructions for her to knit from. Ruz later blocked the knit pieces to further refine the sizing before the garment was assembled and lined.

Two question-mark-shaped facings (left), knit in the ascot pattern, extend from the jacket's bottom edges and are joined at the center back of the neck. The lining is inserted beneath the facings to the garment's front edges and overcast-stitched in place. Shoulder darts accommodate the extra fabric of the silk lining. The cap of the seamed sleeve lining is eased over the shoulder pad and hand-stitched in place. The lining hangs down loosely to the middle of a reinforcing 2½-in.-wide silk strip that keeps the knit fabric from stretching (above).

strictly in the yarn nor in the weave. It's an interaction of both, arising naturally in the cloth's twill configuration. There are various ways of translating this design to knitting. I discovered two possibilities in *The Harmony Guide to Knitting Stitches* (Lyric Books, 1983), but the variation designed by Ruz looks closer to the real thing (see photo and pattern, facing page). Hers is based on a multiple of 4 stockinette sts, where the center of each check is a 2-st, 2-row square, with jagged edges on all sides. The edges are knit in a staggered color pattern: 2 rows of 3 black, 1 ecru, followed by 2 rows of 3 ecru, 1 black, where the pattern begins with a different color on every row. Technically, it is Fair Isle-style knitting, with short floats on the wrong side that form their own not-displeasing horizontal V-pattern, add strength to the fabric, and help minimize widthwise stretching. (It is not out of place at this point to note that Chanel once said: "Elegance means a thing's as beautiful on the wrong side as it is on the right.")

To keep the fabric sturdy, as well as to ensure delicate shaping, we went for a fairly narrow gauge. Each check measures about ⅜ in. across and ½ in. in height.

As for the pocket trim and facing, we wanted them to echo the houndstooth pattern, but we did not want them to be precisely the same. By choosing a slightly contrasting check, we invoked a Chanel trademark of the '20s: the coordination of different, sometimes clashing textures, prints, and even checks—another example of chic poverty. Ruz's trim pattern, which

she called ascot, is a slipstitch design (see photo and pattern, facing page).

Measuring and charting

This suit was to be designed not only to fit me but also to enhance my best features and diminish my flaws. (What more can we ever ask of clothes?) My only unusual features, Ruz's measuring revealed, were particularly narrow wrists and a narrow back. I am also temporarily (ha!) overweight and heaviest in the hip and thigh areas. But basically, Ruz judged, I have a fairly even figure, straight shoulders, and a tendency toward curvaceousness (so I presume that if I were thin, I would have the voluptuous figure of Sophia Loren rather than the straight lines of Twiggy).

With its proportions left relatively unchanged, my knitting strategy can probably be utilized by others with even figures, regardless of size, to chart a similar suit. But a very large bust, for example, would require extra fabric at the front armholes that would be sewn into darts. Sloping shoulders would require additional fabric allowance for large shoulder pads. A big waist would call for square shaping in the skirt, and wide hips would require more gradual decreases to the armholes than in my jacket pattern. There are, as well, many situations that would call for *trompe l'oeil* solutions to mask flaws—for example, the trick of allowing extra fabric ease for extremely thin arms, or diminished ease for heavy arms, and so on.

When she sat down to chart my pattern, Ruz had her indispensable tape measure

around her neck, my gauge swatches, the list of my measurements, and my clipping of the Chanel-Lagerfeld suit nearby. First, she explained, she focused her attention on these elements. Then she mentally inserted me into the suit, as a genie is swept into a magic lamp, and the mathematics and words of the pattern began flowing. Ruz always does her charting in the round, envisioning not a two-dimensional schematic, but rather clothing to be sculpted around the body.

Of course, she did make some computations, and from her charting maneuvers you can begin to learn her techniques. Plotting a jacket, for example—whether it is designed in sizes or custom-fitted—is a series of strategies to move from widest to narrowest to widest points along the route from hip to shoulder—the crucial areas being the waist, bust, and armholes. The pattern is a rendering of the movement among these points. (See drawing, page 21.)

Ruz's customized charting maneuvers were specific to my suit, which is tailored and therefore requires ad lib, ad hoc techniques that deviate from norms and patterns. So the intricacies of her suit instructions are being offered as an insight into her techniques, rather than as a set of hard-and-fast rules.

Making the suit

The Chanel-Lagerfeld jacket is unusually long, with form-fitting hips that accentuate its length. Ruz decided the hips in a knit jacket would require no fabric ease—they'd stretch slightly with use. But above the hips she charted a gently defined, slightly Empire waistline and bustline, and fairly prominent late-'80's shoulders.

Ruz used my hip measurement (43½ in.), taken 8 in. below my waist, to compute the number of cast-on stitches. She multiplied half of it (21¾)—this is just the back of the jacket—by the gauge (8). To the resulting 174 sts, she added 2 sts for each side seam. So the number cast on was 178 sts.

Ruz started plotting her instructions at the lower edge of the jacket, that is, 4 in. below the hips—for me and anyone else of medium height, regardless of girth. For those who are short, Ruz advises starting 3 in. below the hips; for those who are tall, 4½ in. or at most 5 in. below for this design.

Next, Ruz had to get to the waist, a distance, in my case, of 15 in. from the jacket bottom. Within that distance she planned a straight length of fabric that would provide for a ½-in. hem and continue until my hips started curving inward (above the 4-in. measurement she had calculated earlier).

This left 11 in. of hip-contouring from hips to waist. If you're tall, add 1 in. or more; if you're short, subtract. Within this length, Ruz had to decrease in order to taper the fabric inward to the waist. To calculate the number of decreases, she first needed to decide how many stitches she wanted at the waistline, where the Chanel-Lagerfeld design turns from formfitting to gently form-suggesting with extra ease. In my case, Ruz chose 3 in. of ease in the jacket back. For very petite women, she recommends 1 in. or less of ease; for very large or tall women, 1 in. or more. She added the ease to half my waist measurement (15¾ in.) and a ½-in. seam allowance to determine a waist measurement of 19¼ in. (15¾ in. + 3-in. ease + ½-in. seam allowance [2 sts each side]).

So, to decrease to 154 sts for the waist (19¼ in. x 8), Ruz had to get rid of 24 sts from the original 178 sts evenly along the 11 in. up from the hips. In my case, that meant decreasing 1 st at each side of the work every 1 in. 12 times. (The number of decreases and the distance between them will vary according to waist and hip measurements and the length between them.) To emphasize the waist and to suggest, as Lagerfeld did, a slight Empire fullness above it, Ruz allowed for an additional 2 in. of uncontoured knitting with a generous 3 in. of fabric ease.

Over the next 3 in., below the armholes, my back reaches its broadest, so Ruz had to widen the fabric. At the same time, she wanted to reduce the ease and return to a formfitting look. She added a minuscule ¼-in. ease and ½-in. seam allowances to my back width of 19 in. That meant broadening the fabric ¾ in., which she accomplished with increases of 1 st at each end every 1½ in. 3 times. Then Ruz allowed for 2 in. of straight knitting, which brought her to the 22-in. mark—which she had measured on me as the point where the armholes would begin. (For others with even figures, the distance between waist and armhole can be plotted with the same proportions: about 2 in. of straight knitting, followed by 3 in. of increasing, followed by 2 in. of straight knitting.)

In typical sweater charting, armholes start with a bind-off and then taper into a succession of decreases, followed by uncontoured knitting to the shoulders. Ruz's armholes are more complex. Several inches above the initial curves are increase rows that accommodate the natural widening of my back. First she planned the width across my shoulders. She had measured that as 15¾ in. but deducted ¼ in. to get a tight fit at the armholes, because at this stress point the fabric will stretch with use. My shoulders begin to widen about 4 in. above the start of the armhole, so Ruz plotted an inward curve within that space. She reduced from 160 sts to 128 sts (15½ in. of back width at the armhole plus ½ in. in seam allowances x 8). She plotted the curve with an initial bind-off of 1¼ in. (or 10 sts) on each of the next 2 rows. Only the extremely petite and the very large will have to bind off or leave extra stitches.

After that, Ruz planned even decreasing—1 st from each end every other row 6 times—to reach her 128-st goal. Then she allowed for uncontoured knitting until 4 in. above the first bind-off. Every-other-row removals followed by straight knitting are invariable for all women, as the start of the armhole curve is too small to allow for any greater latitude.

For the top of the armscye, Ruz added an extra inch in height for shoulder pads and seam allowances to my armhole length of 8½ in. So, to the 4 in. already knit, she had to work up another 5½ in. and at the same time broaden the fabric a little to allow for the wider back and the wide-shouldered Lagerfeld look. She added a ¾-in. ease and ½ in. in seam allowances to my shoulder width of 15¾ in. That meant increasing to 17 in., or 136 sts, which she plotted as 1-st additions each end every 1 in. 4 times. Then Ruz allowed for uncontoured knitting for the last 2½ in. to reach the shoulder length of 9½ in. This completed the shaping of the sides.

The next task was contouring the neck and shoulders. The shape to aim for was a very shallow U. Unlike the traditional narrow polo neckline, Lagerfeld's is as wide as the shoulders, so Ruz made a convenient division. She split the 136 sts now on the needle into three parts. In shaping each part, she had to accommodate the curvature at the neck edge and the sloping of the shoulders. First she subtracted 2 in. (16 sts) from the total number of stitches. These would be bound off in the center of the next row to start the neck opening. That left 60 sts to be worked at each end, of which 45 sts would go toward shoulder

Knitting information

Materials: Galler's Frivolous, in black: 8 (9, 9, 10, 12) 1¾ oz. (50-g. skeins, each approx. 163 yd.), calculating your store-bought size as 2-4 (6-8, 10-12, 14-16, 18-20).

Crystal Palace's 8-Ply Silk Cord, in ecru (color No. 800): two ½-lb. cones (925 yd./cone) for all sizes.

14-in. size 2 and size 3 straight needles (or sizes to obtain gauge).

Gauge: 8 sts to 1 in. over houndstooth pattern, using size 3 needles, or size to obtain gauge.

7½ sts to 1 in. over ascot pattern, with size 2 needles or size to obtain gauge.

Houndstooth pattern: Multiple of 4 sts plus 2 border sts. Cast on with black.
Row 1 (RS): K1 black (border), *k1 ecru, k3 black; rep from *, end k1 black (border).
Row 2: K1 black (border), p2 black, *p1 ecru, p3 black; rep from * to last 2 sts, end p1 black (instead of p3), k1 black (border).
Row 3: K1 black (border), k2 ecru, *k1 black, k3 ecru; rep from * to last 2 sts, end k1 ecru (instead of k3), k1 black (border).
Row 4: K1 black (border), *p1 black, p3 ecru; rep from *, end k1 black (border).
Rep rows 1-4 for pattern.

Ascot pattern: Even number of sts. Cast on with black.
Row 1 (RS): With ecru, k1 (border), *sl1 p-wise with yarn in back (wyib), k1; rep from *, end k1 (border).
Row 2: With ecru, k all sts.
Row 3: With black, k1 (border), *k1, sl1 p-wise wyib; rep from *, end k1 (border).
Row 4: With black, k all sts.
Rep rows 1-4 for pattern.

The suit is knit in two classic check patterns, variations of which were designed by Ruz: houndstooth for the body, and ascot for the trims at the tops of the pockets and for the edge facings (pattern instructions at left).

shaping; the rest would be sacrificed to the neck opening. Ruz wanted the neck-edge stitches removed in a low curve, which she achieved by binding off 3 sts 5 times at each side of the neck. (If your neck is unusually narrow or wide, Ruz suggests you make your initial bind-off with fewer or more stitches for a neckline of this type.)

After the initial bind-off row, and as she continued the neck shaping, Ruz shaped the shoulders, one side at a time. With 15 sts on each neck edge spoken for, she divided the remaining 45 shoulder sts by 5 to allow for a wide, gradual slope. (For narrower shoulders, she recommends dividing by 4.) These stitches will be bound off 9 sts at a time every other row 5 times on each side. The plotting of the back was complete.

Left front—The side edges of the two front pieces of a cardigan jacket usually align with the side edges of the back piece in order for the side seams to be in the correct position. Because the front of my jacket had to be fuller than the back and in order to accommodate the cardigan overlap, the two front pieces needed a greater total width than the back.

For each jacket front, Ruz calculated a cast-on of approximately half the number of stitches as on the back plus an extra 1½ in. (12 sts), including seam allowances, for the overlap. Ruz followed the same knitting plan for shaping to the waist as for the back, working decreases on the side edge. She kept the center-front edge straight until the neck shaping. By the 15-in. mark, 86 sts were on the needle; 10 side increases (7 more than on the back) were then worked, bringing the stitch count to 96.

To accommodate the bust, Ruz started the armhole shaping at 22½ in., ½ in. higher than on the back. The extra fabric is later eased into the seaming just below the armhole, where the bust is fullest.

In designing the front armhole, to allow for the bust, Ruz plotted an extra 1½ in. of wider shaping than on the back by removing 12 extra sts. At 22½ in., the curve starts with a 6-st bind-off, then 5 sts, 4 sts, 3 sts, and 2 sts. After that, 1 st is decreased every other row 8 times—a total of 28 sts. If you're short or small-busted, plan fewer bind-offs and decreases. If you're tall or have an ample bosom, you'll need to build a wider curve in a longer space. When the armhole measured 4 in. deep, as on the back, Ruz calculated 4 increases for the widening shoulders at 1-in. intervals.

The neckline is deeper in front than in back, so its shaping had to begin at a lower point than on the back. Ruz started the neck shaping at 26½ in., 4 in. above the start of the armhole. Mimicking the gradually deepening curve of Lagerfeld's neck design—which I think he intended as an exaggeration of the round neck of classic Chanel suits—Ruz plotted an initial bind-off of 12 sts and decreases of 1 st every row 8 times and every other row until 45 sts

remained—the number she allowed for each shoulder on the back. If your neck is extra narrow or extra wide, calculate decreases more closely together or spaced farther apart. When the armhole measured 8½ in., she shaped the shoulder to match the back by binding off 9 sts 5 times every other row.

Right front—Ruz worked the right front as she did the left, with all the shapings reversed. We had the buttonholes industrially cut after the suit was finished and lined.

Sleeves—Ruz designed set-in sleeves, for a long, lean look to the arms. Viewed as a flat piece before it is seamed, a set-in sleeve widens into an arch at the top. The arch, or cap, fits into the armhole. Since the cap is firmly attached to the body of the jacket and doesn't stretch, the only ease required is for the wide shoulders. But the sleeve below the cap is notorious for stretching, so Ruz plotted 1 in. less than the distance between wrist and underarm—in my case, 16½ in. of fabric below the cap.

To calculate the starting width for the right sleeve, Ruz added to my narrow 7-in. wrist measurement ½ in. for seam allowances and a generous 2½-in. fabric ease. The resulting 10-in. circumference would gradually broaden to the widest part of my arm, which measures 13 in. just below the cap. Ruz wanted a 1½-in. ease to mask the heaviness of my upper arm, which meant planning for a 15-in. circumference (with ½ in. of seam stitches included), or 120 sts. (For most women, she suggests 2 in. of fabric ease from cuff to cap.)

The Chanel-Lagerfeld sleeve begins as two separate pieces—one of them a button flap that fits underneath the other and serves as an anchoring area for the row of three buttons. The two starting pieces are joined at the 6½-in. mark—making an extremely long "cuff." Both pieces have to widen gradually at opposite edges to form widening sleeves, but their inner edges, where they would overlap, are straight (see drawing of right sleeve, facing page).

The 10-in. circumference of a plain edge would have been accommodated by 80 cast-on sts. But instead, to allow for the gradually widening edge, Ruz planned for the smaller of the two starting pieces to have half the circumference—40 sts, or 5 in. The wider piece needed 52 sts to provide an extra 1½ in., or 12 sts, for the fairly wide underflap.

To widen the sleeve and to join (above the flap) the two pieces, Ruz had to add a total of 40 sts. She plotted them in increments of 1 st at each edge every ¾ in., first along the outer edges of the two pieces, then along each edge of the sleeve above the joining point. This increasing continues to about 1 in. below the cap.

So, for the wider piece, I increased 1 st at the end of the right-side rows every ¾ in. 8 times. After working to 6½ in., I bound off 12 sts at the straight edge and placed the

remainder on a holder. For the narrower piece, I increased 1 st at the beginning of the right-side rows every ¾ in. 8 times, for 48 sts. At 6½ in., I transferred the 48 sts of the wider piece from the holder to the working needle, which held 48 sts from the narrower piece. The bound-off stitches should be under the straight edge of the narrower piece. If necessary, decrease at the joining point to keep the pattern even. Next came increases at each end every ¾ in. for a total of 120 sts and 15½ in. in length.

After I knit straight for 1 in., I began the cap on the wrong side of the work. (This is important because the cap shaping differs on each edge at the start.) The first 1½ in. of the cap follows the shaping of the front and back armscyes—that is, a bind-off slope on the right side of 6 sts, 5 sts, 4 sts, 3 sts, and 2 sts; on the left side, 10 sts bound off once, followed by decreases of 1 st every other row 6 times.

At that point, the cap's edges will no longer match the front and back armscyes but will provide roundness for the shoulder and shoulder pad. Ruz made the cap 8 in. long, approximately 1½ in. less than the armhole length—for generous ease to capture the fullness of the Lagerfeld shoulders.

She allowed for a gentle 3-in. curve, with decreases of 1 st each end every 4th row. For the final 3½ in., she plotted a deeper curve, with decreases of 1 st at each end 8 times every other row and then every row 12 times. That left 42 sts on the needle to be bound off. The result is a cap with a long, flat edge.

The left sleeve is worked like the right sleeve, with all the shapings reversed.

Pockets—The stylish details of this suit—the wide, round neckline; the pronounced shoulders; the exaggerated menswear cuffs—are classic Chanelisms writ large by Lagerfeld. His *coups de grace,* however, are the four huge pockets—reminders of the patch pockets Chanel tacked onto her suits in the '20s.

The width of the hip pockets is about 60% or so of the total width of each front piece. Each pocket has an ascot pattern band across the top; the rest is houndstooth check. The length of the houndstooth portion is 5½ in. or so. In my case, Ruz calculated 58 sts, worked in the houndstooth pattern for 6 in. Then she plotted 2 rows in black stockinette stitch, with 4 sts evenly decreased across the 2nd row. This prepares for the ascot pattern in narrower gauge to be knit at the top of the pocket for 1¾ in. (as little as 1½ in. if you're petite; as much as 2 in. if you're tall). The bind-off row is black—as will be all unturned edges of ascot trim on the suit—to look neat and uniform.

The upper pockets are set 2 in. from the center-front edge and about 3½ in. from the underarm seams directly below the armholes. I worked 50 sts for 5 in. in houndstooth pattern. Then, as in the hip pockets,

Schematic for Linda's Chanel-style suit

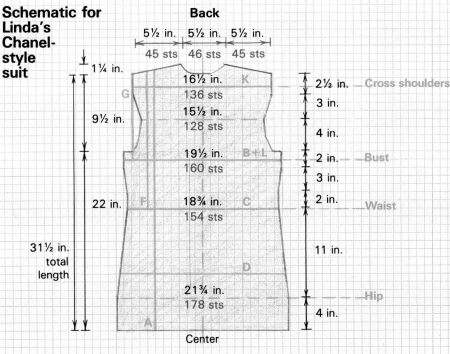

Back

5½ in.   5½ in.   5½ in.
45 sts   46 sts   45 sts

1¼ in.

G

9½ in.

22 in.

F

31½ in. total length

16½ in. — K
136 sts

15½ in.
128 sts

19½ in. — B+L
160 sts

18¾ in. — C
154 sts

D

21¾ in.
178 sts

A

Center

2½ in. — Cross shoulders
3 in.
4 in.
2 in. — Bust
3 in.
2 in. — Waist
11 in.
— Hip
4 in.

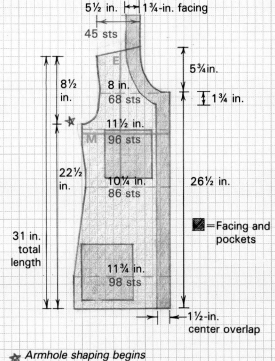

Right front

5½ in. ↔ 1¾-in. facing
45 sts

E

5¾ in.

8½ in.

8 in.
68 sts

1¾ in.

22½ in.

M — 11½ in.
96 sts

10¼ in.
86 sts

26½ in.

31 in. total length

11¾ in.
98 sts

⬛ = Facing and pockets

⟵ 1½-in. center overlap

• Inch measurements reflect desired finished measurement of knit piece after seaming. (Shape alterations from blocking not considered.) 1 sq. = 1 in.

• Stitch counts reflect number of stitches on needles, including ½-in. seam allowances (2 sts each side). Gauge = 8 sts/in.

★ Armhole shaping begins ½ in. higher than on back.

Right sleeve

5¼ in.
42 sts

Back armhole

H

14½ in.
120 sts

8 in.

1 in. — Upper arm

15½ in.

6½ in.

9½ in.

40 sts

52 sts

⬛ = 1½-in. overlap

— Wrist

Skirt

17½ in.
144 sts

1-in. band

D — 22 in.
180 sts

27 in. total length

— Waist

8½ in.

— Hip

8 in.

8½ in.

— Hem
2 in.

23¼ in.
190 sts

Otilia Ruz measured Linda Dyett to develop the knitting strategy (in inch dimensions and stitch counts) for the basic shapes of the suit parts shown here. To devise your own knitting strategy, have someone help you measure your body according to the guidelines below. Add allowances for ease, depending on your body shape and the suit style, as discussed on pages 18-22. After knitting the pieces and basting them together, you can further custom-fit by blocking.

A. **Total jacket length:** Measure from center of shoulder over bust to desired length.

B. **Bust:** Measure around body at fullest point. Make sure tape measure isn't slanted across chest or back. Assistant's thumb should be in front of tape measure; index, third, and fourth fingers behind it, to allow slight additional ease.

C. **Waist:** Waist measurement should be slightly more snug than that of bust. As with remaining measurements, except that of hips, index finger is behind tape measure, thumb in front.

D. **Hips:** Measure hips at widest point, which will be approximately 7 in. to 8 in. below waist. As with bust, thumb should be in front of tape measure; index, third, and fourth fingers behind it.

E. **Length to waist at front:** Tie string around waist. Measure distance from shoulder top at midpoint to waist over bust. (Jacket length will be about 15 in. below this point.)

F. **Length to waist at back:** Use same strategem as for E above, making sure tape measure is straight down back. (Measurement may be about ½ in. less than in front, depending on bust size.)

G. **Armhole:** Measure from top of shoulder to 2 in. below armpit.

H. **Sleeve length:** Bend elbow to form right angle. Place hand straight across midriff. Measure from edge of shoulder to desired cuff length, turning tape measure at elbow.

I. **Arm width:** Three measurements are required: widest point above elbow, widest point below elbow, and wrist measurement.

J. **Neck:** This jacket's wide neckline should start about 2 in. below base of neck.

K. **Shoulders:** Measure straight across back to outer shoulders.

L. **Width at back below armhole:** Measure across back directly below armholes.

M. **Front widths:** Measure from bottom of armhole to center front. Add 1½ in. for this cardigan jacket's center overlap.

Illustration by Deborah Newton

I worked 2 rows of black with 4 decreases evenly spaced on the 2nd row. The ascot pattern followed, for 1¾ in. Again, the bind-off row is black.

Front edge and neckline facing—After the jacket had been sewn together (see "Finishing," below), we decided it needed a little extra structure at the front edges, where the buttons and buttonholes would be. Ruz thought up the idea of knit facings to line the front edge and the neck. Because they were experiments, she knit the bands herself in the ascot pattern, by now the suit's official trim. In addition to reinforcing the edges, they lend a racy, charming note to the inside of the jacket.

The two bands, joined at the center back of the neck during the finishing process, look like question marks facing each other. They are straight along the entire front edge to shortly below the neckline shaping, at which point they widen considerably and curve to follow the neckline.

The facing dimensions can be plotted only after the jacket has been knit and sewn together. To determine the length to the neckline curve, Ruz measured the jacket length from the bottom edge to 1¾ in. below the neckline opening. She decided on 1¾-in.-wide bands—broad enough to accommodate the buttons and buttonholes and add extra firmness—so she cast on 14 sts. (If you are very petite or prefer a narrow band, cast on 8 sts; if you are very large, the bands should be as wide as 18 sts.) She started with the ecru motif, knitting the first and last stitches for seams, and ended on the 2nd row of the ecru motif 1¾ in. below the neckline opening. At this point the band doubles as neckline facing.

Ruz had to cast on enough additional stitches to obtain the length from center front to center back. To calculate the number, she measured half the circumference of the neck at 1¾ in. below the top edge, which was 16 in. It's important to get this lower measurement because it is wider than that of the top. Using a gauge of 7½ sts/in., she cast on 120 sts in black for the neckband's bottom edge, maintaining the pattern. (To be absolutely sure the bands will meet at the center back, add an extra 8 sts, and ease them in when sewing the band onto the jacket.)

Ruz knit straight for about ½ in. over all 134 sts for 7 rows and then planned for evenly spaced decreases across the neck portion of the band to create the curve. She separated the stitches for the 14-st-wide front-edge band with a stitch marker to exclude them from her decrease calculations.

To determine the neckband's top width, Ruz measured half the top width of the neckline. It was 12 in.—4 in. less than the bottom edge, which meant she had to decrease about 30 sts over the next three all-black motifs, where they wouldn't show. Ruz decreased 10 sts per row to gradually narrow the band—2 sts together 5 times evenly

across each row, so as not to disturb the ascot pattern. Again, no decreases are worked on the front-edge stitches. Then, she knit 2 rows of the black motif for a neat edge and decreased a few additional stitches on the final bind-off row, evenly spaced, for firmness.

The right neckline band is worked the same as the left band, with all the shapings reversed.

Skirt—In the Chanel tradition of practical elegance, the skirt is a simple pull-on A-line with an elastic waistband. It is knit in two pieces, which are seamed at the sides. To complement the long jacket, the skirt would have to be short. We decided to end it at my knees.

To calculate the bottom width for each half of the skirt, Ruz added a 1½-in. ease plus 4 seam sts to half my hip measurement (21¾ in.) for a total of 190 sts.

Along the total skirt length of 27 in., Ruz planned a 10½-in. piece of straight knitting at the bottom, including a 2-in. hem. From there, she created a gentle A-line slope that would end at the largest point of my hips—about 8 in. below my waist. To make the skirt formfitting, she allowed for a ½-in. total fabric ease at the hips. Since half my hip measurement is 21¾ in., that meant a total stitch count of 180 for each skirt half, including 4 seam sts. So, to move from the straight knitting to the A-line, 10 sts would have to be decreased along 8 in. Ruz plotted decreases at 2-in. intervals, starting at the end of the straight knitting.

Her next goal was the waistband, 8½ in. above the last A-line decrease. To account for the round curve from hip to waist in the remaining 8½ in., Ruz planned deeper decreases and an ease of about 1¾ in. at each half of the waistband in order to allow for slight gathers. The final stitch count of 144, including 4 seam sts, meant removing 36 sts by decreasing 1 st at each end every ½ in.

To provide a plain black cover that would be turned down over the elastic band to be added later, Ruz added 1 in. of black stockinette stitch. She narrowed the needle size to 2 to account for the slightly wider gauge of the black bouclé; the silk yarn is thinner. Ruz advises binding off loosely.

Finishing
My year of knitting was only the start, setting the stage for the blockings and fittings, basting, and the sewing and lining of the pieces—in other words, fine-tuning and tailoring by Ruz and her lining collaborator, Ilka Damboritz. Through them, the expertise of couture work was revealed to me.

Fine-tuning—Ruz compared the finished fabric dimensions with the ones she had calculated. One skirt piece was slightly wider than the other, but rather than block them to match, Ruz simply designated the narrower piece as the skirt front.

The jacket back was right on target, but the jacket fronts were slightly narrow. Ruz blocked them gently (one of the beauties of knit fabric is that it can be stretched and somewhat manipulated) and made their dimensions identical. With fuschia yarn, she basted the pieces together, matching the checks and everywhere allowing a ¼-in. seam—2 sts from the edge.

Now the suit came alive. It fit well, as a store-bought suit would (the tailoring details were yet to come)—in need of alterations but clearly on the mark. The sensibility of Chanel and Lagerfeld had passed through to Ruz as if she had put a Spockian mind patch on the two designers.

The checks of the unusually large pockets were aligned parallel to the check motifs of the jacket and at the right height—a subtle question of positioning according to the curvature of my torso. The jacket back fit perfectly. The skirt was fine. But the jacket front was still too tight, especially after Ruz pinned in shoulder pads. Also, the sleeves were too wide near the cuffs, and the bottom edges of the jacket jutted out sharply at the sides. So Ruz took the jacket apart, reblocked the two halves of the front about ½ in. wider, and narrowed the sleeves by adding an extra ¼ in. to their seams from elbow to cuff. She took the jacket seams in an extra ¼ in. for 5 in. above the hem.

Before the second fitting, I had bought the buttons and lining fabric. I found the textured gold buttons I was looking for—genuine Chanel knockoffs—at Greenberg and Hammer, a notions store at 24 W. 57th St. in New York City. At $4 each for ten 3¼-in.-diameter buttons and $3.25 each for six ⅝-in.-diameter buttons, I began to think of them as precious jewelry.

After all the efforts that were poured into this suit, only silk would do for the lining fabric. Uptown at Jerry Brown (37 W. 57th St., NY, NY 10014)—where customers swoon with delight over the fabrics and shriek in shock over the prices—I was momentarily seduced by a black cloverleaf print, but had to abandon it at $75/yd. But downtown at B & J Fabrics (263 W. 40th St., NY, NY 10018), New York's best discount fabric house of designer leftovers—I found a 54-in.-wide white-and-black crepe de chine pinstripe, a bargain at $24/yd. I bought 4 yd. It was Italian, the salesman whispered, woven for Bill Blass.

Assembly and lining—Next, I brought the basted suit, buttons, and silk to Ilka Damboritz. Damboritz, who works out of her suburban New York apartment, specializes in lining handknit suits. Born in Vienna in 1913, she started knitting at age 5. During the early 1930s, she apprenticed with a ladies' custom tailor, and in 1939, after she and her husband had left Hitler's Austria, Damboritz worked as a dressmaker in New York's Garment District. In the late '50s, she started free-lance lining for knitting-

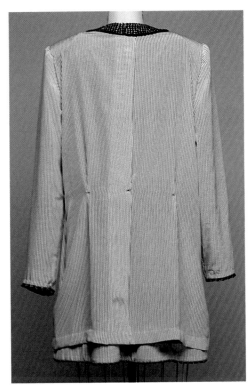

Ilka Damboritz (right), a specialist in lining knit garments, with the partially completed suit. She created a loose-fitting lining for the knit suit (above), pleating it to accommodate the ease in the fabric and tacking it in place throughout the knit garment body with tiny x's. The bottoms of the jacket and skirt linings hang free above the garment hems to allow the knit fabric to move unrestrictedly.

yarn shops in the Bronx, specializing in handknit coats and suits, which, she says, are most in need of a firm lining fabric.

Her techniques, like those of Ruz, seem instinctual. She creates a loose, easy armature of lining fabric and sews and tacks it onto the jacket. Using the basted suit as her guide, she cut the pieces at least ½ in. longer than their knit counterparts in order to add the hems.

For the jacket back, cut on the fold of the silk fabric, Damboritz allowed an extra 4 in. in width at the fold to accommodate a 2-in. double center pleat and two ½-in.-wide waistline pleats. The 2-in. pleat was to give the silk extra leeway—although the knit fabric will stretch, the silk won't. All pleats are tacked with tiny black x's.

For each front piece, Damboritz added 1½ in. for a shoulder dart between neckline edge and armhole (left photo, page 50) and for a small pleat at the waistline. For the sleeves, she cut an extra 3 in. all the way to the widest part of the cap and allowed 2 in. along the shoulder curve for gentle gathers. After rechecking the shoulder pads while I had the jacket on, Damboritz tacked them in place on the seam, center to center at the neck edge at each side of the armhole edge.

Damboritz cut the skirt-lining fabric 2 in. wider than the widest part of the hips, plus a 2-in. seam allowance, and added a few extra inches for a hem. She also cut two

pieces not found in the knit suit to help prevent the knit fabric from stretching: a 2½-in.-wide strip for the jacket bottom; and a 1½-in.-wide bias strip for the skirt hem, To allow the knit fabric to move, the jacket lining hangs loosely to the middle of the bottom edge strip (right photo, page 18).

Damboritz machine-stitched the side seams, and then with the jacket inside out on her mannequin, pinned the lining loosely but neatly in place, right side out, allowing for ease everywhere. Starting about 5 in. from the bottom hem, she tacked the lining in place, side seams to side seams, with running stitches about 1 in. apart next to the knit seams. The front edge of the lining meets the jacket's front edge inside the facing and is overcast-stitched in place.

After machine-stitching the knit sleeve seams and attaching them to the jacket, wrong side to wrong side, Damboritz machine-stitched the sleeve linings and pinned them into the jacket, seam to seam, with a generous basting stitch. She eased the fabric over the shoulder pads and hand-stitched it in place, right side out, leaving puckers along the cap.

The skirt lining hangs loosely inside the knit garment. Damboritz machine-stitched the pieces with 2-in. seams and a 7-in. slit on the left side (for freedom of movement). Then she attached the lining ¼ in. above the bottom of the knit waistband, and the 1½-in. bias strip to the knit hem. Next, she

folded and stitched the lining hem 1 in. shorter than the knit hem (any longer, and it might show if the knit skirt rode up).

When the parts were all attached, Damboritz ironed the lining and sewed on the buttons. The next day, I brought the jacket to the Singer Buttonhole and Eyeletting Corp. (302 W. 37th St., NY, NY 10018) for the final touch: machine-made buttonholes.

Now that it's all done and I've worn it, I've come to an unexpected realization about the suit. Though it fits me easily and comfortably, it has taken on a willful life and unutterably chic personality of its own. It demands special favors—spiky, expensive high heels and a structured Hermès handbag. It's calling out for an ecru silk blouse, it definitely wants a pricey French boater hat, and it expects lunch at La Grenouille. Maintaining finery, I've discovered, has its pitfalls. On the other hand, I possess a supremely elegant business and going-out suit—one that evokes immediate respect from others and awed satisfaction from me.

Although it was time-consuming to knit this suit, it wasn't just a once-in-a-lifetime experience. It has whetted my appetite. I'm contemplating a second one, though not right away. My next projects—for my husband and son—are sport-weight pullovers.

Pieces of cake. □

Linda Dyett is a contributing editor of Threads *magazine.*

Knitting Round on Straight Needles

In which the slip stitch comes between the knits, and the fabric splits asunder for a splendid finish

by Bee Borssuck

I used to pore over the finishing details of my best machine-made sweaters, admiring the way collars and neckbands were attached. I was intrigued by the way the knit stitch at the edge of a ribbed collar appeared to roll over and disappear into nothingness, how it could stretch and stretch and still snap back into place. The completely reversible seam enclosing the neckline puzzled and fascinated me—it seemed the ribbing that made the collar had miraculously dissolved into two thicknesses of stockinette fabric to create the seam. I could poke a bobby pin into the seam and fan the ends about. No threads attached the two layers. I wanted to work these marvels into my hand knits.

I finally visualized the answer to the reversible-seam puzzle. The knit stitches in the ribbing had "floated" to the top, and the purl stitches had "sunk" to create two layers of fabric. Only the knit stitches were worked across the row in one direction, and all the purl stitches were knit on the return pass. The ribbing had turned into a tube, and the rolled edge of the ribbing was also a tiny tube, for I could poke my bobby pin into it too.

If a machine could switch from ribbing to circular knitting, I could do it by hand, I thought. Once I knew what I had to do, it was easy to figure out how to do it. Just pass over, or *slip* the purl stitches. Lo and behold, I could knit round on a pair of single-pointed needles! I could work and slip alternate stitches, and on the return pass, I could work the stitches previously slipped.

Bee Borssuck, of Scottsdale, AZ, was a textile designer in New York City and a tool designer in Syracuse, NY, before she retired. Since retiring, she has written five books on needlepoint design and gives workshops on knitting technique.

The next step was to develop ways to use the technique. Obviously it is a convenient trick when four needles are too awkward or circular needles are too big. But its real value to me is when I'm casting on, weaving off, or picking up stitches. It banished from my knitting the tight and stretched-out ribbed edges and clumsy-looking, picked-up seams that shrieked "homemade!"

Knitting round on a pair of straight needles also brings a third dimension to my knitting. I can *create two layers of fabric* at the same time. Only when I really grasped the significance of this did I realize the full potential of knit-round. In almost any situation where two layers of fabric are required knitting round is unbeatable. What a handknitter can do with the technique goes way beyond what I originally admired in my machine-knit sweaters.

To knit round, you'll need a smooth yarn for making samples—medium- or worsted-weight, firmly spun wool, cotton, or synthetic yarn in a light color. For some samples, you'll also need a small quantity of the same weight yarn in a darker or contrasting color to accentuate the alternate-stitch principle of knit-round and help you see and understand the path taken by the yarn. You'll need a pair of needles that works well with the yarn you selected. You can use single-pointed needles, but for making samples I prefer a pair of double-pointed needles. I like the shorter length, and I find that the other pointed end comes in handy for picking up a row of stitches from the wrong end of a row. In addition, you'll need a tapestry needle, a crochet hook, and a 3-in. by 5-in. piece of woven fabric.

The following samples demonstrate the basics of knit-round as I've developed it. As you begin to apply them, perhaps you'll also find unusual situations in which to use these new tools. My knitting hasn't been the same since I began to use knit-round.

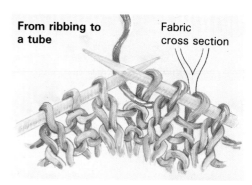

From ribbing to a tube **Fabric cross section**

From ribbing to a tube—Switching from ribbing to knit-round is the easiest way to see how the slipstitch principle works (see drawing above).

1. Cast on an even number of sts (16 to 24) and work a k1, p1 ribbing for a few rows.
2. To knit round, *K1, sl1 wyif (with yarn in front). (In all these samples, slip the sts purlwise, unless otherwise instructed.)
3. Rep from * to end of row, and rep row 1 for about 1½ in.
4. Pull the needle out. The knit and purl sts will spring apart and reveal a small pocket, or tube, that has the same number of sts as the ribbed foundation.
5. To close the tube, reinsert the needle and resume the k1, p1 ribbing.

From stockinette fabric to a tube—The above sample demonstrated the knit-round technique used for stretchy and reversible

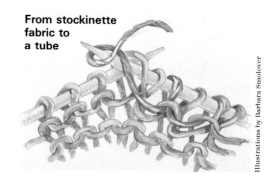

From stockinette fabric to a tube

From *Threads* magazine (August 1987) 12:64-67

The edges and seams on the two lower sweaters at right are knit round (or double knit): The fabric has become a two-layer tube for two or more rows. Knitting needles have been inserted into these tubes so you can see them. The top sweater has been made with waistline casings, as described below.

ribbing. However, when your foundation fabric is stockinette stitch, you must increase the number of stitches for the tube (see bottom drawing, facing page). Here's how to provide and eliminate extra stitches.

1. Cast on an even number of sts (16 to 20).

2. Work a few rows in stockinette stitch, ending on a knit row.

3. On the next row (knit-round pick-up row): P1, *sl1 wyif, with LH needle pick up head of st below st just slipped and purl it. Rep from *, ending with sl1 wyif.

4. Knit-round rows: *K1, sl1 wyif (the new stitch). Rep from *. Rep row 1 for desired length (1 in.). This tube has 2 fewer sts than twice the number of sts in the stockinette-stitch foundation.

5. To close the tube (purl side): P1, p2tog across row, end with p1. Resume stockinette-stitch fabric.

You can apply the techniques in this sample and the first one to details of your knitting that you want double-faced and reversible—hems, pockets, plackets, etc.

From stockinette fabric to a casing—You may want to create a double-thickness fabric, but you may not want to create a vertical tube. A casing like one you would use for a drawstring at the waistline of a hip-length sweater, for example, must be open at both ends. You can make such a casing by working back and forth across one thickness of the double fabric with one ball of yarn, then working back and forth on the other thickness with another ball. Cast on and knit a foundation, as described above, ending on a knit row.

To make the ***casing pick up*** (purl side): *Row 1:* Tie on and use a second color (B), hold the original color (A) in back. Sl1 (A), *sl1 wyif, with LH needle pick up head of st below st you just slipped and purl it. Rep from *, ending with sl1 (A) wyif.

Create a casing by adding a second layer of yarn, shown here in pink, and knitting two pink rows, then two white rows, alternately, to the desired casing size.

B. Borssuck
Original

Return row: Sl1 (A) wyib, *p1 (B), sl1 (A) wyib. Rep from *, ending with sl1 (A). The two yarns, A and B, must never be twisted together. There are two fewer B sts than A sts.

To make the *casing* (left photo, page 25):
Row 1 (purl row with A): Keep B in front. P1 (A), *p1 (A), sl1 (B) wyib. Rep from *, ending with p1.
Row 2 (knit row with A): *K1 (A), sl1 (B) wyif. Rep from *, ending with k2.
Row 3 (knit row with B): Keep A in back. Sl2 (A), *k1 (B), sl1 (A) wyif. Rep from *.
Row 4 (purl row with B): Sl1 (A) wyib, *p1 (B), sl1 wyib. Rep from *, ending with sl2 (A).
Rep rows 1, 2, 3, and 4 for depth of casing, ending with row 1.

To *close the casing* (knit row with A): K1, k2tog across row, end with k1. Continue with stockinette fabric.

You can adapt this back-and-forth principle to other situations. For example, if you use only one ball of yarn, you can close one end of the casing and leave the other open. *Work two rows—a purl/slip row and a knit/slip row (rows 1 and 2), turn and work rows 3 and 4 as a knit/slip row and a purl/slip row. Rep from *. If you work part of the row as a double fabric, you will be able to easily knit an open placket or fly front along the edge of a Chanel-style jacket.

Cast-on and bind-off open-end tube—The tubes described above are all worked from a single fabric foundation and therefore have closed ends. You can also leave either end or both ends open for seamless mittens, leg warmers, doll clothes, cords, or fly fronts—all on two needles.

To make an *open-tube cast-on* (see photo below):
Row 1: Single-cast-on with the thumb method one half the required number of sts (try 6 to 8).
Return row: Hold the yarn in front at all times. Cast on 1 by thumb method. *Sl1 wyif, cast on 1 by thumb method. Rep from *, ending with sl1 (even number 12 to 16).
Knit-round rows: *K1, sl1 wyif. Rep from *. Rep row 1 for desired length (2 in.).

To make an *open-tube bind-off:* You can pull the knitting needle out and bind off the last row of the tube with a row of slip crochet or single crochet. If you're reluctant to pull the needle out of your knitting, transfer the sts to a piece of scrap

You needn't start and end knit-round with a single layer of fabric. This open-end tube was cast on and off in two layers.

yarn on a tapestry needle. Slip the knit st onto scrap yarn, slip the slip (purl) st to a knitting needle, and rep across the row. Turn and transfer all sts to the scrap yarn. Finish off with a crochet hook.

Cast-on and weave-off closed-end tube— There may be no practical use for the tiny, seamless pillow you'll produce in this sample, except perhaps as a Christmas-tree ornament, but it introduces two important techniques: invisible cast-on and invisible weave-off. These techniques are required in many of the practical applications of knit-round because they provide the finish— one that is smooth and elastic.

Invisible cast-on methods are those that give a soft edge to the fabric because the stitches formed for the first row are not twisted or otherwise looped over one another. Other techniques produce a cord-like effect to some degree.

You will want to use invisible cast-on for fabrics that must drape smoothly, for edges that should follow the curves of an undulating pattern without distorting them, or in any situation where you want to eliminate the stiffness caused by other methods.

Although it looks complicated, this method of casting on is one of the fastest of the dozen or so cast-ons I know because the movements are small, concise, easily controlled, and rhythmical. You'll find it easier to see what you're doing as you practice if you use two different-colored yarns, a ball of A and a 24-inch piece of B.

Knot the ends together, clip them, and position the knot within the loop of the starting slip knot. Color A (knit stitches) will alternate with B (purl stitches), and the two yarns will twist around each other between each stitch on the underside of the needle. The trick in this cast-on method is to make sure every stitch is a complete wrap around the needle to bring the twists in line. You'll need to practice a little to do this. You can control the tendency of stitches to turn on the needle by placing your right forefinger over each stitch as you "set" the twist and holding pressure there until you complete the next stitch.

To make an *invisible cast-on* (see drawings at right):
Step 1: Place a slip knot on needle. It counts as 1 st, a knit st. Position left forefinger between B and A, with B in front, grasping both yarns in your fist.
Step 2: *Cast on a purl st with B: First, put tip of needle under A from back to front.
Step 3: Next, slide needle over and then back under B, slipping A loop off needle over B, to front. Place right forefinger on top of this purl st and set twist with slight rolling motion of right hand and a little pull to even up slack in the yarns.
Step 4: Cast on a knit st with A: First, put tip of needle under B from front to back.
Step 5: Next, slide needle over and then back under A, slipping B loop off needle over A, to back. A backward roll and slight

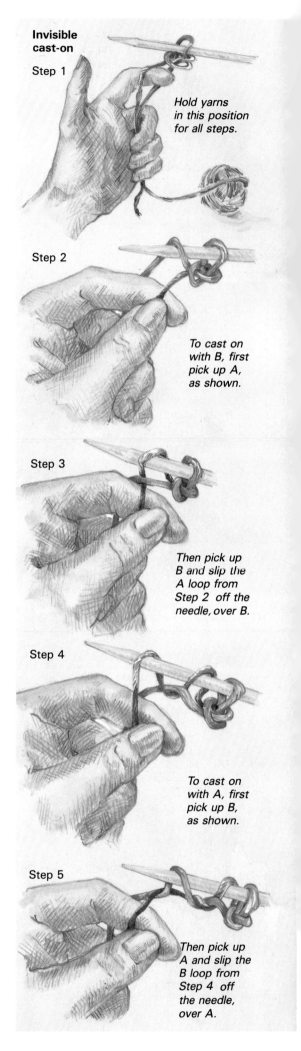

Invisible cast-on

Step 1

Hold yarns in this position for all steps.

Step 2

To cast on with B, first pick up A, as shown.

Step 3

Then pick up B and slip the A loop from Step 2 off the needle, over B.

Step 4

To cast on with A, first pick up B, as shown.

Step 5

Then pick up A and slip the B loop from Step 4 off the needle, over A.

Invisible weave-off

Step 1

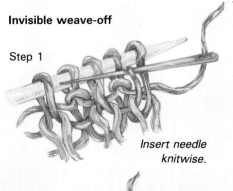

Insert needle knitwise.

Step 2

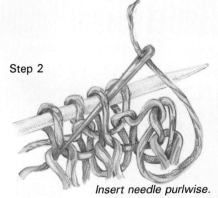

Insert needle purlwise.

Step 3

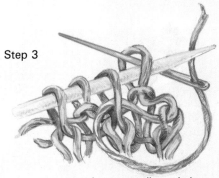

Insert needle purlwise.

Step 4

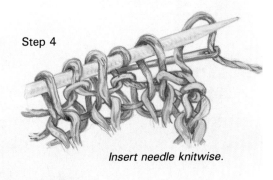

Insert needle knitwise.

Reversible seams

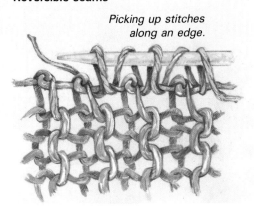

Picking up stitches along an edge.

pull will set that st. Rep from *, ending with a purl st (B) so that you have an even number of sts, including the slip knot (12 to 16). Tie off B.

• Row 1: *K1 through back of loop, sl1 wyif. Rep from *.

• Knit-round rows: *K1, sl1 wyif. Rep from * for desired length (20 rows).

To weave off invisibly in knit-round, you can use the Kitchener method of grafting two pieces of knitting together. The only difference is that both pieces are on one needle. Again, you'll find it easier to recognize the stitches of each fabric if you work the last row of knit-round in another color (B).

To make an ***invisible weave-off*** (see drawings at left): Cut yarn, leaving a 16-in. tail from next-to-last st. Thread a tapestry needle with tail B. Note that the tapestry needle never passes under the knitting needle or through two thicknesses of the fabric.
Step 1: *Swing yarn to front under tip of knitting needle. Insert needle into 1st st (A), as if to knit.
Step 2: Draw yarn through, and slip st off knitting needle. Retain yarn in front and insert needle into 2nd st on needle (A), as if to purl. Draw yarn through toward yourself.
Step 3: Swing yarn to back under tip of knitting needle. Insert needle into 1st st (B), as if to purl.
Step 4: Draw yarn through and slip st off knitting needle. Retain yarn in back and insert needle into 2nd st on knitting needle (B), as if to knit. Draw yarn through away from yourself.

Rep from * to end of row and through last knit st (A), as if to knit. Fasten off.

Ribbing with invisible cast-on and weave-off

—This sample incorporates the techniques used in the seamless pillow in their most useful application, giving elasticity to the edges of ribbing, and shows how the start and finish of ribbing can be made to match perfectly—a big advantage when you're designing your own knitwear.
1. Invisibly cast on and work *rows 1 and 2,* as in the above sample (knit-round).
2. *Row 3 and following:* K1, p1. Rep for desired length of ribbing (2 in.).
3. Create two fabrics by working at least 2 rows of knit-round. Then finish with invisible weave-off.

With the invisible cast-on and weave-off method, the ribbing edge is a double fabric. Each side has half the cast-on stitches. This is the secret of its elasticity, usually sufficient for waist and neckband ribbings of wool or other naturally resilient fibers. But many popular fibers, like cotton, silk, and linen, as well as the beautiful tapes and ribbons now available for knitting, have little or no elasticity. If they need elastic threads added to ribbings, knitting it in with the yarn may create problems with color matching, control, and replacement. When you use invisible cast-on and weave-off, you can thread elastic cord or thread through the channel at the edge and even

supply additional channels at spaced intervals by knitting round for 2 rows.

Reversible seams—Handmade or homemade? The difference is usually in the finish, in the way pieces are attached to each other. It is important to remember that knit fabric cannot fold back on itself sharply as woven cloth can. It does not crease, it rolls. This is no problem when you are seaming pieces together into cylindrical shapes, but it is when you attach trim.

You can make a smooth, flat, reversible seam along the edge of a knit fabric in two ways. You can pick up stitches and then knit edging, collar, or sleeve as desired. This is the finishing touch that started it all for me, and you can see an example of it in the beige sweater on page 25. You can also do it in reverse: Knit the desired piece, and then apply it to the edge. This is an effective technique for trimming woven fabrics with knitting. Each method has its advantages, and both methods deserve a place in your repertoire of techniques.

To make a ***reversible-welted knit-on seam*** (see bottom drawing at left), prepare a garter-stitch strip 8 sts or 10 sts wide and about 3 in. long in yarn B. Mark one side as the right side. On the long edge of the strip, and from the front, insert needle from front to back into first right-hand st. Draw up a knit st in A, leaving a tail that will be worked in later, *yarn over from front to back (yo), draw up a knit st. Rep from *, ending with a knit st and an odd number of sts.
Row 1 (wrong side): Sl1 wyif, * k1 (the yo), sl1 wyif. Rep from *.
Row 2 (right side): K1, *sl1 wyif, k1. Rep from *.
Rows 3 and 4: Rep rows 1 and 2.
Row 5: Rep row 1.
Row 6: K1, * p1, k1. Rep from *. Continue ribbing for 1 in., but don't bind off.

These instructions are basic, and you can adapt them for specific problems. When I apply them to round or V-neck bands, I pick up the neckline with a circular needle or a set of double-pointed needles and work 4 circular rows (2 knit/slip for the outside fabric and 2 purl/slip for the inside) before changing to a ribbing. I also like the pretty touch I get when the pick-up stitches on the right side of the garment are purled for a single row.

To make a ***reversible welted sewn-on seam,*** pick up where you left off on the last sample, switch to knit-round, and make 6 rows. Cut the yarn, leaving a 20-in. tail extending from next-to-last st. To hold sts temporarily, thread a tapestry needle with a 36-in. piece of heavy thread or fine yarn. Transfer all sts from the knitting needle to the thread, leaving about 1 in. of slack between each st. Open the pocket between the layers and insert the woven fabric. Baste in place. Working through the cloth into the st loops, you can now sew or crochet the welt seam closed. □

The Knitted Yarn Over

This simple stitch creates a hole in the fabric

by Shirley W. MacNulty

the yarn-over stitch is one of the simplest to do, yet it can create the most intricate patterns. A yarn over is a new stitch that you form by wrapping the yarn around the right needle. The yarn over will and should leave a hole or space in the knitting.

Since the yarn over leaves a hole, beading (holes for threading ribbon or cord) and delicate lace and eyelet stitches can't be executed without it. These stitches are often used in patterns for baby clothes and lacy sweaters. Although it appears difficult, lace knitting is simple and is the most varied form of knitting. When designing a garment incorporating yarn overs for a lace pattern, choose fine, fingering-weight yarns; the hole created by the yarn over won't show up well in thick yarns. The fabric's texture also changes considerably with different size needles. Because lace stitches tend to be loose, your gauge will be different than if you knit stockinette stitch with the same yarn, so always check the gauge of your pattern stitches.

Because it creates a new stitch, the versatile yarn over is also a method of increasing and can be used to make a decorative hole. For example, in raglan sweaters worked from the neck down (which require increasing instead of decreasing for the raglan seam), the yarn over can be used for the double increase, one on each side of a central stitch.

Yarn overs are also used in many texture patterns. The yarn over is easier to do than a knit or purl stitch. But before attempting it, a beginning knitter must learn how to do the knit and purl stitches, and then how to take the yarn to the front or back between the needles for a rib stitch.

The yarn-over stitch is worked differently depending on whether a knit or purl stitch precedes and follows it. However, many instructions give only the abbreviation *yo* or just *o*, so knowing which way to wrap the yarn can be difficult. European instructions often use *wf* (wool forward), which means simply to bring the yarn to the front of the work.

Generally, the yarn over should lie in the same direction as the other stitches on the needle, with the stitch slanting down to the right in front of the needle. The stitch is completed in the following row, when it is knit, purled, or slipped, just like any other stitch.

Yarn over between two knit stitches—When the stitches before and after the yarn over are knit stitches, just bring the yarn from the back of the work (where you held it for knitting) to the front between the needle points. Then take it back over the top of the right needle and continue knitting, as shown in the drawing on the facing page. For the next stitch, you'll be knitting with the yarn held as if to purl.

In the following row, work the yarn over as a regular stitch, whether it is a knit, purl, or slip stitch—this will create the hole. The abbreviations for this yarn over include *yo* (yarn over), *yf* (yarn forward), *wf* (wool forward), *yfon* (yarn forward and over needle), and *wfon* (wool forward and over needle).

Yarn over after a knit stitch and before a purl stitch—Bring the yarn from the back to the front between the needle points. Wrap it around the right needle and again bring it between the needles to the front. Purl the next stitch. The abbreviations are *yfrn* and *wfrn* (yarn or wool forward and around needle).

Yarn over between two purl stitches—Take the yarn from the front over the right needle to the back, and then bring it between the needle points to the front again. The abbreviations are *yrn* and *wrn* (yarn or wool around needle).

Yarn over after a purl stitch and before a knit stitch—Take the yarn from the front, over the right needle to the back, and knit the next stitch. The yarn is not brought between the needle points, as in the previous three methods. The abbreviations are *yon* and *won* (yarn or wool over needle).

Yarn over before working a first stitch—When the first stitch in a row is a yarn over, the techniques are slightly different.

For a yarn over before a knit stitch, put the right needle under the yarn and begin to knit. For a yarn over before a purl stitch, put the right needle under the yarn, bring the yarn from the back to the front between the needle points, and purl.

If a yarn over is not to be an increase, it must be accompanied by a decrease in the same row or in one of the following two or three rows so that the established number of stitches is maintained. Several decreases can accompany yarn overs; the method used will alter the appearance of the work. One of the most common is *k2tog* (knit 2 together), which is a right-slanting decrease. If your pattern calls for just one type of decrease, it is usually *k2tog*. *Ssk* (slip, slip, knit), *sl, kl, psso* (slip 1, knit 1, pass slipped stitch over), and *k2tog tbl* (knit 2 together through back loop) are all left-slanting decreases. *Ssk* means to slip two stitches one at a time knitwise onto the right needle, then to insert the tip of the left needle into the fronts of the two stitches and knit them together. This is the neatest of the left-slanting decreases and the one that most nearly matches the right-slanting *k2tog* decrease for a symmetrical decrease on either side of a central stitch. It can be used any time *sl, k1, psso* is called for.

When executing a yarn over followed by an *s1, k1, psso* decrease, make sure you pass the slipped stitch, not the yarn over, over the knit stitch. Slipping the yarn over is an easy error to make.

Another form of yarn over used in pattern stitches is an elongated stitch. This stitch is made when the yarn is wrapped two or more times around the needle. The yarn overs are dropped in the following row to create a long stitch. The instructions for this stitch are *y2on, y4on* (wrap yarn two times, or four times, around needle), or *OO, OOO* (wrap the yarn once for each *O*). The instruction to drop the yarn overs is *drop yo* or *drop wf*. For an elongated stitch, the yarn should be wrapped as for a regular yarn over, based on the stitches that precede and follow it. □

Shirley W. MacNulty is a knitting designer and instructor in St. Mary's City, MD.

From *Threads* magazine (April 1987) 10:38-39

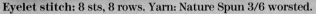

Eyelet stitch: 8 sts, 8 rows. Yarn: Nature Spun 3/6 worsted.

Row 1: Purl.
Row 2: K3, yo, ssk, k3.
Row 3: Purl.
Row 4: K1, k2tog, yo, k1, yo, ssk, k2.
Row 5: Purl.
Row 6: Repeat row 2.
Row 7: Purl.
Row 8: Knit.

Yarn-over increase: Yarn-over increases are commonly used in raglan sweaters worked from the top. In this double increase, the stitch in which the increases are made will be the "seam" stitch. Always work the k1, yo, k1 directly above the yo of the previous rows. Yarn: Paton's Beehive Double Knitting by Susan Bates.

Row 1—Work to position of seam stitch; k1, yo, k1 all in next stitch; work across row.
Row 2 and all wrong-side rows: Purl.
Row 3 and all right-side rows: Work to seam stitch (yo from previous right-side row); k1, yo, k1 all in next (seam) stitch; work across row.

Photo by Michele Russell

Yarn over between two knit stitches
yo, o, yf, wf, yfon, wfon

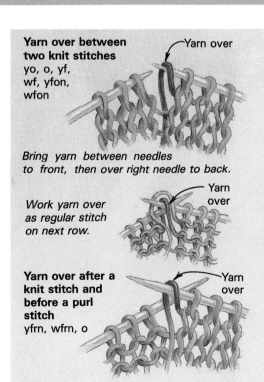

Bring yarn between needles to front, then over right needle to back.

Work yarn over as regular stitch on next row.

Yarn over after a knit stitch and before a purl stitch
yfrn, wfrn, o

Bring yarn between needles to front, around right needle to back, and between needles again to front.

Yarn over between two purl stitches
yrn, wrn, o

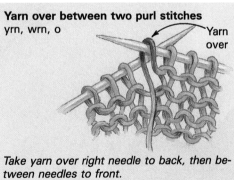

Take yarn over right needle to back, then between needles to front.

Yarn over after a purl stitch and before a knit stitch
yon, won, o

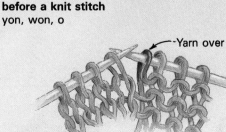

Take yarn over right needle to back.

Yarn over before first knit stitch

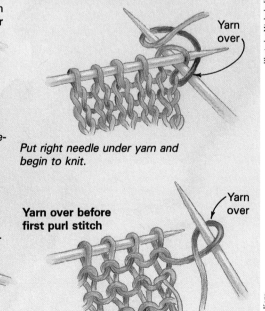

Put right needle under yarn and begin to knit.

Yarn over before first purl stitch

Put right needle under yarn, take yarn over right needle to back, and then bring yarn between needles to front.

Illustration by Mark Kara

Textured Knitting on Circular Needles

Convert wrong-side rows to their right-side equivalents and knit around

by Marilyn Moss

Circular knitting needles have many advantages. Probably the main reason people love working in the round is that they have fewer seams to sew up after they finish knitting, but there are other good reasons. It's harder for a child to grab a circular needle than a straight one and run off with it. Also, if you knit while in the passenger seat of a small car, a circular needle doesn't keep jabbing the car door or driver.

When I began searching for textured-knit directions written for circular needles, I discovered that there are precious few. However, with a little ingenuity, you can convert directions for straight-needle patterns to circular-knitting directions.

Preparing the pattern for conversion—Before converting a pattern, determine if the odd- or even-numbered rows are on the right side. Make a swatch on straight needles. This will also help when you start your conversions, since you'll be able to relate the actual knitting to the printed instructions.

Write down every step in this process, and begin by copying the original directions, one row per line and only one repeat of the pattern. Be sure to write down the "end whatever" part of the directions, as you would if you were knitting only one repeat of the pattern. Although the logical place to note the beginning and end of a pattern repeat might seem to be between the asterisks, they aren't always placed at the same point from one row to the next in the pattern, so don't jump to conclusions about how the pattern works yet.

Next, recopy the right-side rows from left to right, just as they appear in the original instructions. But write down the wrong-side rows from right to left, copying in the

Marilyn Moss knits seamless garments with complicated-looking textured-stitch patterns in the round. She translates wrong-side pattern directions to their right-side equivalents. (Photo by Michele Russell Slavinsky)

reverse order. Begin with the "end whatever" stitches. Then draw arrows from each stitch on a lower row to the stitch in the row above into which it gets worked, and circle the "end whatever" stitches. These are the same as the "plus y" stitches added to any pattern multiple. The conversion example below illustrates this process clearly. Rewriting the wrong-side rows and drawing the arrows may seem like a lot of extra work, but it cuts down immensely on the confusion that might arise when you're making the conversions. The only time I don't make this diagram is when all of the wrong-side rows are knit or purl stitches in very obvious places, such as the purl wrong side on a cable stitch.

Converting the pattern—After you know which is the right side of your pattern and which stitches get worked into which other stitches, you're ready to begin the conversion process. If you're planning to use the pattern completely around the garment, you must change "multiple of x plus y" to "multiple of x plus nothing." The "plus y" stitches are for a border on each side of the pattern, so when you knit in the round, you don't want them. When preparing your diagram, make sure that you mark the "plus y" or "end" stitches so they'll be easy to eliminate later. If you're planning to use the pattern as a vertical section on the garment, you'll probably want to include the border areas to set one pattern off from another.

As you write out the new directions, the right-side rows remain the same, minus the "plus y" stitches, if you've decided to omit them. You can begin your directions at any point within the pattern, but if you start with a solid area, you'll avoid awkward, lacy stitches at your change-of-round point. Just don't omit any of the pattern stitches. Refer to the conversion chart on page 32 to get the right-side equivalent for each wrong-side stitch. Simply substitute the equivalents in the same order that you've written the wrong-side directions.

When you've completed your conversions, you'll need to work a gauge swatch. Knitting done in the round, only on the right side, results in a slightly different gauge than knitting worked back and forth on both sides. You can use double-pointed needles to make a small cylindrical swatch. Three repeats of the pattern often work well, since you'll have complete patterns on each needle. The disadvantage of a cylindrical swatch is that it may be difficult to measure accurately unless you put more repeats on each needle.

Making a flat swatch on circular needles is quicker and more reliable when I use this method: Cast on a sufficient number of stitches, and knit one row to give yourself a firm base. Include the "plus y" border stitches for an edge on this flat swatch, even if you won't be using them in your garment. Then work the first "round" of your new pattern directions. At the end of the round, cut the yarn and slide the work around to the other end of the needle to start the next "round." Each "round" begins with the same stitch, and you always have the right side of the knit fabric facing you. To reduce the number of cut threads, pull out enough yarn to work the second "round" and other even-numbered "rounds" from the middle of the strand toward the tail. Then, when you push the swatch around to the other side of the needle, work the third "round" and other odd-numbered "rounds" from the middle of the strand (where you began the previous "round") toward the ball. Cut the yarn at the end of each odd-numbered "round." This leaves all loose ends on the same edge of the work. If necessary, adjust your gauge by changing the needle size so unbroken patterns go around your garment's circumference.

Knitting the garment—Once you've worked out the conversions and gauge, you're ready to begin your garment. This technique is good for skirts, dresses, and sweaters. You can design your own sweater in the round

---

Steps in conversion

First copy repeat and "end" of pattern.	*Next, invert wrong-side rows, writing directions from right to left, and draw arrows to show how stitches are related. Circle "plus y" or "end" sts.*	*Translate wrong-side rows to right-side equivalents, using chart on p. 66, and eliminate "plus y" or "end" stitches.*
Multiple of 7 sts + 2		
Row 1 (right side): *P2, k3, k2tog, yo*, end p2.	**Row 1:** P2, k3, k2tog, yo, p2.	**Rnd 1:** P2, k3, k2tog, yo.
Row 2: *K2, p1, yo, p2tog, p2*, end k2.	**Row 2:** K2, p2, p2tog, yo, p1, k2.	**Rnd 2:** P2, k2, k2tog, yo, k1.
Row 3: *P2, k1, k2tog, yo, k2*, end p2.	**Row 3:** P2, k1, k2tog, yo, k2, p2.	**Rnd 3:** P2, k1, k2tog, yo, k2.
Row 4: *K2, p3, yo, p2tog*, end k2.	**Row 4:** K2, p2tog, yo, p3, k2.	**Rnd 4:** P2, k2tog, yo, k3.
Row 5: *P2, k5*, end p2.	**Row 5:** P2, k5, p2.	**Rnd 5:** P2, k5.
Row 6: *K2, p5*, end k2.	**Row 6:** K2, p5, k2.	**Rnd 6:** P2, k5.

Conversion chart

Wrong-side stitches	Right-side equivalents
P (purl).	K (knit).
K (knit).	P (purl).
Pb (purl in back).	Kb (knit in back).
Kb (knit in back).	Pb (purl in back).
Increases	
P into back and front.	K into front and back.
P into front and back.	K into back and front.
K into back and front.	P into front and back.
K into front and back.	P into back and front.
Yo (yarnover).	Yo (yarnover).
Decreases	
P2tog.	K2tog.
P2togb.	Sl k psso (slip, knit, pass slip st over), or work SSK (slip, slip, knit 2 slip sts together).
K2tog.	P2tog.
K2togb.	P2togb.
Sl k psso.	P2togb.
P3tog.	K3tog.
K3tog.	P3tog.
P2tog pnso (pass next st over). *Work:* P2tog, sl next st to RH needle k-wise, replace on LH needle in new orientation, replace p2tog on LH needle, pass sl st on LH needle over p2tog, transfer p2tog back to RH needle.	Sl k2tog psso.
Sl k2tog psso.	P2tog pnso.
Twist stitches	
Cross L, knit (skip 1st st, k 2nd st in back, k skipped st in front, slip both sts tog to RH needle). *Alternative method:* Skip 1st st and k 2nd st in back, k2togb skipped st and 2nd st, slip both sts to RH needle tog.	Cross L, purled.
Cross L, purled.	Cross L, knit.
Cross R, knit (skip 1st st, k 2nd st in front, k skipped st in front, slip both sts tog to RH needle). *Alternative method:* K2tog, leaving sts on LH needle; insert RH needle from front between 2 sts and k 1st st again; sl both sts from needle tog.	Cross R, purled.
Cross R, purled.	Cross R, knit.

Moss checks her pattern conversion by comparing the original swatch (left) knit back and forth with the new one (right) knit in the round. Her flat-swatch technique allows her to knit only on the right side and keeps all the cut ends on one edge.

by using Elizabeth Zimmermann's percentage system (see pages 33-35), Jean Dickinson's method for a top-down raglan (pages 40-41), or B. Borssuck's technique for a designer raglan (pages 42-43). Raglan sweaters are the easiest to knit completely in the round because all the parts—yoke, sleeves, and body—lend themselves to this type of construction.

You can convert a straight-needle pattern to circular knitting by working the front and back together, minus the edge stitches, up to the armholes. You can work shaping with a knit-in steek and continue to knit in the round, or you can redesign the upper body with raglan shaping. Work the body up to the underarms; then knit each sleeve up to the underarm. You may have to lengthen or shorten the body a little so that it ends at the same place on the pattern as the sleeves. Place the completed parts on stitch holders until you're ready to connect the sleeves to the body.

You can avoid seams entirely by binding off the sleeve and body underarm stitches together. Work one round more of the pattern on the sleeves than on the body. When you get to the point in your garment body where you would normally bind off for the underarm, bind those stitches off together with the corresponding sleeve stitches. On the next round, knit in the remaining sleeve stitches from their holders. If you decide that you would rather work regular bind-offs and sew the underarm seams later, work the sleeves and the body to the same pattern round.

To shape a round neckline, figure out how many inches higher than the front neck you want the back neck to be, and convert this number to rounds. When you're one round short of where you want the front-neck edge to end, begin shaping. Work from the beginning of your round across the front-neck edge for as many stitches as rounds you'll be doing. Turn and slip the first stitch, and work the remaining front-neck edge stitches. Continue across the back, and work the same number of front-neck edge stitches on the other side. Turn and slip the first stitch. Continue short-rowing in this way, working 1 st fewer on each side of the front-neck edge, turning and slipping the edge stitch. Remember that when you knit short rows, every other row will be wrong-side stitches, so you may need to consult the original pattern. After you've worked the number of short rows you calculated, the back will be the desired number of inches higher than the center front, with the front-neck edges curved down to the center. Knit one complete round. Then finish the neck edge with ribbing or whatever you desire. □

Marilyn Moss of Lincoln, NE, says that this technique has given her a new sense of freedom and innovation, and she urges continued experimentation.

Knitting a Seamless Sweater

It's easy with circular needles

by Elizabeth Zimmermann

the circular needle is a wondrous implement, a direct descendant of the four, and sometimes five, needles used for making prehistoric socks and stockings (the earliest known hand knits). Like four needles, it enables one to avoid those two bugbears of so many knitters, sewing up and purling. With it, one achieves that miracle, a seamless garment, possible only in knitted fabric.

Circular needles come in several lengths. I use a 24-in. needle for garment bodies, skirts, blankets, and afghans, and a 16-in. needle for sleeves, hats, and baby sweaters. Cuffs and socks are more easily made on four needles or on the dinky 11½-in. needles that have reappeared on the market after a sad lapse of many years. All very well, you say, circular bodies and sleeves make sense, but they still must be sewn together.

Surprise. They don't.

When both sleeves and body have been worked to the wanted length to the underarms, the pieces can be assembled on the body's 24-in. needle and continued in the round to the neck; all that's left to sew up are the underarms. My daughter Meg and I have devised, or revised, shoulder-shaping methods over the past 20 years, and some of them are pretty involved. The raglan, however, is one of the simplest and best-looking, and this is the one I will give you.

Start off with a swatchcap (a swatch the size of a cap) to measure your gauge. With the wool you have chosen for your sweater, cast on about 80 sts on a 16-in. circular needle of the size you estimate will give you the fabric you want. (Worsted weight uses about a size 5 or size 6 needle for 4 sts to the inch, while a bulky handspun may need a size 10½ needle to get 2½ sts to the inch.) Join, being careful not to twist the stitches on the needle, and work around for an inch or so in k2, p2 rib. If you are anxious to start your sweater, you may skip the k2, p2 rib and launch right into the stitch you want for your sweater. Whether it be plain stocking stitch, two-color pattern knitting, Aran, or texture stitch, the stitch you knit is a factor in determining your gauge.

After 3 in. to 4 in. of knitting, pull the needle out. Lay the swatch flat, and puff at it gently with a steam iron—don't iron it, just puff. Get out a stiff ruler (measuring tapes are notoriously unreliable) and place two pins vertically in the knitted fabric, exactly 4 in. apart. Now honestly count the exact number of stitches (even the fractions of a stitch, if necessary) between the pins. Divide the number of stitches by 4. You guessed it. The result is your personal and private gauge of stitches to 1 in., with this wool and this size needle. At this point you may either finish your cap or, armed with the knowledge of your gauge, charge into the seamless sweater.

The body—Use one of the recipient's favorite-fitting sweaters to determine size information. Lay the sweater out flat and measure it across the chest. Double the number of inches, and you have the circumference of the sweater. Multiply this number by your gauge, and you have the key number of stitches, or K, for your sweater body.

All sweater measurements are percentages of this number, thus the term Elizabeth's Percentage System (EPS) for this method of designing sweaters. For example, let's say we're knitting a sweater 40 in. in circumference, and our gauge is 5 sts/in. Our K number is 40 x 5, or 200 sts.

I will, however, start by casting on 10% fewer than K, or 180 sts, because the lower edge of the sweater is to be in k2, p2 rib, which should be close-fitting. If the recipient is very slim-hipped, I might go to a smaller size needle for the ribbing. If subtracting 10% from K leaves you with a number of stitches not divisible by 4, add or subtract one or two stitches to make it so. Now your calculations are all but done, and you can sail into the knitting. On the 24-in. needle, cast on K less 10%. Check carefully to see that the stitches are not twisted on the needle, join, and work around in k2, p2 rib.

Rib for as long as you can stand it—at least 4 in. to 5 in. for an elastic lower edge. Now change to your pattern stitch. Increase to 100% of K in the first round after the ribbing by increasing 1 st every 9 sts (k9, m[make]1). Mark the sweater's exact side "seams" with safety pins and start working up the body. You can add elegant refinements, such as short rows across the back, slight side shaping, and phony seams as you work the body; my third book, *Knitting Workshop*, gives instructions for doing these things. After you have worked up the body for 5 in. or 6 in., slip the work off the needle, lay it out as flat and unstretched as possible, and measure it across to determine if your gauge is accurate. If your sweater is an inch or two too large, don't worry, as sweaters should be loose, and you can make it slightly narrower by blocking it longer. If your sweater is too narrow, increase the necessary number of stitches

Double increase for sleeve

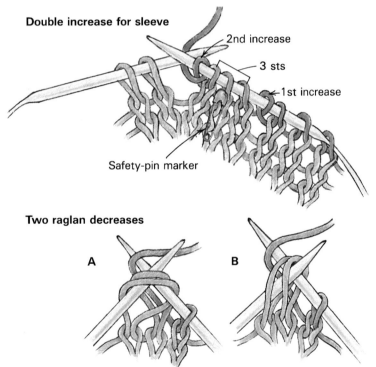

Two raglan decreases

*A. Knit 2 together (k2tog). K1. **B.** Slip, slip, knit (ssk): Slip 2 sts separately knitwise, insert tip of left needle into them, and knit together.*

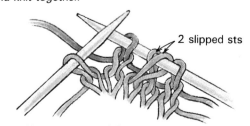

Slip 2 together (sl2tog) knitwise; k1; pass 2 slipped stitches over (p2sso).

Elizabeth's percentage system for yoke sweaters

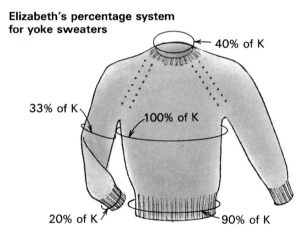

K = number of stitches in body circumference.

Joining sleeves and body
With 24-in. needle, knit across front of sweater, around one sleeve, across sweater back, and around other sleeve.

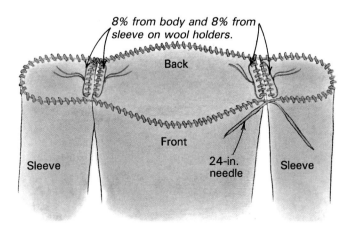

evenly on either side of the marked side stitches. Continue knitting, and when the body is long enough to the underarm, set it aside and start the sleeves.

Sleeves—Cast on 20% of K (in our example 40 sts) on an 11½-in. circular needle (or on 4 needles), and rib perhaps 50 rounds for a turned-back cuff. Change to stocking stitch (or to your pattern stitch), and mark the center of the first 3 sts with a safety pin. Using any method you like, increase 1 st on each side of the 3 sts every 5th round, to gradually widen the sleeve to the upper arm. I prefer to make a firm backward loop over the right needle before and after the 3 sts. I twist each loop in opposite directions (see drawing at top left, facing page), but you don't have to. Continue increasing 2 sts every 5th round, changing to the 16-in. needle when there are enough stitches to go around it, until you have 33% of K (66 sts in our example). Work straight to the wanted length of the underarm.

Make the other sleeve.

Assembly—Now comes the most fascinating part of the whole procedure. At each underarm of body and sleeves, place 8% of K on pieces of yarn, to wait. These under-arm stitches will be woven together later, forming seamless underarms.

With the 24-in. needle, knit across the front of the body to the 8%s at one underarm. Now knit the sleeve off its 16-in. needle onto the 24-in. needle. Work across the back until you bump into the other 8%s, and knit the other sleeve onto the needle. All body and sleeve stitches, except the four 8%s at the underarms, are now on the 24-in. needle (see drawing at bottom right, facing page). Work straight for 1 in. to 1½ in. With safety pins, mark the four points where body and sleeves meet.

Now begin the raglan shaping. Work a double decrease (decrease 1 st on each side of the marked stitches every 2nd round), making sure the center stitch remains constant. Use any double decrease you like. I like k2tog, k1, ssk (slip, slip, knit) or sl2tog knitwise, k1, p2sso (pass 2 slipped stitches over), shown in the photos below and the drawings on the facing page. When the sleeve stitches have been reduced to 5% of K (10 sts in our example), it is time to shape the back of the neck.

Place the neck-front stitches on a piece of wool, except for 2½% of K (half of the remaining sleeve stitches, or 5 sts in our example) at either side of the front. These 2½%s will be decreased away on successive back-and-forth rows, forming vertical selvages at each side. As you knit and purl back these rows, continue the raglan decreases every 2nd row. When the sleeves and the 2½%s at the neck-front edges have been used up, the end is near.

Knit up the neck-side selvage stitches, knit the neck-front stitches from the piece of wool back onto the needle, and you are ready to continue around on all stitches in k2, p2 rib for a good inch. (You may want to switch back to the 16-in. needle for this.) The neck opening will be roughly 40% of K (80 sts in our example). Cast off loosely in k2, p2. It is a good idea to ease elastic thread through the inside of the neck to keep it snug. Weave (or Kitchener-stitch) the underarms, darn in all ends, and wear with pride.

Now listen: This is knitting, which is by nature elastic. The percentages I've given are guidelines; one or two stitches too many or too few don't matter. Good knitting. □

Elizabeth Zimmermann is the author of Knitting Without Tears, Knitter's Almanac *and* Knitting Workshop, *which is also on VHS videotape. All are available from Schoolhouse Press, 6899 Cary Bluff, Pittsville, WI 54466.*

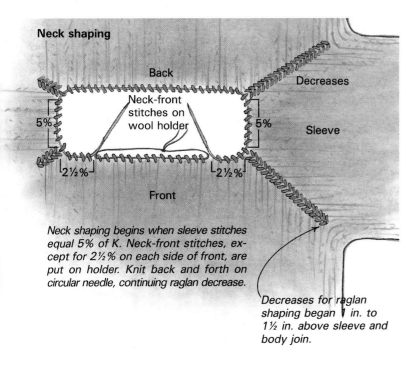

Neck shaping

Back

Neck-front stitches on wool holder

Decreases

Sleeve

5%

5%

2½%

2½%

Front

Neck shaping begins when sleeve stitches equal 5% of K. Neck-front stitches, except for 2½% on each side of front, are put on holder. Knit back and forth on circular needle, continuing raglan decrease.

Decreases for raglan shaping began 1 in. to 1½ in. above sleeve and body join.

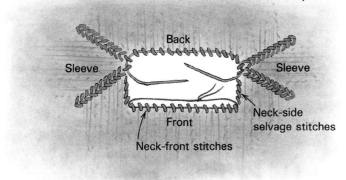

When sleeve stitches have been used up, pick up neck-side selvage stitches and neck-front stitches, and knit around in k2, p2.

Back

Sleeve

Sleeve

Front

Neck-side selvage stitches

Neck-front stitches

Two double decreases for raglan shaping: K2tog, k1, ssk (top); sl2tog knitwise, k1, p2sso (bottom).

Knitting for Kids
Versatile designs

by Judith Eckhardt Greer

Judith Greer likes the challenge of designing clothes for kids. Clockwise from left: Blue sweater featuring kangaroo pouch with inner pocket; yellow cable sweater with attached gnome hat; girl's version of multicolor vest with hood framed by picot ruffle; and baby's "boiler suit" with practical stretch velour inserts. (Photo by Bobbie Sue Palmer)

We sometimes assume—incorrectly—that "small" means "easy." But, when designing knits for children, we must take two hard facts into account: Kids grow, and kids play. If we forget these realities, our investment in time and materials can be wasted. But these facts can also serve as challenges to inspire imaginative and sophisticated knitting solutions.

Creative approaches

There are many ways to build flexibility of size and appearance into a child's sweater. While it is important to design a sweater that will fit one child for several years, it is also wise to think of ways to make it suitable for others. Since children lose and damage clothing, these facts should also be considered in the design.

Designing for growth—The first and most obvious way to handle growth is to make the garment expandable. Stretchability is one of the beauties of knitting, and length usually becomes a problem before width. Wrists and belly buttons are often visible long before a child outgrows a sweater sideways. Make your ribbing extra long at the waist and wrist; a flat, inconspicuous seam, like mattress stitch or circular knitting, which has no seams, will enable you to turn cuffs up in the beginning and down later. If the child is available for frequent fittings, a "top-down" design (see page 40) is a good idea, as it will allow you to unravel and reknit a longer waist and wrist later.

Tucks are also an option. You can make widthwise tucks by knitting twice into several evenly spaced stitches, which creates vertical increase stripes. The tuck is formed when you pull the stripe closed with embroidery—anything from a cross stitch to elaborate smockings and bullion knots, in matching or contrasting yarn. Lengthwise tucks are even easier to make. Knit extra rows in matching or contrasting yarn (see blue sweater, facing page). After you've assembled the sweater, pull the tucks together with an overhand stitch (top-left drawing, page 38). When more length or width is needed, you can release them for another season of wear and additional decoration. Check the chart at right to determine how much growth allowance you might want to add, and where.

Another way of dealing with growth is to make the item versatile as a hand-me-down. Hand-me-downs have two basic problems, though: The second child sometimes feels the item is a castoff, and the potential recipient is often the opposite sex.

A solution to both problems is to design the item to be "renewable" before it is passed on. Changing the buttons can help considerably to make a sweater seem new again, as can the addition of embroideries, such as a duplicate-stitch monogram or "re-tucked" growth tucks. You can do a lot to change the appearance of a garment by removing, adding, or altering edgings and borders, especially lace. Buttonholes should be worked in both front edges of a cardigan so neither sex will feel slighted. In a placket sweater, you can leave the bottom of the inner placket edge free to make the button transition easier, as I did in the girl's ski vest on the facing page.

But in the end, psychology is all, and hand-me-downs should be approached as if it is a privilege to wear an older child's clothes. Considering this, it's fun to give the item to both children in the beginning, with a special note to the younger one on what changes will be made for him or her.

Withstanding hard play—Children are active, heedless, and headlong. They are especially tough on their outerwear, which handknits tend to be. They get so involved in games and activities that they are careless of what is happening to their clothes. They will snatch off a mitten to pick up something interesting, tuck a hat or scarf into a back pocket, and take off a cardigan when the game gets heated. Thus, your designs should take potential loss and damage into account.

Consider giving mittens in sets of three—or even five! Attaching them to strings for threading through coat sleeves is an option, but it's frequently resisted. Those who disdain mittens are often charmed by a kangaroo-pouch pocket (see blue sweater, facing page) to put their hands into while they're waiting to catch the ball.

Another interesting approach is to make sleeve cuffs into mittens that can be turned back when not in use (center-left drawing, page 38). Cuff mittens are easiest to work round from the top down. Continue the cuff to the base of the thumb. For larger sizes, you'll probably want to add a few stitches for a thumb gusset. Put the thumb stitches on a holder and continue knitting until you reach the fingertips. Bind off half the stitches, and work the other half back and forth to form a flap 2 or 3 in. long. Fold it back on itself so both sides of the mitten are the same length, and stitch the edges to the sides of the hand. Fold the flap over the fingertips to close the mitten. You can sew Velcro strips on the flap, hand, and cuff for extra security. To complete the thumb, work the stitches on the holder, picking up others as needed.

Make hoods to keep hats from being lost, or knit hats into the collar, like the gnome hat on the yellow sweater, facing page. Like the cuff mitten, this hat is a continuation of the collar ribbing. Bind off a few stitches at the collar's front edges. Then cast on additional stitches for the front sides of the hat. For a firm, rolled hem, add 3 or 4 more stitches on the front sides and work them in stockinette. Work the hat stitches to 3 or 4 in. from the top of the head, and finish the hat in stockinette. Use Kitchener stitch to graft the top seam together (top-right drawing, page 38). Then roll the hem, and seam it with mattress stitch (see the articles on pages 108-110).

To knit the hood ties, pick up the cast-on stitches for the hat front, excluding the hemstitches, and work them in stockinette. For a strong tubular edge, use the technique for switching from stockinette fabric to a tube, described in the article on pages 24-25, to begin the flap. Then knit the flaps in stockinette. Decrease on the back edge, keeping the front edge straight, to the desired width for the ties. Work them in seed stitch so they'll stay flat and tied.

Potential damage can be minimized if you design for easy repair, particularly if you knit the garment from the neck down to make the vulnerable cuffs and elbows easy to replace. You can reinforce elbows by adding knit or woven material patches or cross-stitch embroidery, or more interestingly, by working a doubled-yarn stripe or woven color pattern at elbow level. A slip-stitch pattern is good, too, because it produces a double-knit fabric.

Measurements for children's sweaters

	6 mo.	12 mo.	2 yr.	3 yr.	4 yr.	5 yr.	6 yr.	7 yr.	8 yr.	10 yr.	12 yr.
Chest	to 20*	to 22	21	22	23	24	25	26	27	28.5	30
Waist	19	20	20	20.5	21	21.5	22	22.5	23	24	25
Hip	20	21	22	23	24	25	26	27	28	30	32
Back waist length	7	7.5	8.5	9	9.5	10	10.5	11.5	12.5	14	15
Across back	7.75	8.25	8.75	9.25	9.5	9.75	10.25	10.75	11	11.5	12
Shoulder	2.25	2.5	2.75	3	3	3	3.5	3.5	3.5	3.75	4
Back neck	3.25	3.25	3.25	3.25	3.5	3.5	3.5	3.75	3.75	4	4
Underarm sleeve	6.5	7.5	8.5	9.5	10.5	11	11.5	12	12.5	13.5	15
Armhole depth	3.5	3.75	4.25	4.75	5.5	5.5	6	6	6.25	6.5	7
Upper-arm width	7	7.25	7.5	7.75	8	8.25	8.5	8.75	9	9.5	9.75
Wrist width	5	5	5.25	5.25	5.5	5.5	5.5	5.75	5.75	6	6
Head	15	16	17	18	18	18	18	18	18	18	18

*All measurements are in inches.

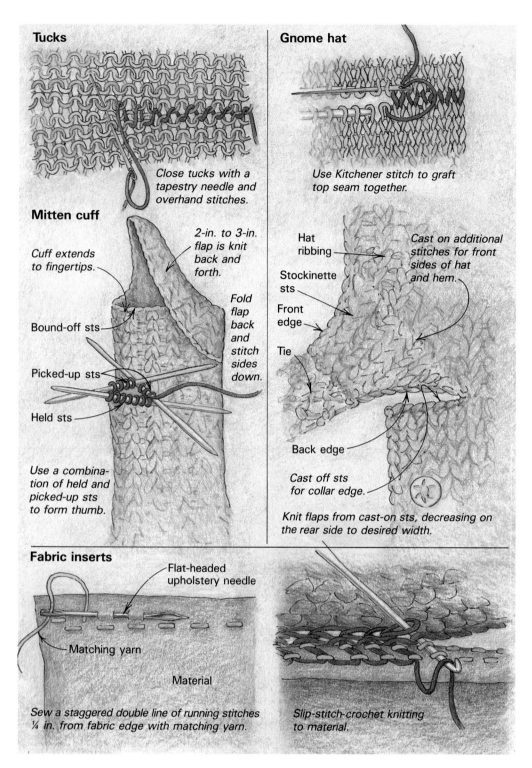

Tucks

Close tucks with a tapestry needle and overhand stitches.

Mitten cuff

Cuff extends to fingertips.

2-in. to 3-in. flap is knit back and forth.

Bound-off sts

Fold flap back and stitch sides down.

Picked-up sts

Held sts

Use a combination of held and picked-up sts to form thumb.

Gnome hat

Use Kitchener stitch to graft top seam together.

Hat ribbing

Cast on additional stitches for front sides of hat and hem.

Stockinette sts

Front edge

Tie

Back edge

Cast off sts for collar edge.

Knit flaps from cast-on sts, decreasing on the rear side to desired width.

Fabric inserts

Flat-headed upholstery needle

Matching yarn

Material

Sew a staggered double line of running stitches ¼ in. from fabric edge with matching yarn.

Slip-stitch-crochet knitting to material.

You can even attach knit pieces to sturdier cloth sections placed at strategic heavy-wear locations with a simple crochet stitch. If you want to insert fabric at the elbows or knees, bind off the knitting at those points. Knit the cuffs and lower arm or leg pieces separately and bind them off too. Prepare the fabric pieces by finishing the edges to prevent fraying. Then, using a flat-headed upholstery needle, sew a staggered double line of running stitches about ¼ in. from the edge with matching yarn, as shown in the bottom-left drawing above.

Use a crochet hook to slip-stitch the knitting to the material. Fold the material along the edge of the second line of stitches. Insert the crochet hook into the wrong side of the knit edge, then into the first stitch on the fold and the stitch diagonally below

it. Yarn over and draw the hook through all the stitches, as shown in the bottom-right drawing above. Repeat until the knitting and material are joined. You can detach material from the knitting by "zipping back" all the crochet loops or by cutting the running stitches if you want to replace the fabric with a larger or new piece. Sew the seams in the knitting and material separately for easy removal.

Buttonholes need to be firmly reinforced. Make them larger than necessary in the knitting, as the reinforcement will fill in the opening. Button attachments need to be very strong too. Make the button bands firm, perhaps in a double-twisted rib, to give good anchorage. Back the buttons with "mates" to help prevent them from ripping out and to provide for replacements later.

Pockets must also be sturdy, both in material and attachment. Knit fabrics are notorious for allowing tiny belongings to work their way out. One idea for preventing such loss is a doubled-fabric pocket (see drawings, facing page), one side in stockinette stitch, the other in garter or seed stitch.

To minimize the damage that dirt can cause, consider dark colors for bottom edges, particularly cuffs. Tweedy and textured yarns can also help hide dirt, but avoid loopy yarns that catch on desk hardware and fence nails. You might think about giving a set of matching "gauntlet-top" cuff covers with your sweater, to be worn during the grubbier activities, like learning to print.

Making it comfortable—Making kids' knits wearable is a delicate balance between providing enough room for movement and making clothes so big that they get in the way. They must be firmly put together and easy to get on and off. Avoid small, spherical shank buttons—they slip through buttonholes easily and are always coming unbuttoned. Novelty buttons shaped like ducks and stars can be cute but are often a pain to button or unbutton, especially when one is in a hurry, which children always are.

Kids also move so quickly from quiet to rough-and-tumble activities that they always seem to be either too hot or too cold in their clothes. The reason sleeveless ski-vest designs are popular with children is that they're ideal for retaining "core" body heat while allowing the active arms freedom and muscle cool-down. Layers are good, and the best layer combination is cotton inside and wool outside—perhaps a slim-ribbed cotton "long-john" sweater topped by a coordinating sweater-jacket in a loosely knit doubled chunky wool. The combination breathes, but the wool is surprisingly warm and light. An ensemble of ski vest and matching undersweater is also ideal.

Special notes for different ages

Although these general suggestions will help you design a practical and interesting sweater, you must also take into account special considerations for different age groups. Remember that children's tastes change almost as fast as their bodies grow.

Babies—Be exceedingly careful about buttons that can come off and get caught in little throats. Ribbons should be avoided, or at least be short and firmly attached. Instead, work with zippers, Velcro, or even snaps, which can be attached to ribbon strips and sewn into closure bands. Clothes with back fasteners are a hassle, since babies who can't sit up by themselves must be laid on their stomachs to be done up.

Ensembles are especially prized if they include everything. If you're working on a coat, also do a pair of leggings, a hat, and some thumbless mittens. Try balaclava-style hat designs to avoid the struggle of tying twisted cords under tiny chins. Overalls are good for crawlers if the knees are reinforced or designed for quick-and-easy repair (perhaps knit from the waist down or with a separate woven material section around the knee). This is the fastest growing age group, so include provision for growth or handing down.

Toddlers and potty trainers—Separates and "dress-myself" clothes are essential here. This is one place where simplicity can pay off. If you make fronts and backs the same, sweaters can't be put on backward. Stitch your color patterns after knitting, rather than letting the unworked yarn trail across the inside of sweaters to catch little hands and noses. Make armholes and necklines generous, perhaps by incorporating the "overlap shoulder" of baby underwear into the designs. Pants should be pull-ons. Zippers are much beloved by this age group, and Velcro fasteners are quick for kids and their adult dressers to manipulate.

Nursery-school kids and kindergarteners—Preschoolers love pockets, but they're hard on them. Pockets with flaps that fold down over valuable contents, perhaps with a Velcro fastening, are much admired. How about knitting a "safari jacket"? These kids are learning to button their clothes, and big, easily handled buttons are good choices. Thumbless mittens are not only warmer, but easier to make and replace with extras. Using inexpensive string, you can also quickly knit up some simple tubes that can be pulled on like socks over boots or shoes to help prevent slipping on ice.

Avoid putting young children's names visibly on their clothes. Even after safety talks, these young ones can be disarmed by strangers who "know their names."

Six- to eight-year olds—Personal taste begins to play a bigger role when kids reach the first grade. At this age, they love clothes that display their interests. Dinosaurs, tigers, and other creatures are often big hits. The offbeat is genuinely appreciated—this age group even enjoys such unlikely decorations as snakes and turtles or armadillos and skunks. You can delight a budding artist by knitting one of his or her own drawings into a sweater front or transferring it in duplicate stitch to a tabard-style vest.

Preteens—Sophistication sets in with a vengeance during the preteen years, and it becomes harder to determine what will appeal to a child. At this age, kids are more conformist—they like things that are at most just barely different from current trends—and they are very fussy. Considering this, perhaps the simplest thing to do is to teach them to knit for themselves. □

Judith Eckhardt Greer of Honolulu, HI, is a knitwear designer and political-science instructor. She is currently designing smocked knit-lace christening gowns.

Double-knit handwarmer with seed-stitch pocket

The handwarmer on the blue sweater on page 36 is a double-knit fabric flap that joins to the sweater body at top and bottom. Besides being warmer, double-knit fabric allows you to insert a seed-stitch pocket between the layers near the top of the double-knit section. To close the pocket, you can add a button flap. Although this pouch and pocket may seem like a lot of work, a child's delight will make it all worthwhile. Here's how you construct the handwarmer.

Picking up and knitting the handwarmer pouch—Knit the sweater front up to the place where the top of the handwarmer will be. Mark the stitches at the top of the ribbing that will be the bottom edges of the handwarmer. Using the same size needles, pull up a loop in the first marked stitch and yarn over; repeat to the last marked stitch and yarn over. Let's assume you have 40 sts. On the next row, knit the yarn overs and slip the pulled-up loops with yarn in front. Then knit the loops and slip the stitches, with yarn in front. This makes two layers of fabric on your needle. Repeat these two rows until the double knit is as high as you want the top of the pocket opening to be.

Making the pocket—Before you make the pocket, you have to separate the layers of double knit, as shown in the top drawing below. The pocket will be knit on the central group of stitches of the front layer. Put both layers of the side 10 sts on a holder. Alternately slip the next 10 sts of the front layer onto a

needle half as thick as the one you've been using, and slip the 10 sts of the back layer onto a holder. Then put both layers of the last 10 side sts on a third holder.

Since you're using much finer needles to knit the pocket, which is actually a flap that gets folded over later, you'll have a nice tight fabric. But you'll have to double the number of stitches so it will fit the opening in the looser knitting. Knit in the front and back of each loop on the first row. Then knit a seed-stitch flap twice as long as the desired depth of the pocket. On the last row, k2tog across.

Finishing the double knit—You're almost finished. Put the 10 sts from the first holder back on the larger needle. Then alternately slip 1 st from the pocket and 1 st from the middle holder onto the needle. Finally put the 10 sts on the third holder on the needle. Continue knitting double knit until the pouch is the same length as the front of the sweater. Weave the handwarmer stitches, two at a time, into the corresponding center-front stitches, and finish the sweater front.

Inserting the pocket and knitting the button flap—Sew the sides of the pocket together, leaving the top, where it joins the double knit, open. Invert it, and push it between the two layers of double knit. To knit the flap, pull up loops at the top of the double knit, as shown in the lower drawing. Start and end 2 sts past the pocket opening. Knit to the desired length in stockinette, and, if you like, work in a buttonhole. —*J.E.G.*

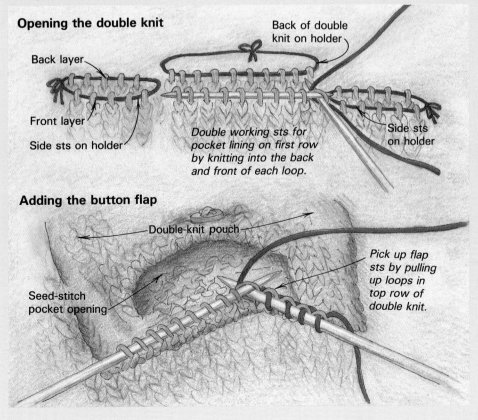

Opening the double knit

Back of double knit on holder

Back layer

Front layer

Side sts on holder

Double working sts for pocket lining on first row by knitting into the back and front of each loop.

Side sts on holder

Adding the button flap

Double-knit pouch

Pick up flap sts by pulling up loops in top row of double knit.

Seed-stitch pocket opening

The Magic Raglan
A sweater that almost knits itself

by Jean Dickinson

the top-down raglan sweater is an almost perfect pattern. It has no seams; requires almost no stitch or row counting; fits anyone; and is adjustable for growing children, insufficient yarn, or figure problems. It is made with circular needles and any yarn, its stripes always match, and it seems to knit itself after it is set up. Over 40 years ago I found the basic plan in Ida Riley Duncan's *The Complete Book of Progressive Knitting* (Liveright: 1966, 1961, 1940) and, with modifications, I've used it ever since.

The raglan starts at the neck and grows quickly in both length and width because you increase in each of eight increase points every other round until you reach the underarm. Since the sweater has a dropped front neck, you cast on the back, sleeves, and only two of the front-neck stitches. You work back and forth, adding front-neck stitches at each end and increasing in the increase stitches to the base of the neck. Then you cast on the center front-neck stitches, join the edges, and continue knitting in the round. At the underarm, you separate the sleeves from the sweater body. You knit each of these sections in the round and finish them with ribbing or an edging. Now all you have to do, besides burying the ends and steaming the sweater, is to finish the neck, which you may edge however you wish.

Getting started—You'll need two different color stitch markers and two sizes of circular needles appropriate for your yarn. For the body, use 16-in. and 27-in. lengths; for the neck and body ribbing, use the same lengths two sizes smaller. The lower portion of the sleeve requires 11-in. circular needles; the sleeve ribbing is made on a set of double-pointeds in the smaller size.

You'll also need some basic measurements. Measure the neck of the person for whom you're knitting, holding your tape measure snugly around the center of the neck. (A man's shirt-collar measurement would be correct.) The diagonal raglan measurement from the neck edge to the underarm is also required, as well as the body length of the sweater below the underarm, the sleeve length, and the wrist measurement.

Unless you're knitting for someone with unusual figure problems, the normal rate of increase from the neck measurement to the underarm will produce a comfortable-fitting sweater with just the right amount of ease. If the recipient has a large bust or rounded back, you'll probably need to work a few extra increases over several inches in the front or back section of the sweater.

To find the stitch gauge, knit a 4-in. x 4-in. swatch, and lay it flat to measure 2 in. of stitches several times. Don't disregard fractions of stitches. The gauge is half the number of stitches you count in 2 in.

Calculate the total neck stitches by multiplying the neck measurement by the stitch gauge. Don't worry that the sweater won't go over your head this way, because the design has a dropped front-neck edge.

Once you know the number of neck stitches, you must apportion them. The back takes one third of the total, and each sleeve has one fourth the number of back stitches. There are also eight increase stitches. Calculate the front stitches by adding the back, sleeve, and increase stitches and subtracting this number from the total neck stitches (see "Sample calculations," facing page). The front must always have more stitches than the back because of the lower neckline. If this is not the case—possible if your gauge is 4 sts/in. or less—move enough stitches from the back to the front to correct it.

To begin, sketch the neck with only one front stitch on each edge. Place the increase stitches at the beginning and end of each section (see top drawing, facing page), and indicate the number of stitches allotted each sleeve and the back neck.

Casting on—While you're casting the stitches onto the 16-in. circular needle, don't count the total stitches. Instead, count (aloud if possible) as you cast on:
- 1 front-neck st.
- Marker (use color A to separate front-neck sts from body of sweater as you add remaining front-neck sts).
- 1 inc st (for building left side of front).
- Marker (use color B for next 4 markers—to denote inc sts).
- 1 inc st (for building front of left sleeve).
- Sleeve sts.
- 1 inc st (for building back of left sleeve).

Jean Dickinson's miniature striped raglan sweater (above) is in perfect proportion, and the stripes match exactly.

From *Threads* magazine (April 1988) 16:28-29

- Marker.
- 1 inc st (for building left side of back).
- Back sts.
- 1 inc st (for building right side of back).
- Marker.
- 1 inc st (for building back of right sleeve).
- Sleeve sts.
- 1 inc st (for building front of right sleeve).
- Marker.
- 1 inc st (for building right front).
- Marker (use color A).
- 1 front-neck st.

Now if you count your stitches, you'll find that you have two more than the total for sleeves, back, and increase stitches. When you cast on like this, you're setting up each part of the sweater on the needle as well as in your mind. Invariably, if you count total stitches, you'll misplace the markers, forget an increase stitch, or leave out a whole section. After making hundreds of these sweaters, I still start: "One front-neck stitch, marker, one increase stitch, marker, one increase stitch. . . ."

Purl back and recheck your casting on and marker placement. The hardest part is over. As soon as you add the front-neck stitches, the sweater will just grow.

Planning the front neck—To figure out how to add the front-neck stitches for a round neck, divide the remaining number of front-neck stitches in half (for each side), then in half again. Increase one fourth by adding 1 st at each end of the knit rows, and cast on the other half all at once at the base of the neck (see bottom drawing).

Knitting—When you begin knitting, don't count to check your work; just look to see if you increased where you should have— before and after each increase marker. Work back and forth, knitting the right side— where all the increases are made—and purling the wrong side. Increase at the ends of each knit row and in each increase stitch on the knit rows until you've added the stitches along the front-neck edges. At the end of the next knit row, cast on the remaining neck stitches all at once, and connect the knitting to make it circular. Remove the two front-neck markers when you come to them, and knit the first circular row without increasing at the increase stitches.

You'll now increase at the markers every other round until you've reached the raglan measurement. When there are too many stitches on the 16-in. needle, knit onto the 27-in. needle.

After knitting to the length of the raglan, slip the sleeve stitches onto a stitch holder (I use a piece of yarn). Now, cast on up to 1 in. of stitches at the underarm and continue knitting around to the next sleeve. Place these sleeve stitches on a holder, cast on the same number of stitches as you did at the first underarm, and continue knitting.

To complete the body, continue knitting without increasing until you've reached the length you want. Do the ribbing on a circular needle two sizes smaller than the one you used for the body of the sweater. I prefer the elasticity of k2, p2 ribbing. To calculate the number of stitches in the ribbing, decide on the width you want, and multiply it by your gauge on the needles you used for the body. Subtract this number from the number of stitches you have, and decrease the difference evenly around. Remember that k2, p2 ribbing is a multiple of 4. Bind off, and only the sleeves remain.

Using the 16-in. circular needle, pick up a set of sleeve stitches from the stitch holder as well as the cast-on stitches at the underarm, and knit the length of the sleeve to the ribbing for a very full sleeve. For a tapered sleeve decrease gradually. Place a marker at the center of the underarm to mark the "seam," and decrease on each side of it every inch or so, starting 3 or 4 in. down the sleeve. To see if the sleeve is the right width, measure it and adjust your decreasing to achieve the taper you desire. You may also decrease stitches at the bottom of the sleeve before the ribbing. When the knitting gets too small for the 16-in. circular needle, switch to the 11-in. one. At the ribbing, decrease to the desired tightness and change to double-pointed needles two sizes smaller. Bind off, and knit the other sleeve to match.

For ribbing at the neck, pick up 1 st in each stitch across the top of the sleeves, back, and front; allow 3 sts for every 4 rows as you pick up along the sides of the front neck. Use a 16-in. circular needle or double-pointed needles in the smaller size. Bind off loosely, bury the yarn ends, steam or block the sweater, and you're finished.

The variations to this basic formula are endless. For starters, you can knit hems instead of ribbings, using the smaller needle and decreasing a few stitches to make it lie smooth. You can form a cable along the raglan edges if you move some of the neck stitches to between the increase markers. You'll get an open raglan seam if you use yarn overs as the increase stitches. For a cardigan, open the sweater down the front and knit it flat. The sweater can be striped, as shown in the photo on the facing page, or you can have complex color or texture patterns, to name just a few possibilities.□

Jean Dickinson has been knitting since she was five years old. Her aversion to following patterns, sewing seams, and finishing in general led her to teach for a time. Knitting is now simply her way of life.

Beginning the top-down raglan

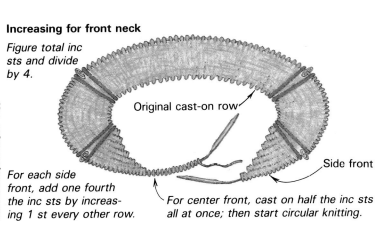

Inc markers
Inc sts

Cast on for back and sleeves

Sleeve (6 sts)
Back (25 sts)
Sleeve (6 sts)

Start front neck with only 1 st per side.

Front (1 st)
Front (1 st)

Increasing for front neck

Figure total inc sts and divide by 4.

Original cast-on row

Side front

For each side front, add one fourth the inc sts by increasing 1 st every other row.

For center front, cast on half the inc sts all at once; then start circular knitting.

Illustrations by Christopher Clapp

Sample calculations

Take measurements and figure stitch gauge:

- Neck: 15 in.
- Raglan: 12 in.
- Body: 13 in.
- Sleeve: 15 in.
- Gauge: 5 st/in.

Multiply neck measurement by gauge to get total neck sts: (15 x 5)=75. Then calculate the back and sleeves, as shown in the top drawing at left.

• Back neck: (⅓ x 75)=	25
• Sleeve: (¼ x 25)=	6
• Sleeve: (¼ x 25)=	6
Inc sts:	8
Total	45

For the front, subtract the total that you have just calculated from the number of neck sts: (75-45)=30. Remember that the front neck should have more sts than the back, even if you have to fudge a little bit. The front neck has 30 sts; but since you cast on 2 sts at the beginning, you need to add only 28 sts. Divide the 28 sts by 2 to give the 14 sts that are needed for each side. Dividing 14 again by 2 gives 7, to be added gradually at each side. So on the next 7 knit rows, add 1 st at the beginning of the row and 1 st at the end of the row and work the purl rows plain. At the end of the 8th knit row, cast on the remaining 14 sts and connect the knitting to make it circular. —*J.D.*

Designer Raglans

The difference between the back and sleeve widths determines the sweater's proportions

by B. Borssuck

the raglan is named for Lord Raglan (1788-1855), a British field marshal, who, having lost his sword arm at Waterloo, had special shirts and jackets made. Because of their comfort and classic lines, raglan-style slipovers, cardigans, and coats retain an enduring popularity. All have sleeves that extend up to the neckline of the garment, resulting in four slanted seamlines from underarm to neck opening.

When you're knitting a raglan garment, it's a great advantage to start from the top so you can test and perfect the fit at the shoulders and bust before you're committed to the width and length of the body. However, formulas based on percentages or fixed proportions of the body or neck opening (see the articles "Knitting a Seamless Sweater" on pp. 33-35 and "The Magic Raglan" on pp. 40-41) are rather inflexible, restricting the knitter to classic, relatively form-fitting shapes. These are acceptable for children's clothing and menswear, but current fashions for women feature looser armholes and wider sleeves, as in the popular Shaker-style slipovers.

Since I prefer raglan shaping but don't want to be restricted to classic styles, I've developed a technique that lets me work to *desired dimensions* rather than in *fixed proportions*. Thus, my raglans can incorporate the comfort of traditional sweaters with exciting new shapes and elegant designs.

Fundamentals of the design—When working a raglan from the top down, the knitter forms the four slanted seamlines typical of raglan-sleeve construction by making *one increase on each side of each seamline every other row*, a total of 8 sts every two rows.

The workmanship here is very important, as these seams are more obvious structural details than in other styles. Choice of method (samples on p. 46) depends on the design of the garment, but the cardinal rule for all paired increases and decreases must be observed: A right-hand or left-hand slant must be paired with its mirror image for a professional look.

Seamlines may be narrow or wide, plain or patterned, ribbed or cabled. Wide bands between the paired increase stitches also allow you to reapportion the body and sleeve stitches at the base of the armhole (photo, p. 45). You can divide the seamline stitches equally between sleeves and body or put most or all in the body or sleeves. Even if each seamline is only 4 sts wide, you can vary the size of the body by up to 16 sts and the width of each sleeve by 8 sts to further refine the proportions.

I always use markers at the four seamlines and next to front bandings. I find them essential, at least until the seamlines are well established and recognizable. I prefer to use a 5- or 6-in.-long piece of crochet or perle cotton. I double it over the knitting needle and slip it from the left-hand to the right-hand needle as I come to it. If you always slip it with the knitting yarn in front when you're knitting back and forth or with the yarn alternately in front and back when you're knitting in the round, the long tail will be woven over and under the bar between stitches. It serves as both a row-counting and stitch-counting aid.

Basic proportions—When planning a raglan, I decide on the width of the sleeves and back (in inches) and determine the gauge of my yarn. From these three figures I can plan any knit-from-the-top-raglan-sleeve project and be assured of desired fit even though different styles have different proportions. For example, I might want a topper for evening wear with short, rather tight, cap sleeves and a loosely fitted bodice; or I might prefer a tunic with the same bodice size but bat-wing sleeves (see drawings, p. 44). The difference in the width of the sleeves of these two garments will affect the way I apportion the stiches around the neck for the placement of the four seamlines. Clearly, the same percentage formula can't be used for both styles.

Instead, I apply this arithmetical truth about raglan-sleeve construction: *The back is always greater than the sleeve by the difference between the largest dimensions of back and sleeve.* With this rule, you can change a sleeve size—and thereby garment proportions—without changing body size. Thus, the formula for my designer raglans is:

$$Back = Sleeve + D,$$

where *D* is the difference between the desired circumference of the sleeve and the desired width of the back, each measured at the underarm seam. This formula can be applied on any row of the raglan-sleeve area, including the cast-on. For example, if the back of your sweater is to be 20 in. wide, and the circumference of the sleeve at the underarm will be 18 in., the difference is 2 in. The back will always be 2 in. wider than the sleeve while you're working the raglan seam area. *D* does not determine the size of the neck opening, nor is it affected by it. It just positions the seamlines, establishing the garment's proportions.

Theoretically, the number of stitches in the width of the back and front is the same, but you may want to make the front wider. And it's necessary to add extra stitches to the front for the lap-over or bandings of an open sweater or coat.

Planning the neckline—The formula works with any size and almost any style neckline—closed or open, square or boat, round or V—with or without collar, turtle, or cowl. And the finish may be a single row of crochet, a ribbed band, or a shawl collar. You can start with any number of stitches, but here's my game plan. I measure the length of the back of the neckline from the top of one shoulder to the top of the other; it's usually just a curved line measured right below the desired finish or pick-up edge. Then I multiply by the gauge. The actual cast-on will have more stitches, since it will extend from one front seamline, around the back to the other front seamline. It's better to have too many stitches than too few. I can always pull in or fill in the neck opening when finishing the sweater if it's too large. Starting with too few stitches or casting on with a tight, cordlike or inelastic edge can create greater problems, so I use

From *Threads* magazine (February 1989) 21:58-62

B. Borssuck knit both raglans according to a mathematical formula she devised. It allows her to vary sleeve and armhole styling as she desires rather than use a fixed-percentage system that produces only the classic shape. The dressy, boat-neck sweater had to be started in two pieces to provide a wide enough neck opening when the full sleeves were as wide as the back. (Photo by Robert Marsala)

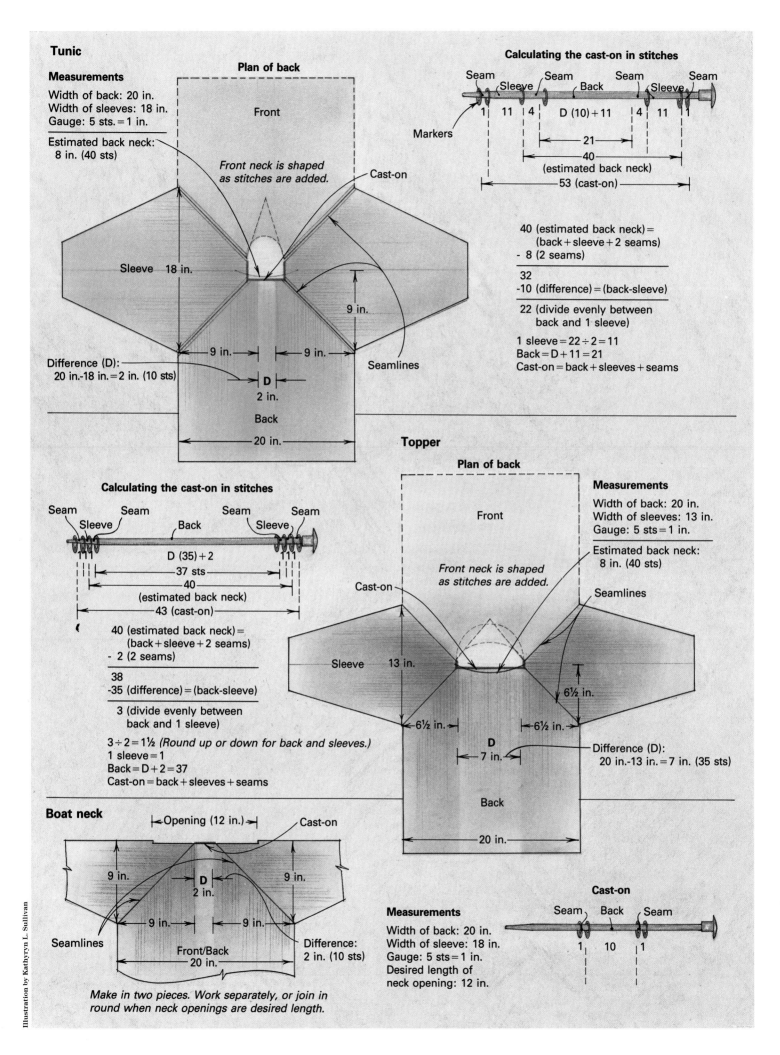

Tunic

Measurements

Width of back: 20 in.
Width of sleeves: 18 in.
Gauge: 5 sts. = 1 in.

Estimated back neck:
8 in. (40 sts)

Plan of back

Front

Front neck is shaped as stitches are added.

Cast-on

Sleeve 18 in.

9 in.

9 in. → ← 9 in.

Seamlines

Difference (D):
20 in.-18 in. = 2 in. (10 sts)

D
2 in.

Back

20 in.

Calculating the cast-on in stitches

Seam Sleeve Seam Back Seam Sleeve Seam

Markers

1 11 4 D (10) + 11 4 11 1

21

40
(estimated back neck)

53 (cast-on)

40 (estimated back neck) =
(back + sleeve + 2 seams)
- 8 (2 seams)

32
-10 (difference) = (back-sleeve)

22 (divide evenly between
back and 1 sleeve)

1 sleeve = 22 ÷ 2 = 11
Back = D + 11 = 21
Cast-on = back + sleeves + seams

Calculating the cast-on in stitches

Seam Sleeve Seam Back Seam Sleeve Seam

1 1 1 D (35) + 2 1 1 1

37 sts

40
(estimated back neck)

43 (cast-on)

40 (estimated back neck) =
(back + sleeve + 2 seams)
- 2 (2 seams)

38
-35 (difference) = (back-sleeve)

3 (divide evenly between
back and 1 sleeve)

3 ÷ 2 = 1½ (Round up or down for back and sleeves.)
1 sleeve = 1
Back = D + 2 = 37
Cast-on = back + sleeves + seams

Topper

Plan of back

Front

Front neck is shaped as stitches are added.

Cast-on

Seamlines

Sleeve 13 in.

6½ in.

← 6½ in. → ← 6½ in. →

D
7 in.

Difference (D):
20 in.-13 in. = 7 in. (35 sts)

Back

20 in.

Measurements

Width of back: 20 in.
Width of sleeves: 13 in.
Gauge: 5 sts = 1 in.

Estimated back neck:
8 in. (40 sts)

Boat neck

← Opening (12 in.) → Cast-on

9 in.

D
2 in.

9 in.

9 in. 9 in.

Seamlines

Front/Back
20 in.

Difference:
2 in. (10 sts)

Make in two pieces. Work separately, or join in round when neck openings are desired length.

Measurements

Width of back: 20 in.
Width of sleeve: 18 in.
Gauge: 5 sts = 1 in.
Desired length of
neck opening: 12 in.

Cast-on

Seam Back Seam

1 10 1

the thumb (single cast-on) or invisible (loops over scrap yarn) method. (See *Mary Thomas' Knitting Book*, Dover, 1972, pp. 60 and 66.) Both produce stretchy edges that are easily adjusted to the correct size in finishing.

Planning the cast-on—When I've decided on the design—yarn and gauge, the width of the back and sleeve in inches, and the style of the neckline—and I've estimated the number of stitches needed for the back of the neck from shoulder top to shoulder top, I'm ready to plan the cast-on.

By honoring the formula for the back (Back = Sleeve + D) at the cast-on stage, I can be sure my sleeves will be the width I planned when I work the body to the necessary width. The estimate for the back neck from shoulder top to shoulder top can be any number of stitches. It depends on the style only—anything from a close-fitting crewneck to a loose peasant-blouse effect. My system merely dictates how to divide those stitches into body, sleeves, and seamlines, according to the proportions I want. The rule of thumb for this formula is: The greater the *D* figure, the narrower the sleeves will be, and the higher the armhole.

Before you start to cast on, notice that the estimated number of stitches from shoulder top to shoulder top will give you the cast-on for one half-sleeve, a seamline, the back, another seamline, and another half-sleeve. In other words, these stitches will give you the back, two seamlines, and one sleeve. But you must include another sleeve in the cast-on. To figure out exactly how many stitches to add for the second sleeve: Subtract the number of seam stitches and *D* from the estimated number of back-neck stitches, and divide by 2, as shown in the drawings.

The design examples—tunic and topper—in the drawings on the facing page illustrate the arithmetic involved in positioning the seamlines. Make a line sketch, as shown by the knitting needles, and fill in the numbers as you calculate them. I always recheck my calculations with my design in mind. Deviation in the estimated number of stitches will affect only the size of the neck opening, not the sweater proportions. Small changes are sometimes needed and always allowable. If a stitch pattern is involved, the number of stitches for *D* must be a multiple of the pattern repeat so it will be centered.

Casting on—Now I can cast on according to my line sketch. I usually start and finish the cast-on with a single stitch for each of the two front seamlines. If more than 1 st is needed for the seamlines, as in the tunic, I add the stitches one at a time at each end of the knit rows. After I've added enough stitches for the seamlines, I place markers at each end of the row to flag the starting place of the cast-on for the front panel as

well as the beginning of the increases along both sides of the front seamlines.

The shape of the neck opening in your design will determine how the stitches for the garment front must be added. Most styles require an opening that's lower in front than in back. The stitches you originally cast on for the front halves of the sleeves begin the vertical drop. It's continued by the bias edge of the front seamlines if they're more than 1 st wide. Further single increases at the end of every other row will produce an angle suitable for a round neckline. Increases every 4th, 5th, or 6th row will result in a V neckline. Successively larger steps (1, 1, 2, 2, 3, 4) will produce an oval or rounded neckline. Or you can reverse the instructions in your favorite pattern book, substituting *increase* for *decrease*.

At some point for oval- and round-necked sweaters, you'll cast on all the remaining front-neck stitches. When you've completed the shaping of the opening, the number of stitches between the two front seams must equal or exceed the number of stitches between the two back seams on the same row. If more stitches are needed, cast on the required number across the center front. You may now work the garment in the round; or you can add extra stitches for bandings or lap-over for an open style, and you can continue to knit back and forth.

More about casting on—Designer raglans can be started with any style neckline if *D* has been determined and will be maintained. Instead of starting by casting on stitches for the back of the neck, you can complete a hood, a turtleneck or mock turtleneck, a turned-down collar, or bandings first. After you've cast on and knit the neck treatment, you're ready to begin the raglan apportioning. The estimated number of stitches that are needed across the back, from top of shoulder to top of shoulder, will come from the center-back portion of the collar stitches already on the needle. Place markers for seamlines, as previously discussed. You may pick up the remaining stitches from the collar at the end of short rows; or you can place the front collar stitches on a cord and seam them to the front of the neck later.

Boat-neck or shoulder-line button styles can also be made, but they must be started in two pieces—front and back—as would any style where the difference between back and sleeve is a figure close to zero (i.e., very full-sleeved styles). In these situations it isn't necessary to estimate the number of stitches from shoulder to shoulder. Start the back with the difference number (between two markers), plus 1 st at each end for the back seamlines (bottom drawing, facing page). If seamlines are to be more than 1 st wide, add them 1 st at a time at the ends of every other row, and add two more markers. Then add another stitch at each end of the row for the sleeves. After

this, increase on each side of the seamlines, but not at the ends of the rows.

Continue to work back and forth, increasing at the four markers until the length of the selvages and cast-on, measured from the first stitch on the needle along the cast-on stitches to the last stitch on needle, is the length of the desired opening across the back of the neck.

You can make the front a duplicate of the back, or you can make it wider by increasing the number of stitches in the difference. The number of rows in the two pieces must be equal if the pieces are joined and knit in the round. Or you can work them separately and seam them.

Parting of the ways—When the body of the garment reaches the desired size—in tunic and topper, 100 sts between the back markers—try it on for fit. Then shape the area at the bottom of the armhole to suit your design. For relatively narrow sleeves, I recommend the classic construction method of adding a few stitches for a short horizontal seam under the armpits so the sleeve will hug the underarm comfortably. For wide sleeves and a loose fit, you can work the seamlines to the bottom of the armhole and divide them between body and sleeves. Or, in the case of wide seamlines, you can decrease them in pairs with one of the methods suggested on p. 46 to give a bias line, like a gusset between sleeve and body.

There are no rules for making designer raglans. Just remember that four seamlines extend from the neckline to the underarm to divide the body from the sleeves and that on any row the difference between the number of stitches in the back and sleeve is the same figure as at their widest.

B. Borssuck, who wrote about a special ribbing in "Knitting Round on Straight Needles" on pp. 24-25, brings an engineer's eye to the art of knitting.

Borssuck's multicolor, striped V-neck pullover demonstrates an advantage of knitting from the top—exact color-stripe matching. Borssuck wanted high, tight armholes; she added fullness to the sleeves by putting all the seamline stitches into them and casting on another 3 sts in the underarm area.

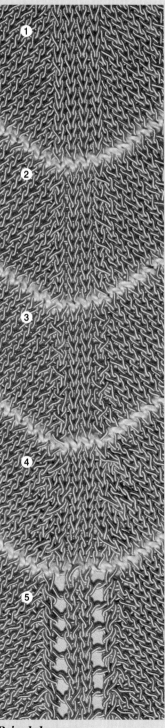

Paired increases and decreases

It is essential to use paired increases when you knit the shoulder area of a raglan from the top down and paired decreases for the sleeves from armhole to wrist. The complementary slants produced give the garment an elegant, professional look.

Paired increases—Although I worked all the paired increases shown here with a single-stitch seamline, you can work some with multiple seam stitches in a ribbing or cable pattern. All pairs shown are repeated every other row. Work one method at each of four seamlines for the eight increases of a raglan sweater.

1. Bar increase: Single or multiple seam stitches. Produces a small bar across the stockinette side. Increase (knit in front, knit in back) in the stitch before the seamline, and increase (knit in front, knit in back) in the only (or last) seamline stitch.

2. Double increase in single stitch (open). Knit, yo, knit in single seam stitch.

3. Double increase in single stitch (closed). Knit seam stitch, knit in seam stitch in row below, knit seam stitch.

4. Double increase in single stitch (invisible). Knit in seam stitch in row below, knit seam stitch, knit in seam stitch 2 rows below.

5. Yarnover increase: Single or multiple seam stitches. Yo, knit seam stitch(es), yo.

6. Raised method (visible): Single or multiple seam stitches. Work to first seam stitch. With LH needle pick up running thread between needles from front and knit from front. Knit seam stitch(es). With LH needle pick up running thread between needles after last seam stitch from front and knit from front.

7. Raised method (invisible): Single or multiple seam stitches. Work to seam stitch. With LH needle pick up running thread between needles from back, and knit from front (RH slant crossed stitch). Knit seam stitch(es). With LH needle, pick up running thread between needles after last seam stitch from front, and knit from back (LH slant crossed stitch).

8. Lifted method (invisible): Single or multiple seam stitches. Work to stitch before seam stitch. Knit in stitch below 1st st on LH needle. Knit stitch before seam stitch. Knit seam stitch(es). Knit stitch after seam stitch. Knit in stitch 2 rows below stitch on RH needle.

Paired decreases—Paired decreases are shown on each side of a 2-st seamline. You can also use them on edges to be seamed together: Put a left-side decrease near the beginning of the row and a right-side decrease near the end of the same row. In raglans knit from the bottom up, make paired decreases as shown.

1. Popular decrease: RH/LH slants. These smooth decrease lines are used for full-fashioning and vertical darts.
  Right of seamline: Work to 2 sts before seamline, K2tog, knit seam st(s).
  Left of seamline: SSK (slip 2 sts knitwise; knit together).

2. Accented decrease: LH/RH slants.
  Right of seamline: Work to 2 sts before seamline, SSK, knit seam stitch(es).
  Left of seamline: K2tog.

3. Easy-match decrease: RH/LH slants. This technique is better if your K2tog and SSK decreases aren't a good match.
  Right of seamline: Work to 2 sts before seamline, insert RH needle into 2nd st on LH needle as if to purl and lift it over the 1st st, k1, knit seam stitch(es).
  Left of seamline: Slip 2 sts to RH needle as if to knit, pass 1st slipped stitch over 2nd, transfer remaining stitch to LH needle, k1.

4. Feather decrease: Double LH/Double RH slants. This technique adds attractive detail and texture. Repeat every 4th row for a 45° angle. You may do triple decreases in the same way, repeating them every 6th row for the same angle.
  Right of seamline: Work to 4 sts before seamline. Slip 1st 2 sts as if to knit onto a cable needle (CN), and hold in front. *Knit 1st st on CN and 1st st on LH needle together. Repeat from *. Knit seam stitch(es).
  Left of seamline: Slip 2 sts as if to knit onto CN, and hold in back. *Knit 1st st on LH needle and 1st st on CN together. Repeat from *.

5. Yarnover decreases: RH/LH slants (decrease 2, add 1). This style adds a decorative touch to smooth fabric or blends well with yarnover and fagotted patterns.
  Right of seamline: Work to 3 sts before seamline. K3tog, yo.
  Left of seamline: Yo, sl 1, SSK, psso. —B.B.

Paired increases

Paired decreases

No-Sew Set-in Sleeves
Shaping the drop-shoulder sweater

by Jean Baker White

Living on a tiny island 70 minutes off the coast of Maine makes it necessary for one to become a self-reliant knitter. Many of the women (including me) knit for the "summer people," and we often collect yarns without having an end product in mind—an insurance, perhaps, against the winter season, when weeks, if not months, go by between stocking-up trips to the mainland.

It was to offset the frustration of having no pattern to correspond to the yarn in hand that I offered to teach a series of classes on knit design. My goal was to teach anyone—from novice to expert—how to turn yarn into something of her own choosing that would suit the yarn and fit the wearer. I also teach the importance of finishing garments neatly, with a minimum of fuss.

While teaching this class, I devised a method to work set-in sleeves that elimi-

Jean White's Aran, p. 47, is constructed like a drop-shoulder sweater but has the better fit and appearance of a set-in-sleeve sweater.

nates all the common sleeve problems—figuring out the perilous sleeve caps and corresponding armholes, which can be difficult to plan and sew together well. It involves almost no calculations and no sewing in the cap area. After you have completed the front and back of the sweater and have joined the shoulders (I knit flat pieces from the bottom up), you pick up stitches and knit the sleeve cap right into the shoulder of the sweater; then you continue knitting the sleeve down to the cuff.

First I have my students design, plan, and execute a simple drop-shoulder, boatneck sweater with its inevitable success; then they're ready (and generally brave enough) to attempt something more complicated. As you, too, will discover, it's not that difficult to plan a set-in-sleeve sweater with a round, a Johnny, or a turtleneck collar. The initial steps are the same: Experiment with the chosen yarn and various needle sizes to obtain the desired appearance, calculate the gauge, and sketch the shape and features of the desired sweater.

Planning set-in sleeves—Figuring out the wearer's shoulder width measured across the chest at the underarm (drawing below) is the key to good fit. This measurement, when combined with your gauge information (number of sts/in. x number of in.), will tell you how many stitches to decrease at the underarm so the garment will fit the shoulders properly. Sweaters for young children generally require a 1½-in. to 2-in. reduction per side; larger sweaters need to be reduced 2 in. to 3 in. per side.

In a drop-shoulder garment, you determine the sleeve length by measuring the wearer's underarm length. The "sleeve cap" is formed by the sweater's unshaped upper body, so it doesn't enter the sleeve calculations. Now, since you're eliminating that "overhang," you must figure in the sleeve cap as part of the sleeve length. To do this, measure the arm length on top, from shoulder joint to wrist. Just as you need to add ease to the chest measurement when planning a sweater, you must also increase the sleeve length—usually 1 in. for a young

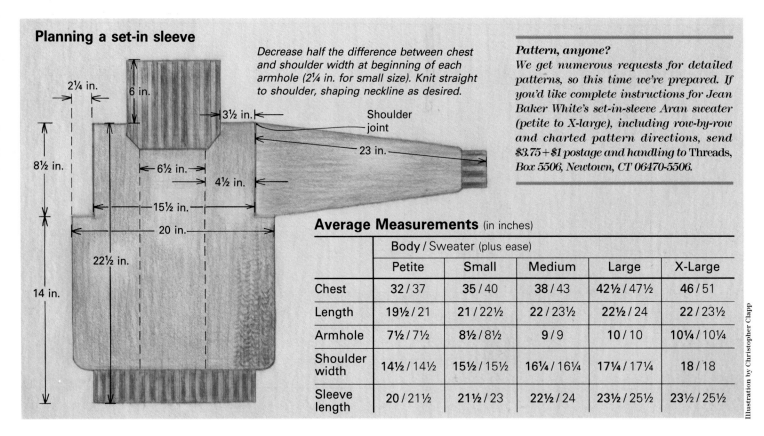

Planning a set-in sleeve

2¼ in.
6 in.
8½ in.
3½ in.
6½ in.
4½ in.
15½ in.
20 in.
22½ in.
14 in.

Shoulder joint
23 in.

Decrease half the difference between chest and shoulder width at beginning of each armhole (2¼ in. for small size). Knit straight to shoulder, shaping neckline as desired.

Pattern, anyone?
We get numerous requests for detailed patterns, so this time we're prepared. If you'd like complete instructions for Jean Baker White's set-in-sleeve Aran sweater (petite to X-large), including row-by-row and charted pattern directions, send $3.75 + $1 postage and handling to Threads, Box 5506, Newtown, CT 06470-5506.

Average Measurements (in inches)

	Body / Sweater (plus ease)				
	Petite	Small	Medium	Large	X-Large
Chest	32 / 37	35 / 40	38 / 43	42½ / 47½	46 / 51
Length	19½ / 21	21 / 22½	22 / 23½	22½ / 24	22 / 23½
Armhole	7½ / 7½	8½ / 8½	9 / 9	10 / 10	10¼ / 10¼
Shoulder width	14½ / 14½	15½ / 15½	16¼ / 16¼	17¼ / 17¼	18 / 18
Sleeve length	20 / 21½	21½ / 23	22½ / 24	23½ / 25½	23½ / 25½

Illustration by Christopher Clapp

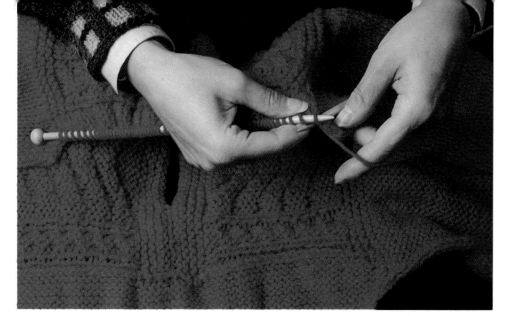

White knits a set-in sleeve cap right into the armhole of her sweater. After joining the shoulders, she picks up the armhole stitches. At the end of each row, she knits or purls the next stitch on the bound-off edge and passes the last armhole stitch over it to maintain the stitch count.

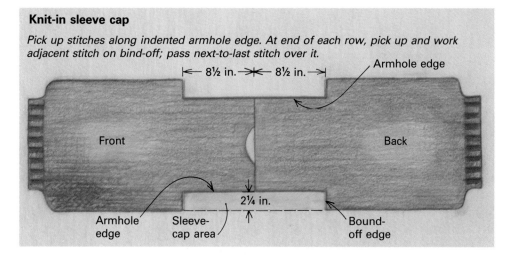

Knit-in sleeve cap

Pick up stitches along indented armhole edge. At end of each row, pick up and work adjacent stitch on bind-off; pass next-to-last stitch over it.

← 8½ in. →←← 8½ in. →

Armhole edge

Front

Back

2¼ in.

Armhole edge

Sleeve-cap area

Bound-off edge

---

child and 2 in. for a larger person. This extra will take care of the way sleeves tend to shorten from being bent and crimped at the elbows, and it will compensate for the riding up that occurs when arms are moved.

Planning the neckline—Now is also the time to plan the front-neck shaping. I find that if I begin a neck opening 2½ in. below the shoulder seam for a young child, 3 in. for a teen or average-size woman, and 3½ in. to 4 in. for a man, it will allow for a successful crewneck or Johnny-collar finish. For a turtleneck, I allow ½ in. less depth to the neck opening for a smaller sweater and 1 in. less for a larger size. Draw the base of the neckline on your sketch in the center third of the upper-chest area (see drawing, p. 48), and sketch the desired neck treatment. Shape the neck opening evenly on both sides of the bound-off edge at its base by decreasing 1-in. worth of stitches on each side of the opening at a rate of 1 st each edge every other row. Then work straight up to the shoulder seam.

Knitting set-in sleeves—I knit my sweaters back and forth in flat pieces, but this technique would also work for sweaters knit in the round. I subtract the shoulder-width measurement from the chest measurement to determine the amount I need to decrease at the base of the armholes. I bind off half of that at the base of each underarm. The underarm decrease on a woman's *average-size* sweater is usually about 2¼-in. worth of stitches per side. I find that it's better to take off a hair more than the exact difference you calculate, since steaming will relax the fabric a bit. (If you're knitting in the round, you can bind off these stitches and work the front and back separately from here. Or you can bind them off or put them on holders, create a knit or wrapped "steek," and continue working in the round to the neck shaping.) After binding off, I continue working straight with no more decreases until it's time to divide for the neck opening.

On my woman's small-to-average-size sweater, I knit across about the first 4½ in. of stitches. This, plus the 2¼ in. bound earlier, represents about one-third of the width of the sweater front. I loosely bind off the center third and knit the remaining 4½ in. Actually, the sides are a little more than one-third, and the center is a little less to ensure a comfortable neck opening,

but even thirds generally work acceptably. Working one side at a time, I reduce 1 in. more on each side of the neck, decreasing 1 st at the neck edge every other row. Then I work straight until the armhole is the desired length. I work the remaining shoulder to correspond, leaving both 3½-in. groups of shoulder stitches on safety pins.

I work the back like the front *but with no neck shaping*. When the armhole is the correct total depth, I work across 3½ in. of stitches for the first shoulder, bind off the center stitches, and work the remaining 3½ in. Then I join the front and back by placing right sides together and binding off the corresponding shoulders by knitting them together. After a gentle pressing, the joined pieces will look like the drawing at left.

To work the sleeves, I pick up the stitches along the armhole edge with the right side facing me, just as I'd do on a drop-shoulder sweater—3 sts for every 4 rows. This ratio always gives a smooth, unpuckered join. I pick up between the selvage stitch and the second stitch, never right on the edge. I don't pick up any stitches along the bound-off edges of the underarm yet.

First, I form the "sleeve cap," which fills in the indented area on the drawings. I do this by working in the bound-off stitches at the base of the armhole front and back gradually, one per row, as shown in the photo at left. Row 1 is the pick-up on the right side. On row 2, purl to the end of the row. Then purl 1 st into the base of the bound-off edge. Pass the stitch worked immediately before it over this new, extra stitch to keep the stitch count constant.

On subsequent rows, continue building the cap out along the bound-off edge by working a new stitch into it and passing the previous stitch over the new one until the indented area is filled. If you've been knitting in the round, you'll have to work the sleeve cap back and forth. When the cap is completed, you can resume circular knitting if desired. Don't do any sleeve shaping until the sleeve is half the length from shoulder to elbow; then start decreasing according to your calculations to reach the desired number of stitches at the cuff.

Work the second sleeve to match; then knit the neck finish. That's it! Press the work lightly again, sew up the underarm and side seams, and your set-in-sleeve sweater is ready to be worn—without the extra calculating and sewing that such sleeves usually require. □

Jean Baker White of North Haven, ME, is the island's director of Adult and Community Education. In addition to devising creative solutions to knitting problems, she teaches a refresher English/word-processing course to prepare students to take advantage of the interactive television university courses that are available on the island.

Dazzling with Sequins

Whether you knit or crochet, you can add sparkle to clothing

by Barbara Shomer Kelsey

aybe it's the magpie in my blood, or the fact that as a child I never had a spangled tutu, but the current fashion for sequins touches me to the core. They're all out there, in cellophane packets, waiting to adorn some fabulously flashy outfit—shiny, concave couvettes and sparkling, flat paillettes, shaped like snowflakes, leaves, and stars.

During the first part of the century, sequins were associated with bawdy, barroom garb and theatrical costumes. But in the 1930s, Norman Norell created elegant evening gowns with handsewn sequins. Os-

car de la Renta added sequins to evening pajamas, and Suzy Perette attached them to paisley prints. Constance Rivemale, a designer of wearable art, creates quilted collage fabrics with sections outlined in sequins. Today, sweaters, shoes, dresses, even hairpieces are sequinned—the list is limited only by the imagination.

Sequins are usually sewn onto knitted garments, but I like to make them an integral part of the fabric. You can add paillettes with large, off-center holes over the needles one at a time as you work, but small-holed couvettes must be threaded onto the yarn before you knit.

Threading couvettes is easy if you buy them strung together. Tie the thread to the yarn with a single knot, and slide the sequins over the knot onto the yarn. The cup, or front, of the couvettes should face the ball of yarn so they'll be cup side out on the knitted fabric to catch the most light. Work with a smooth knitting yarn so the sequins will thread easily.

Push the sequins far enough onto the yarn so that you can cast on and knit at least two rows of stockinette stitch. To attach sequins to the right side of the garment, you must be on a knit row. Slide a sequin up close to the right needle, insert

From *Threads* magazine (October 1985) 1:60-62

the needle into the next stitch, yarn over, and push the sequin through the old stitch before taking the new one off the needle. Knit the next stitch through the back of the loop to keep the sequins lying flat and in diagonal lines, as shown in the drawings at right.

Another way to add couvettes—and one I find faster—is with the linen stitch. With the yarn in front, slip any knit stitch and slide a sequin onto the yarn that is carried. This method gives you a different effect. Instead of dangling vertically, the couvettes are positioned horizontally across the fabric, and they don't lie as flat as they do when they're threaded onto the yarn.

Never put couvettes on the first or last two stitches of a row, as they'll interfere with the seams. In circular knitting, alternate plain-knit and sequinned rows so the sequins won't overlap. On flat and circular work, stagger the sequins in consecutive rows to obtain an even coating of shine. You can get a lot of dazzle by patterning just one area or by creating stripes.

To cover a medium-sized, long-sleeved sweater with 8mm couvettes, you'll need about 10,000 of them; but if you use 20mm paillettes and don't overlap them, you'll need only about 500 for a sleeveless shell.

To add a large-holed paillette to a row (see photos below), knit to the stitch where you want to place it, and hang the paillette on the tip of the right needle. Knit the next stitch, lift the paillette over the needle so that it hangs on the new stitch. The paillette will lie flat, so you don't need to knit into the back of the

next stitch. This technique was so easy when I discovered it that I was certain it couldn't work. But it does.

As a "continental" knitter—I hold the yarn in my left hand—I preferred this technique, but depending on how you knit, you may find that it's faster and more comfortable to attach large-holed paillettes in this way: Insert the tip of the right needle into a paillette and then through the next stitch. Yarn over and pull the new stitch through both the old stitch and the paillette.

If you're a machine knitter, you can't add couvettes or small-holed paillettes to your knitting (they won't fit onto the needles or the double thickness of yarn), but you can add large-holed paillettes (see photos, p. 52). You'll be adding them to the wrong side, or purl side, of the fabric. Machine-knit one row beyond the row you want to sequin, select the needles to which you want to add paillettes, and then push the needles all the way forward to holding position. Hang a paillette on a latch hook, and use the hook to grab the stitch below the one on the needle. Now push the needle back to nonworking position so the stitch drops and unravels one row. Slide the paillette off the hook and onto the stitch. Then push the latch hook into the dropped stitch so the yarn is behind the latch. Rehang the stitch onto the original needle, lifting the dropped stitch at the same time. It isn't necessary to reknit the dropped stitch—hanging it back on the needle creates a tuck stitch. Add paillettes across the row. Then knit at least one row

Knitting with couvettes

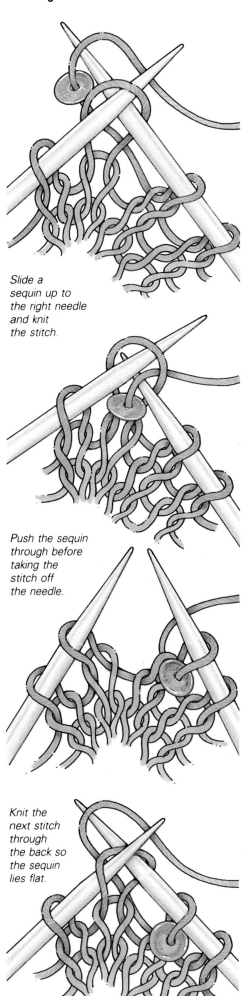

Slide a sequin up to the right needle and knit the stitch.

Push the sequin through before taking the stitch off the needle.

Knit the next stitch through the back so the sequin lies flat.

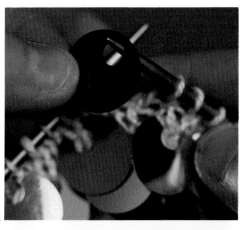

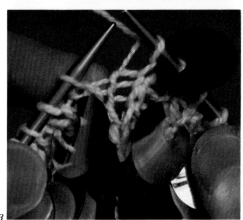

To add a paillette as you work, hang it on the right needle (A), and make the stitch (B). Then lift it over the tip of the needle (C) so that it hangs on the new stitch.

To add a paillette on the machine to the purl side of a garment, hang it on the latch hook, and grab the stitch below the one on the needle (A). Then push the needle back so one stitch drops (B). Slide the paillette onto the stitch (C). Then push the hook into the stitch until the yarn is behind the latch. Tip the hook to pick up the dropped stitch, and hang both stitches back on the needle.

plain and repeat the process. Stagger the sequins in alternate rows.

You can also crochet with sequins. If you're using couvettes, slide them onto the yarn with the cups facing the ball. I alternate rows of single- and double-crochet stitches, with sequins on the latter. To add a sequin with a double-crochet stitch, slide the sequin up close to the hook and lift it over the hook with the first yarn over. Then put the hook into the top of the single-crochet stitch below, pull a loop through, yarn over, and pull it through two loops behind the sequin, twice.

When working on a knit or crochet project, always make a sample swatch that includes the sequins, measuring carefully to determine the stitch and row gauges. When working with couvettes, check your work frequently—ripping out is a nightmare, because each sequin must be passed back through a stitch. After you've finished, be sure to block the pieces. Place them between wet towels, and when they're saturated, push them into shape with your fingers. Never use steam or a hot iron for blocking, or you will have a melted disaster. I prefer to hand-wash sequinned garments, but if you decide to have them dry-cleaned, test a swatch first. Some sequins dissolve in the chemicals.

As I write, I find a paillette in my shoe. I wonder how sequins would look on socks?□

Barbara Shomer Kelsey, of Bethel, CT, is an ardent knitter, and a lover of shiny objects.

Sources for sequins

In the 15th century, European embroiderers attached metal sequins to their handwork. In the late 19th century, the wings of rose beetles were used as spangles, as were the clear, shiny, boiled and dried bones from the heads of cod and haddock. Nacre (mother-of-pearl) is still used in a stitchery technique of that name, but in the main, today's sequins are made of plastic.

Some sequins are sold loose, to be attached one at a time. Others are sewn on trims made of braided or stretch fabric (some wide enough to form a bodice), or on net-backed appliqué pieces, many of which have beads. You can also buy sequinned fabrics by the yard.

Local craft, yarn, and fabric stores are good places to hunt for sequins. For $1, Sheru Enterprises offers a generous packet of sequins in assorted sizes, shapes, and colors. I found packages of 20mm paillettes, 5mm and 8mm couvettes in bright metallic and opalescent colors, and multi-colored stars, leaves, and snowflakes. I also found the best deal here for large-holed paillettes—$4.50/1,000. At M & J Trimming, I saw all colors of small-holed paillettes, 30mm large-holed paillettes in gold and black, three sizes of gold and silver stars (ranging from $3.98 to $11.98 for packets of 500). Prestrung 6mm and 8mm couvettes on twine start at $1.98/100. You can also purchase sequins and trims through mail-order catalogs (see list at right).

The most expensive way to purchase sequins is attached to yardage, whether domestic or imported. On a backing of chiffon, jersey, and sometimes silk or lace, sequins can frost the whole surface, be randomly scattered, or swirl in wave, fan, or geometric patterns. The fabric stores listed here do not regularly handle mail-order business, but they will help if you know what you want. Prices begin at about $35/yd. and go up to as much as $125 for a multi-colored yard.

B & J Fabrics
263 West 40th St.
New York, NY 10018
(212) 354-8150 or 8212
Sequinned fabrics. No catalog.

Fero Textiles, Inc.
147 West 57th St.
New York, NY 10019
(212) 581-0240
Sequinned fabrics. No catalog.

Florida Supply House
P.O. Box 847
Bradenton, FL 33506
(813) 756-1831
Sequins. Catalog $1.

G Street Fabrics
11854 Rockville Pike
Rockville, MD 20852
(301) 231-8960
Sequinned trims, fabrics, appliqués. For information about their custom-sample service, send a self-addressed envelope with $.44 postage. No catalog.

The Greatest Sew on Earth
P.O. Box 214
Fort Tilden, NY 11695
Sequinned trims. Catalog $1.

Guildcraft
3158 Main St.
Buffalo, NY 14214
(716) 837-9346
Sequins. Catalog $2.50.

House of Crafts & Stuff, Inc.
409 North Gall Blvd.
Zephyrhills, FL 34248
(813) 782-0223
Sequins. Catalog $2.

Jehlor Fantasy Fabrics
Pavilion Outlet Center
17900 Southcenter Parkway
Suite 290
Seattle, WA 98188
(206) 575-8250
Sequinned trims, fabrics, appliqués. Catalog $2.50. Request an order form for custom-sample service.

M & J Trimming Co.
1008 Sixth Ave.
New York, NY 10018
(212) 391-9072
Sequins and trims. No catalog, but will fill a mail or phone order.

Sheru Enterprises, Inc.
49 West 38th St.
New York, NY 10018
(212) 730-0766
Sequins and trims. No catalog, but will fill a mail or phone order.

Weller Fabrics, Inc.
54 West 57th St.
New York, NY 10019
(212) 247-3790
Sequinned fabrics. No catalog.

Knitting with Cotton
Stitch maneuvers help sweaters stay in shape

by Linda Dyett

One of the legacies of the hand-knit sweater boom of the early 1980s is the widespread availability of cotton yarns. Durable and comfortable to wear, cotton has become a versatile fashion staple, whether treated to a polished surface or textured like a rough-hewn homespun. The natural fiber takes wonderfully to dyes. Its subtle, lustrous hues will have you mistaking it for silk, while with a matte finish, it becomes the essence of casual wear.

Cotton has the virtue of being incredibly absorbent. The fiber can store large amounts of moisture—up to 65% of its own weight—and then release it slowly. Thus, cotton clothes function like air conditioners for the body. Even on the hottest days, heat never builds up, and there's no scratch or itch. In winter, richly textured cottons turn around as thermal blankets.

For all its good qualities, cotton has a poor reputation among handknitters. Unlike wool, cotton is not elastic. It's notorious for stretching without springing back until it's washed, whereupon it's known to shrink. Many knitters overcautiously avoid it. Why waste time with cotton, they reason, if it's going to lose its shape?

But there are ways—simple tricks and common-sense techniques—of knitting with cotton and caring for cotton handknits, which will produce beautiful, long-lasting garments. You should know, first of all, which type of cotton yarn to choose for the sweater you're about to knit.

Cotton yarns—Some cotton yarns are processed to be stronger than others and to remember their shape. These are the mercerized cottons. Mercerizing, a chemical process involving a soak in alkaline caustic soda, was developed 140 years ago by John Mercer, a Scotsman (thus called *fil d'Ecosse,* or Scottish yarn, by the French). Mercerizing adds smoothness, luster, and strength; allows for optimal dye saturation; and reduces the potential for shrinkage. Most mercerized cottons are relatively thin, though recent additions knit up about 5 sts/in. And, of course, the thinner ones can be doubled. For all but the most casual sweaters, I prefer thin cottons knit on size 2 or size 3 needles. Knitting tightly is the best way to prevent stretching.

The type of yarn that's least likely to stretch is *cable cotton,* which is plied exactly like standard, multiple-strand wool-crepe yarns. The ends are individually twisted in one direction, then twisted together in the opposite direction. Chat Botté's Loto and Galler's Cannelé Grande Vitesse are cable cottons. Also frequently mercerized and eminently durable is high-twist *perle cotton,* which can be double-mercerized for extra strength and luster—DMC's Pearl Cotton or Bernat's Cassino, for example.

Cable, perle, and most other plied cottons, particularly when they've been mercerized, are "flat" yarns with almost no "loft"; that is, they lack the fuzz that stands away from the strand in wool and other animal fibers. These yarns won't hide stitch irregularities, so they are not for beginners or uneven knitters, but they are a joy to handle once you have learned to knit them evenly. They are unlikely to pill quickly and are perfect for twin sets or other sweaters that are meant to be neat, tailored, and elegant.

Another type of cotton has recently come into its own as a fashion yarn that gives garments a matte, sporty look. *Cotton string* is a multi-ply, low-twist unmercerized yarn. It is available in a wide variety of thicknesses; examples are Aarlan's Cotonova, and Tahki's Creole. In its bulkier version, some of the plies sometimes come loose and snag at the tops of knitting needles. You can overcome this hazard by knitting slowly until you develop an accurate aim. String yarn will knit up into wonderfully loose and comfortable outdoor cardigans or winter turtlenecks.

Finally, there's what I call *batting-like cotton,* which is really a loosely spun yarn or roving plied with a strong binder thread (not necessarily of cotton). The result is a slubby yarn, a thick-thin, or a bouclé, depending on the spinning process. This is the most rustic-looking cotton (Ole-Oaxaca's Handspun Mexican Cotton, for example). If it's a good quality yarn, it will age marvelously and acquire a nice patina, like untreated leather. It's ideal for oversized novelty sweaters.

Knitting the ribbing—When you're knitting with cotton, ribbing is the first problem you'll encounter. Because the fiber is inelastic, the fabric will sag, though the job of the ribbing is precisely to remain elastic and buoyant. The remedy is simple: Cast on as you ordinarily would, or try a wider needle than your instructions call for. Then immediately, for your first row, switch to needles that are three to five sizes smaller than those indicated for the body of the sweater. If, for example, the pattern calls for size 8 needles, knit the rib on size 3, 4, or 5. I also suggest that you knit into the backs of all your rib stitches, as shown in the drawing on page 54. This creates an extra twist, which gives added support. You may also want to try a cable rib or reverse cross-stitch rib (see swatch, page 54) for extra elasticity.

Alternatively, or in addition, you can add stretch by knitting cotton-covered hat elastic along with the cotton yarn for the ribbing. Since elastic usually comes in white or black only, you'll have to dye it to match the color of your cotton. One supplier, Cotton Clouds, offers a translucent elastic thread that's almost invisible. However, I've found that any elastic will show slightly, so you may prefer to tack it inside the ribbing, after you finish the sweater. Just sew it on by picking up each stitch of the ribbing all the way around.

For the body of the sweater, switch back to wider needles to get the gauge indicated in your instructions. If the pattern calls for a simple stockinette, you may once again prefer to knit into the back of each knit stitch, as shown in the swatch at left on page 55. Be sure you've used the same back stitch in your gauge swatch. If you twist the purl stitches as well, the fabric will deform; thus, if you're working on circular needles, knit into the back of the stitches on alternate rounds only. The overall effect is much the same as ordinary stockinette, though the stitches are slightly raised.

In *Mary Thomas's Knitting Book,* a classic published in 1938, the British knitting scholar recommends two types of stockinette that prove to work very well with cotton yarn. One is the elastic right-over-left crossed knit stitch. For a somewhat denser fabric, Thomas suggests what she calls knit stitch—plaited, an uncrossed Western knit stitch combined with an Eastern European purl stitch. I call it plaited stockinette, as

Ribbings for cotton

Rib with crossed knit stitch

Ribbing knit with right-over-left crossed knit stitch.

Row 1—*k1-b, p1; rep from *.

All subsequent rows: k and p all sts as they stand on the needle; knit all k sts from the back, as explained below.

Cable rib

Multiple of 5 sts plus 2 sts.

Rows 1 and 3 (wrong side)—K2, *p1-b, k1, p1-b, k2; rep from *.

Row 2—P2, *k1-b, p1, k1-b, p2; rep from *.

Row 4—P2, *sl next 2 sts to dpn (double-pointed needle) and hold in front, k1-b, sl the purl st back to left-hand needle and purl it, k1-b from dpn, p2; rep from *.

Rep rows 1-4.

Reverse cross-stitch rib

Multiple of 4 sts plus 2 sts.

Row 1 (right side)—P2, *k2, p2; rep from *.

Row 2—K2, *skip 1 st and purl 2nd st, purl the skipped st, sl both sts tog off needle, k2, rep from *.

Rep rows 1 and 2.

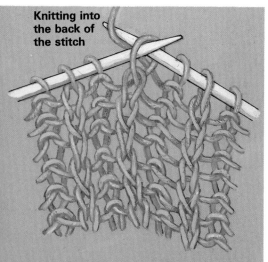

Knitting into the back of the stitch

Knitting into the back of the stitch (k1-b) means inserting the needle through the back, instead of the front, of the loop. This causes the loop of the stitch to cross right over left. Wrap the yarn around the right needle, as you normally would. You can also cross purl stitches (p1-b) by inserting the needle through the back of the loop. For the rib stitch shown above, knit into the back of all knit stitches; work the purl stitches as usual.

shown at right on the facing page. I suggest you experiment with both of these stitches and compare them with your own stockinette. Choose whichever gives your knitting the greatest firmness as well as elasticity.

Some knitters find that garter and seed-stitch patterns lend themselves especially well to cotton knitting. But there are many stitch patterns that will add body and elasticity to knitted fabric, so experimentation is worthwhile.

Cotton knitting can similarly be strengthened via Fair Isle and jacquard patterns, in which the additional colors float behind the fabric. And because cotton colors are unusually vivid, these techniques are particularly desirable. On the other hand, cotton is a dense fiber, and the extra yarn will weigh it down—a boon for winter garments, but not ideal for breezy summer knits.

Choosing a sweater pattern—A well-charted set of instructions can also add longevity to a cotton sweater. If they're geared for cotton, the instructions should allow for a greater-than-usual reduction of stitches at points of body contact and control—at the underarms and wrists, for instance. Ac-

cording to several expert pattern writers, the length of the underarm decrease for a set-in sleeve in a cotton sweater should always be a half inch greater than for wool. It's fairly easy to recalculate such decreases when you're substituting cotton yarn in a wool pattern. But if you're reluctant to try this, you can still hunt down a pattern specifically calling for cotton yarn. When you later block it, or after one initial wearing, it will stretch to fit you.

If you like knitting absolutely by the book, you can test the shrinkage of your cotton yarn in advance of producing a sweater. Simply knit up a square swatch somewhat larger than the 4-in. gauge swatch called for in the instructions. Measure it carefully at its borders. Then machine-wash it in warm water and tumble-dry. Repeat this wash-and-dry routine for any yarn that isn't mercerized. (If you know the yarn is mercerized, you don't need to wash and dry it more than once). Block the swatch by pressing it on the wrong side with a steam iron. Then measure your gauge. When you later wash your sweater, simply use the same water and dryer temperatures as you did for the swatch. Many knitters fol-

Body stitches for cotton

Crossed-knit stockinette stitch
Knit into the back of each stitch; purl as in regular stockinette.

Seed stitch
Even number of sts.
Row 1—*K1, p1; rep from *
Row 2—*P1, k1; rep from *
Rep rows 1 and 2.

Plaited stockinette stitch
Row 1 (right side)—k all sts.
Row 2 (wrong side)—p all stitches b, with yarn looped under needle.
Rep rows 1 and 2.

low this rigorous swatch testing no matter what the fiber.

Good cotton will not shrink much, if at all, especially if it has been mercerized. Not-so-good cotton may shrink 10% or more, but if you've tested it properly, you still shouldn't have problems. Shrinkage is caused by a combination of high heat (over 105°F) and agitation. To avoid shrinkage, you don't have to hand-wash your cotton knits in cold water. Warm water will not only get them cleaner but will keep the dyes from running, whereas cold water may bring out the dyes.

Unless you plan to have your sweater dry-cleaned every time, the advance testing system is essential when you're knitting with more than one color (in which case the swatch must contain all the colors). Add a few drops of white vinegar to the final rinse water to stabilize the multicolors. If they run, at least you'll have found out sooner than later. You can still go ahead and knit the sweater, but you'll have to consign it to a dry cleaner whenever it's soiled.

It's better to use a liquid laundry detergent than a powder to wash cottons, as powders tend to get caught in the ribbing. And it's perfectly okay to put them in the washing machine, on the gentle cycle; add a fabric softener to the last rinse. To keep colors bright, you can add 6 tsp. or 7 tsp. of white vinegar to the rinse. By all means, tumble-dry your cotton sweater at low heat. This will make it extra soft and will cut down on stretch. It's a good idea to toss a wet bath towel into the dryer with your cottons. It will absorb excess heat.

If your cotton sweater is meant to be tailor-fitted, you may want to reblock it after each washing. In that case, dry it 20 to 30 minutes. Then pin it to shape on a blocking board. One clever knitter I know experiments with her cotton sweaters each time she washes them. She'll elongate them one week or widen the sleeves the next week. It's like having a new sweater each wash day. After 20 or more reshapings, her sweaters still look and feel great. King Cotton may not be the most elastic yarn you'll ever meet, but it's surely the most versatile—and obliging. □

Contributing editor Linda Dyett frequently writes about knitting.

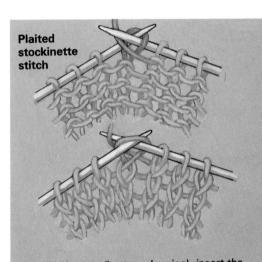

Plaited stockinette stitch

On all knit rows (bottom drawing), insert the right needle through the front of each stitch. Loop the yarn under the needle (Western style). On the first row only, the result is ordinary uncrossed knit stitches. On all purl rows (top drawing), insert the needle through the back of the stitch and loop the yarn beneath the right needle (Eastern style). The purl maneuver combined with the ordinary knit stitch crosses the knit rows below and prepares as well for the succeeding knit rows to be twisted.

Bead-Knitting Madness
Treat yourself to a dazzling purse

by Alice Korach

Alice Korach's tour de force is knit on size 00000 needles, with seed beads strung on Gudbrod silk thread. String beads waiting to be knit are wound onto an empty yarn spool. On the inside you can see the increases, made before the floral pattern was begun.

One day, while paging through *Mary Thomas's Knitting Book*, I came across a picture of a tiny bead-knit jacket and bead-embellished cap. I was hooked and decided that I'd teach myself bead knitting. A neighbor told me that the Cooper-Hewitt Museum in New York City has a fine collection of bead-knit purses, so my first step was to view their undisplayed collection.

Curator Gillian Moss, an expert knitter, and I spent hours poring over bags made between the late 18th century and the 1930s. We put some of the more fascinating ones under the microscope to study the fiber, direction of work, and knitting techniques. The purses were usually knit in the round on very fine steel needles. There were bags knit with simple strands of single-colored beads looped between plain stitches; isolated patterns of beads knit onto fine-cotton stockinette fabric; Fair Isle-type stranding with beads; and elaborate pastoral scenes and florals of solid, bead-knit fabric. The image of those bags stayed with me for a year as I trained myself in bead knitting, preparing to attempt something similar.

Getting the hang of bead knitting— The first step is to learn how to knit even bead fabric. Solid bead fabric, whether knit flat or in the round, is worked on a ground of twisted, or crossed, stitches, which lock the beads into position on the front of the work.

Before you can begin knitting, you must string the beads on the knitting thread. The largest size thread over which the beads can pass easily is best. Historically, silk "purse twist" was the thread of choice, probably because it resists tangling and abrasion, and the beads slip along it easily. The fine Victorian work called for steel needles in multizero sizes. Try 5/2 perle cotton, 6mm beads, and No. 2 needles for your first attempt, but don't use this soft cotton for anything large or heavy—it abrades easily.

If you knit a flat piece, as I did for the blue purse on p. 59, you work a row of knit-in-the-back twisted stitches, pushing a bead through the loop onto the front of each stitch. The beads sit nicely on the front of the work. On the return row, you purl in the back, popping the bead through the loop onto the front side of the work as you form each stitch (drawings, p. 58). Twisted garter stitch with a bead on each stitch is unsatisfactory, as a garter ridge forms between every other row, making the thread too prominent. Working through the instructions in "A bead-knitting lesson" (p. 58) will help you get started. Develop a system of manipulating the beads, and master the intricacies of tension before you start your bag. Bead knitting is slow and difficult. It's important to feel confident before you start a project you might be working on for a year or more. Fortunately, bead knitting becomes easier and faster with practice.

Planning a purse— Before you even pick up a knitting needle to make a bead-knit purse, you must make a lot of decisions. What kind of bead decoration do you want? What shape do you want the bag to be? Do you want a string-gathered reticule, or do you want to use a purse frame? What size beads should you use? What kind of thread and what size needles should you use? Not least important, can you get the beads and colors you think you want? Should you knit flat or in the round? How will you line and finish the bag? And where will you find the design you want to knit?

The first choice was easy for me. I wanted a picture purse. And, of course, the more elaborate, detailed, and elegant the picture, the better. But I'm not crazy—yet—so I knew I had to try something simpler first.

I looked at cross-stitch books and needlepoint patterns. Both abound in patterns on square grids. And it seemed that if I were knitting a fabric of spherical units, my gauge would be square or nearly so. Then I looked at Oriental rugs and graphed Oriental-rug needlepoint patterns. I studied a number of the Dover design books, finally selecting one with Celtic patterns—Co Spinhoven's, *Celtic Charted Designs* (1987). I adapted design No. 253 to my requirements.

I sent for bead catalogs (see suppliers, p. 61). Then I measured and calculated the number of beads per inch of the various sizes. Eventually, I decided that 3mm beads would be a good compromise between fine detail and manageability. These gave me about 8 beads per inch. I found I could get some beautiful cobalt-blue 3mm glass beads from Shipwreck Beads. I went to the bead area of New York's Garment District and found some lovely strands of opalescent Japanese plastic beads and a good selection of Gudbrod silk at Sheru Enterprises. I chose size E, black. Size EE or F also would have worked for my beads (the further along the alphabet, the thicker the thread). I don't recommend combining plastic and glass, because they probably won't wear evenly over time; but that's what I did.

Gauge in bead knitting has almost nothing to do with yarn or needle size. The size and shape of the beads determine the number of bead stitches and rows per inch. You want to knit tight enough so that only beads show. To determine the best needle size, I gathered sets of knitting needles ranging from sizes 00000 to 1. After transferring about a 1-yd.-long strand of beads to my silk, I started with my 0000's and cast on 20 sts. I knit a row, then purled a

An irresistible urge to possess a knit purse like these two bags set Korach on her bead-knitting odyssey. Tricky though it is to learn, the work can easily become an obsession.

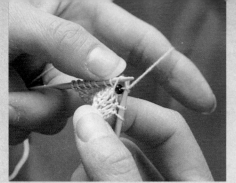

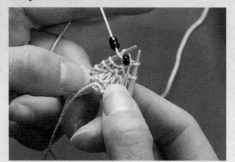

The first knit bead stitch.

The first purl bead stitch.

Knitting flat

Knit bead stitch **K1b**

Knit in back, wrap counterclockwise, pop bead through to front, pull loop over new stitch to complete.

Purl bead stitch **P1b**

Purl in back, pop bead through to back, complete stitch.

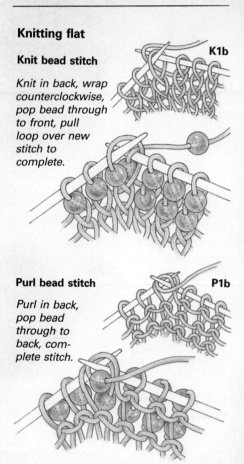

Illustrations by Phoebe Gaughan

A bead-knitting lesson

According to Mary Thomas, the key to bead knitting is an active left hand. If you knit Continental style (yarn in left hand), you're at an advantage in bead knitting. Another key is to ignore the bead; knitting with beads is like knitting without them. Just remember to pop a bead through as you complete the stitch.

Here's how—Start with a small, flat piece with 10 beads to the row. String 60 6mm beads on 5/2 perle cotton. If they're on a hank, and the holes are large enough, transfer them to the knitting thread by knotting the ends together with a square knot and slipping them over the knot and onto your thread. If the beads are loose, thread a beading needle with the end of your knitting thread, and collect them that way. Tie a bit of yarn on your thread after every 10 beads to double-check your count.

You should plan 2 sts on each edge without beads, so cast on 14 sts on size 2 needles. Knit the first selvage stitch uncrossed and the second crossed (k1b, in back of loop) to keep the yarn snug around the beads. Knit the first two rows without beads. This will give you a chance to practice the crossed stitches:
Row 1: k1, k12b, k1.
Row 2: p1, p12b, p1.
Keep these two rows, as well as the subsequent selvage stitches, very loose.
Row 3: k1, k1b, and now for the first knit bead stitch (k1b-b): Insert RH needle into stitch from back, and use both needles to open loop as wide as possible. Slide first bead into position up against knitting, and push it through loop from back to front as you wrap around RH needle counterclockwise to knit stitch (top drawings at left). When bead is through loop, pull loop over new stitch to complete it. Repeat this stitch nine times. For last 2 sts, k1b without a bead, k1.
Row 4: On return row, p1, p1b. Now for the purl bead stitch (p1b-b): Insert RH needle into stitch from back, open loop, wrap yarn counterclockwise around needle; then snug next bead up and pop it through to back (right side), and complete stitch (bottom drawings at

left). Repeat p1b-b nine times to last 2 sts. P1b (without bead), p1.

Repeat rows 3 and 4 until your beads are gone; then knit 1 row of crossed stitches and cast off.

Some useful tips—At first it often took me a minute or so to make one stitch. But I kept practicing, and it got easier. I also discovered two essential tricks: Control the silk or cotton with a very tight tension so it can slide only with effort. This way, you can pull against it when opening the stitch loop and pushing the bead through. To get the necessary resistance, wrap the silk around your little finger three or four times.

Try using the tip of your left thumbnail to separate the desired bead from its fellows and to slip it into place, and the side of your left index fingernail to push the bead through the loop from the back on the knit side. On the purl side, you may need help from your right index finger to push the bead through.

Invariably, some of the beads on the stitches on your LH needle will slide around the needle to the wrong side. Be careful that each bead is pushed into position on the front surface of the work before you knit the new stitch. If the beads are on the wrong side of the fabric when you knit, or if you fail to pop the new bead completely through the loop as you form the stitch, you'll find beads misaligned in your completed fabric. Even if you do everything perfectly, some of those annoying little critters will get out of place. This isn't a disaster. Use the point of your knitting needle to coerce the bead along the thread to its proper place. You'll sometimes have to pull a loop open to slide the bead into place.

Work patiently and systematically, and you can make the fabric perfect. If you make a knitting error, correct it right away. It's better not to have to jockey the beads into place later, but it's comforting to know that you can if you must. It's easier to make these corrections several rows past the error because the fabric is more flexible. *—A.K.*

row in the back, and was ready to work beads on row 3. The loops were too small for me to push a bead through. After three false starts, I found that the 00's were the right size.

Having settled on the beads, silk, needles, and pattern that I would use, my first project began to take form. I decided on a clutch-purse shape, but with a long shoulder strap. I would knit it as a flat piece of fabric approximately 11 in. x 14 in., to be interfaced with a stiff hair canvas, lined, and folded into an 11-in. x 5-in. rectangle

with a 3-in. flap. I would need about 12,500 beads for the body and another 2,675 for the crocheted strap—about ½ kilo.

Stringing the beads—The most important step in knitting a bead purse is stringing the beads. You must be meticulous about this, following the charted pattern in the reverse order that you'll knit it. Even a single error will destroy the design completely. Knitters of the past had two methods of compensating for their errors. If they'd inadvertently strung an extra bead, they'd

slip it so it tended to go to the wrong side because it wasn't involved in a stitch. If they'd left out a bead, they'd just knit a plain twisted stitch to keep its place. You can occasionally get away with both of these tricks if the beads are very tiny, but for large beads, like my 3mm ones, only perfection in stringing will do.

It isn't possible to string all the beads for a purse at one time. Instead, you'll string as many as you can handle, knit those, string some more, and join the new batch with a knot. You're sure to tangle your silk if you try to string more than 20 or 30 rows of beads at once. For the same reason, never unwind more that 3 or 4 yd. of silk. String a few rows of beads. If a long tail remains, you can leave the silk in the bead needle; otherwise, knot the end to keep the beads from sliding off while you unwind a few more yards of silk, slide the beads down to the spool, and string some more. I use an empty spool from by weaving to store my strung beads (photo, p. 56). I hang the silk spool inside the weaving spool and wrap the strand of beads around the outside. Sliding the beads abrades the silk, so it's safer to tie a few more knots than to risk excessive damage to the thread.

For your first group, thread 10 or 15 rows. You might be able to thread more rows next time, after you've found out how difficult it is for you to handle this amount. Begin threading with the last bead in the group that you'll knit. End with the first bead to be knit. If you're stringing an even number of rows for flat knitting, start with the upper-right-hand corner of the chart group, row 6 in the example below (see drawing). When you reach the left edge of the row, tie a piece of wool yarn onto the silk, move down to row 5, and start with the left side. Moving along and down the rows in this way, you'll end at the right-hand corner of row 1. If you're stringing an odd number of rows, start at the upper-left-hand corner.

Making the purse—Remember to cast on 4 extra sts for your 2 selvage sts on each side. You can start knitting bead stitches immediately above the cast-on. Knit the selvage stitches without beads, and work all of your bead stitches by knitting or purling in the back.

When you've used up your first batch of beads, you must knot the first stitch of the newly strung group to the last stitch of the knitting as unobtrusively and securely as possible. For flat knitting, the nonbeaded selvages are the best places for this. I use a surgeon's knot and then weave the ends into the selvage fabric.

As you knit the strung beads, keep referring to the chart to make sure that there are no errors. If you find a mistake, you can cut the strand, correct it, and knot the ends to resume knitting. Too many knots are highly undesirable, and it's crucial to have an extra spool of silk so that you'll always have many yards available for emergencies, such as knots in the thread that force you to restring. After you've strung and knit through your entire chart, knit a final row of twisted stitches, without beads, and bind off.

Crocheting a matching round cord is easy (drawing at far right). I strung my beads in a 4-blue, 1-white repeat. I started by chaining 5 and closing the loop, using a size 10 steel crochet hook. Then I slip-stitch-single-crocheted around, always working into the

Korach stitches the lining to the edge of her Celtic purse after couching the beadwork to a double layer of hair canvas. The final step will be to secure the crocheted strap.

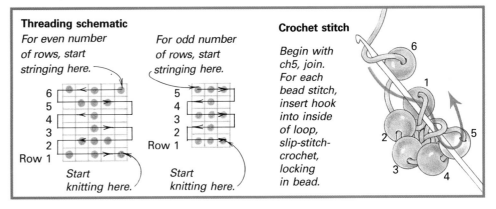

Threading schematic

For even number of rows, start stringing here.

For odd number of rows, start stringing here.

Row 1

Start knitting here.

Start knitting here.

Crochet stitch

Begin with ch5, join. For each bead stitch, insert hook into inside of loop, slip-stitch-crochet, locking in bead.

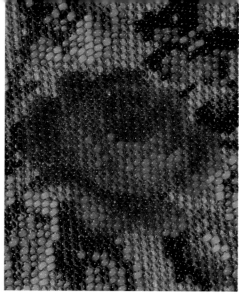

Plaited bead knitting in the round

Round 1: *Plain, uncrossed Western knitting.*

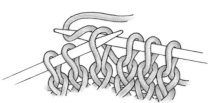

Round 2: *Plain, uncrossed Eastern knitting. (Yarn thrown clockwise.)*

To work a traditional knit-in-the-round beaded bag, you knit in the back of every stitch. The fabric biases slightly (above), but all the beads slant in the same direction.

Plaited, knit-in-the-round fabric is worked in alternate rounds of uncrossed Western and uncrossed Eastern knitting. The fabric (left) won't bias. On one round, beads slant up to the left; in the next, they slant up to the right.

inside of the loop below, and locking the bead into place with the slip stitch.

To block out most of the bias, I soaked the finished rectangle in cool water for about 15 minutes. I laid it out wrong side up on a fluffy towel on my ironing board, and using a yardstick to make sure the sides were equal lengths and the piece was square, I stretched and pinned repeatedly until everything was even. I placed pins at ½-in. intervals and let it dry for several days.

I interfaced and stabilized the purse shape by couching a double layer of hair canvas, cut on the straight grain, to the inside (as shown in the photo on p. 59). I placed pins at the corners, then at the side centers, and finally along the edges to keep the bag aligned on the straight of the canvas. I pinned all over the inner portion of the rectangle to keep it square during couching. As I couched in zigzags round and round the bag, I was very careful to go between beads and not to split the knitting silk.

The lining is a heavy silk charmeuse that exactly matches the blue beads. I cut it with generous seam allowances all around and staystitched. I carefully measured the amount of pouch to be folded up and the place the flap would fall across the back. Then I cut a mirror pocket double, sewed right sides together almost all around, inverted it, and folded in the unsewn seam. I placed it on the center back of the lining so the mirror top would be a scant ⅛ in. below the flap fold and topstitched the pocket sides and bottom in place close to the edge. Then I sewed the lining pouch, leaving an allowance to be folded in and handsewn at the front top. I tacked in the bottom corners.

I handsewed the bead pouch with an overhand stitch, folding in the selvage. Then

I worked a blind hem along the top edge of the pouch and lining. I blind-hemmed the flap sides and top (photo, p. 59).

Finally, I attached the strap. I found some lovely silver metal tassels at the M & J Trimming Co. in New York. I ran the threads from the cord ends through the loops on top of each tassel and the center of the cord for several inches. An overhand stitch holds the cord invisibly along the edges of the side pouch seams up to the flap fold.

Knitting a bead purse in the round—Now for my next adventure: All of the older bags that I've seen were knit in the round, probably to avoid purling. Knitting in the back of each stitch and pushing the bead through from back to front is relatively easy, but there's still a major problem: All twisted stitches bias. Some of the bags I studied looked like beaded bias tubes with pastoral scenes spiraling around them.

Adjusting gauge, tension, and materials can help, and you can block out a lot of the distortion, but it seemed that there ought to be a way to control the bias by alternating it. That technique is known as plaited knitting; it was much more common centuries ago, particularly in the East, in the Middle East, and in Northern Africa. *Mary Thomas's Knitting Book* (Dover reprint, 1972) explains how to produce it in flat knitting and notes that it was sometimes used for bead knitting.

In order to work plaited knitting in the round, you must alternate a plain, uncrossed round of Western-style knit with a round of plain, uncrossed Eastern knitting (drawing above). The opposite methods of entering the stitch and throwing the yarn cause the stitches on each round to alternate the direction of twist.

All choices have consequences, and choosing to eliminate the bias in bead fabric by zigzagging it this way involves trade-offs. Most of the bags I saw were knit with a single direction of cross and its consequent bias; so, if you want to knit something typically authentic, your bag should bias. If your beads are transparent or semitransparent, you'll see them aligned on the thread diagonally. Most were also knit with a Western crossed stitch, so the thread slants upward to the left. On plaited fabric, one round slants upward to the left, and the next slants upward to the right. The beads also tend to nestle into each other. These effects (detail photos above) can be distracting or attractive, depending on your design and point of view.

I decided it was very important to knit my elaborate floral purse in the round, without bias, so my first step was to practice plaited bead knitting in the round. The odd-numbered rounds are plain, uncrossed Western knit (left drawing, above), with a bead inserted on each stitch. The even-numbered rounds are plain, uncrossed Eastern knitting and beads. If the left-hand (front) leg of the stitch is closer to the tip of the needle, you know the stitch was knit Western; if the right-hand (back) leg is closer to the tip, the stitch was knit Eastern.

I was ready to find my floral pattern. I considered tracing a picture onto fine graph paper and coloring it. If a friend hadn't come up with the antique chart on the cover, that's what I'd have done.

With the chart in hand, I made a list of the colors and numbers of shades of each that I needed. Then came the hard part—finding 32 different colors of the same size seed bead. I didn't need large quantities of any of the pattern colors, so I didn't want to buy half kilos. At Beadworks I found almost all the colors and shades I needed in tubes. I'd been hoping to knit with size 12° seed beads, but size 11° was the smallest I could find that offered excellent color ranges. I ordered small quantities of the three other colors I was lacking from Eagle Feather Trading Post. I wanted gunmetal-colored faceted beads for the background, but no one seemed to have them, at least in size 11°. Finally, I went to Elliot Greene & Co. in New York, where I could see the bunches of seed beads, and selected a kilo of green iris—40,000 beads for the background.

When I'd finally gotten all the beads and had bought two spools of white Gudbrod silk, size D, I was ready to plan the shape of the bag and calculate my cast-on. I wanted almost the entire floral bouquet to be on the front of the bag—150 sts—and I wanted the bag to have a bowl-shaped bottom.

The bags I studied were rectangular, had curved sides caused by rapid increasing at the beginning and middle of the round, or were increased in segments. I chose the last method, but I decided to make my bottom edge slightly longer than usual. That's why the bottom curves like a frown when the bag is laid flat. Some of the bags were begun with a pinhole cast-on, but managing 1 or 2 sts on four double-pointeds is really difficult. Others began with a cast-on several inches long and then increased out to the straight sides of the bag body. Seams were rare or nonexistent, which meant that a tubular cast-on was normally employed.

I decided to cast on 112 sts and to increase to 288 sts in 34 rows with eight segments (photo, p. 56). I worked two increases in each segment every third round. And I decided that, since the main pattern was very elaborate, I wouldn't work a design there. Many of the old purses and bags used a wheel pattern similar to those on traditional Scottish tammies.

I wrote out a list of my 34 rounds and calculated the number of beads that each would have. Then I strung the 34 rounds,

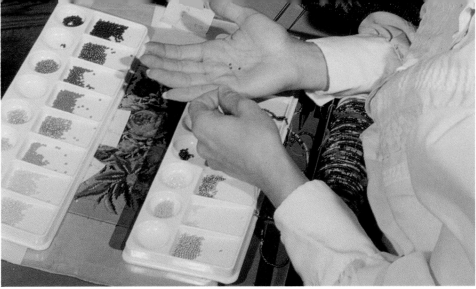

Accurate stringing is nine-tenths of the battle. Korach strings 20 rounds (5,760 beads) at one time, using a twisted-wire beading needle. The chart is protected by a plastic sleeve so she can mark her place. She triple-checks the count for each row, as an error can ruin the pattern.

starting with the 34th and tying a wool yarn marker on the thread between rounds. I found that a twisted-wire bead needle works better for me than a conventional long steel bead needle because the eye is much bigger, but flexible, so I can thread the silk directly through it.

To avoid a seam in the bottom of the bag, I worked a tubular cast-on. I used two-strand cast-on to put 112 silk sts on one size 00000 steel double-pointed needle. I knit four tubular plaited rows back and forth with two needles as follows: *K1, inserting a bead; sl1 wyif* to end of row. Turn work over (since there's an even number of stitches, the last stitch is slipped). *K1, inserting a bead; sl1 wyif* to end of row to complete round 1. I worked round 2 similarly, except that I knit the bead stitch Eastern. On round 3 it was time to make the first set of increases. I placed split rings for jewelrymaking every 14 sts, remembering that slipped stitches didn't count on each side of the needle. I found that the most invisible way to increase was to pick up the running thread between stitches and work a crossed Western knit bead stitch in it.

By the time I'd reached the fourth round, I was getting pretty nervous. It would have been fatally easy to knit a slip stitch or to slip a knit stitch, so I transferred the work to eight size 00000 double-pointed needles and knit with the ninth needle. My friends dubbed my work "Ninja knitting" and begged me not to do it at lunch because it made them nervous. After about ten rounds, I cut back to six holding needles and a seventh one for knitting.

When I completed the 34 rounds of background color that I'd strung for the increases, I was finally able to start stringing for pattern. While stringing, I count each round at least three times and double-check the pattern part. This way, I know that if I run out of beads before the end of the round, I've slipped that many extras by accident. I have to check back along the row to the error, unknit, and redo the row. It's a lot easier to count carefully and work slowly and precisely than to find and fix mistakes. I hope to have the purse completed in a year. I'm sure the next one will go much more quickly. □

───────────

Alice Korach is an associate editor of Threads.

Books

Kliot, Jules and Kaethe, eds. *Bead Work.* Berkeley, CA: Lacis Publications (2982 Adeline St., Berkeley, CA 94703); 1984, $5.95 + $2 P&H.
The knitting and crochet information provided is very sketchy, but the pictures and charts are good. See

Thomas, Mary. *Mary Thomas's Knitting Book.* New York: Dover, 1972 (reprint), $4.50.
This book is unsurpassed by modern knitting books in quantity and quality of bead-knitting information.

Suppliers

Au Ver a Soie (manufacturer)
Kreinik Mfg. Co. (distributor)
Box 1966
Parkersburg, WV 26101
(304) 422-8900
Silk yarns: Soie Gobelins, Soie perleé, Soie 303.

Beadworks
139 Washington St.
South Norwalk, CT 06854
(203) 852-9194
Beadwork supplies; catalog, $10.

Eagle Feather Trading Post
168 W. 12th St.
Ogden, UT 84404
(801) 393-3991
Beadwork supplies; catalog, $3.

Elliot, Greene & Co., Inc.
37 W. 37th St.
New York, NY 10018
(212) 391-9075
Beads; color bead chart (free).

Gudebrod
Box 357
Pottstown, PA 19464
(215) 327-4050
Silk threads; call for the nearest distributor.

HARMAN Importing Co.
16 W. 37th St.
New York, NY 10018
(212) 947-1440
Beads, silk thread; catalog (free), to be requested by mail.

M & J Trimming Co.
1008 6th Ave.
New York, NY 10018
(212) 391-9072
Embellishments; no catalog.

Promenade
Box 2092, Boulder, CO 80306
(303) 440-4807
Beadwork supplies; catalog, $2.50.

Sheru Enterprises Inc.
49 W. 38th St.
New York, NY 10018
(212) 730-0766
Silk, beads (not in catalog).

Shipwreck Beads
5021 Mud Bay Rd.
Olympia, WA 98502
(206) 866-4061
Beadwork supplies; catalog, $3.

Knitting with Furs and Feathers

How to enliven commercial yarns with handspun exotic fibers

by Helen von Ammon

Confetti, a typical Helen von Ammon hand-spun yarn, starts as a balanced assortment of fibers. In this case, from left to right: 3-in. lengths of scrap yarns, ramie sliver, and equal parts gray and camel-colored wool roving. Below, von Ammon uses a drum carder to blend the fibers together and comb them into alignment with each other.

Once off the carder, the resulting batt is ready to be spun (below). At the wheel, von Ammon (right) slowly feeds the batt through the ori-fice and onto the spinning bobbin, both of which are sized to handle bulky, one-ply yarns.

From *Threads* magazine (August 1989) 24:52-55

*t*he lady who lived in the house next to ours when I was little was of such heroic proportions that she couldn't wear most clothes from stores, so she knit her own. She taught me to knit when I was about as tall as a pogo stick. That skill has stayed with me, involving me in then undreamed-of pursuits. It would never have occurred to me that decades later I'd be raising Angora bunnies for wool or that I'd be part of a team doing research in Alaska on the Arctic musk-ox, whose superb down I now spin and knit.

Years later, while I was immersed in a busy life as a painter, a friend gave me a Turkish drop spindle as a birthday gift. Neither of us suspected what he was about to start. Another friend showed me how to use the drop spindle, introduced me to the world of fibers, and invited me to visit her weavers-and-spinners guild. Then I took a course in silk preparation and spinning, and that did it. My life hasn't been the same since. Spinning overtook painting forever, as well as any social life I might have had. I learned to combine silk with wool, llama, alpaca, cotton, and angora. I knit swatch after swatch of experimental combinations and soon was designing and knitting garments with my own handspun and home-designed yarns.

Without attempting here to teach the craft of spinning (spinners' guilds are still good places to go for that), I'd like to share how I approached the design of a few of my own knitting yarns and how I use them. If you've ever tired of the yarns you can buy, the possibility of producing your own may be as revolutionary for you as it has been for me.

My design process—I always plan my yarns as combinations of fiber and color, never using just a single element, as if I were mixing colors with fibers instead of in paint. In fact, even after a yarn is designed and spun, I usually combine it in a garment with other yarns, either knit together or in stripes. This way, I can contrast and combine commercial yarns with the qualities I designed into my own yarn, which look as little like commercial yarns as possible. Fibers and textures that wouldn't normally be used for knitting are stimulating to me, and I enjoy incorporating unlikely materials into my work.

Even when I use only commercial yarns, I combine them to create a new material. The knitting can get difficult, but I've combined up to ten commercial yarns into a single new yarn, knitting from all the cones and balls at once (left photo, p. 64). Because I don't ply these yarns together on the spinning wheel before knitting (I prefer the random color changes from just knitting the strands together), the different textures have a tendency to tangle and snag as they twist together, and I have to stop frequently to smooth them out. I still

feel that the results are worth the effort, and no spinning is involved at all.

Whether the yarn is commercial or handspun, I think first of color, and then of texture, feel, weight, and purpose. My procedure for developing each handspun yarn is always the same: I keep detailed notes in case I ever want to duplicate an effect. I record the date, source, and percentages of each fiber in each experimental mix, and all the steps I took in the process.

Several experiments are invariably necessary before I settle on a mix I like enough to make into a production yarn. I gather small quantities of the fibers that I think will work, and I blend them together into a batt by carding them, as I'm doing in the center photo on the facing page. I spin each small test batch into 1-yd. or 2-yd. lengths, plying them if necessary. Then I hand-wash the yarn in soap flakes, adding some hair conditioner or lemon juice to the final rinse to get out all the soap. I spin the wet yarn for about 15 seconds in the washing machine—spin cycle only—and hang it over dowels to dry. If the yarn is bulky, I sometimes have to set the twist by hanging a weight on the drying yarn.

When the samples are dry, I knit small swatches with several sizes of needles until I find the size that allows the yarn to breathe and loft and the knit fabric to drape. I hate to see handspun yarns knit under such tight tension that they're suitable for jousting bouts—too heavy and bulky. I measure each swatch before and after washing it to check for shrinkage and (Heaven forbid!) fading or bleeding. When I'm satisfied, I card and spin the full amount I need.

One way to spin—My careful record-keeping is about as scientific as my spinning ever gets. I do all my measuring of percentages by eye. I don't have any idea what the difference is between woolen and worsted yarns, and if I had to know what RPM's were, I'd quit. I've become very conscious, like any experienced spinner, of how the speed and tension of the spinning affect the results, but I try to keep the whole process intuitive and instinctive. Because my batts are usually full of odd bits and strange combinations, I spin slowly, with a medium tension and medium twist. Fluffy yarns like angora need slack tension to produce high twist and hold together. I always spin the wheel clockwise, which turns out a Z-spun yarn, so when I ply delicate yarns like angora and silk, I S-ply. The orifice, bobbin, and hooks on my wheel are all large enough to accommodate the bulky, single-ply yarns that I tend to prefer.

I sometimes find it helpful to wear close-fitting surgical or cloth gloves while spinning, especially if I'm working with large amounts of silk or a very textured yarn; both can be rough on the hands when you're spinning in quantity. I also have a carefully chosen spinning wardrobe, which

I'm wearing in the right photo on the facing page. For long bouts of treadle-pumping, I find the wooden-soled clogs comfortable, and my slacks and shirt are made of Qiana, which works like Teflon—nothing sticks to it!

Wool blends—Described below are a few of the yarns I've designed. Sweaters from these yarns can be hand-washed in warm, soapy water, rinsed at the same temperature, with hair conditioner or lemon juice in the final rinse, and dried flat on towels.

Confetti: When I was a child, I loved to get grab bags; I always waited until I got home to see what surprises were inside. Recently I realized that I do the same thing when I design Confetti, one of my favorite yarns. Weaver members of the fiber guild I belong to save their trimmed yarn thrums for me in bags; when I return home from our meetings, I eagerly spill the contents onto the floor and examine the colors, textures, and quantities of each. Sometimes the grab bag contains such a perfect selection of colors that I use them just as they're combined. More often I separate the contents into seasonal family groups: yellows for spring; white, beige, pale violet, rose, and light blue for summer; brown, tan, orange, and green (my least favorite) for autumn; strong red, purple, dark blue, and black for winter. If a yarn isn't appropriate for Confetti, I use it for wrapping gifts. I've also spun Confetti out of my own yarns and threads that have slipped off their cones and gotten hopelessly entangled.

Keeping the colors in separate piles, I cut all the yarn into about 3-in.-long pieces. I use a sharp knife instead of scissors so the ends are less blunt and blend better with other fibers. I take a percentage from each color and mix them by hand. Then I add the softest gray and camel wool I have and white ramie sliver. I use about one-third each of thrums, wool, and ramie. Then I run the usual experiments. If the percentage of thrums is too high, the yarn won't stay together properly; it may be too intense or too scratchy; or I'll run out of thrums before I have enough yarn for a sweater. Once the combination of fibers is right, I drum-card the entire amount I plan to spin. Confetti holds together best at a medium twist. I don't ply it, but I do weight the washed hanks to set the twist.

Confetti is the most versatile yarn I've designed. I use it alone, as in the sweater in the right photo on p. 64, and knit it together with commercial yarns. Since it's bulky, I use a large needle for knitting—size 13 or 15. If a commercial yarn is being knit along at the same time, I may use a size 17.

Easton: Some years ago, I made an autumn visit to Easton, located on Maryland's Eastern shore. This area is a flyway for wild geese, with legal hunting carefully controlled at certain times of the year. As I walked around my friend's property, I was

Von Ammon blends commercial yarns by just knitting, or crocheting, them together (left). Her cone rack helps keep yarns untangled, but she still must stop often to smooth them out. The rich, random contrasts make it worth the effort. Her sweaters are simple structures designed to focus attention on the unusual yarns. The one above in Confetti (also shown in the detail) is finished with crocheted trim in blended commercial yarns. (Photo above by Robert Aude)

saddened to come upon a wild goose, alive but wounded by a hunter. My friend humanely dispatched the goose, and we plucked it soon thereafter. To see a wild goose this closely was a new experience. The breast and underdown beneath the large feathers were pearl gray, and the small, curled feathers were smoky gray. I examined the feathers and down tufts under a ten-power hand lens, awed by the perfection of each tiny, feathery frond. It was essential to find a way to incorporate this natural, ethereal resource into my work.

When I got back to San Francisco, I stuffed the down and small curled feathers into three pillowcases, which was like trying to package snowflakes. A face mask helped, but there was no way to prevent the down from whirling and drifting into every crevice of my clothes and the workroom. Setting the washing machine on the gentle cycle, I washed the feathers in the pillowcases, one case at a time, in warm water and soap flakes. Unfortunately, the last load was expensive. The pillowcase seam split, spilling feathers and down throughout the washing machine and motor. Once order was restored, I fluffed wet feathers and down onto a large towel, turned them from time to time, and soon the material was dry and more beautiful than before.

With clean down and feathers I began experimenting in earnest. I carded them together in varying percentages with black alpaca, chocolate llama, and brown Cots-

wold wool and spun several different combinations, but the yarn continued to lack that life-giving spark. Remembering advice from a former instructor that a painting should always have a surprise element, however small or subtle, I added a small percentage of rich midnight-blue batt. The subtle, deep blue, mixed with dark brown fibers and pale-gray down, was the element it needed. The final recipe was one-fourth each of alpaca, llama, down, and blue wool.

Pleased with the mix, I carded down, feathers, and fibers on my drum carder, filling a big basket with lofty batts. I wanted only down in the yarn, and carding was a fairly efficient way to separate the feathers. Large feathers and some down fell under the carder. As I spun the batts, I pulled out most of the other feathers. I pulled out persistent feathers that got caught in the yarn as I knit. I spin Easton, like Confetti and most of my bulky yarns, with a medium twist, and I don't ply it. After I wash it, I hang a 6-lb. to 8-lb. weight (depending on skein size) at the bottom of each skein to set the twist. As I knit the yarn, a bit more down comes out, but most of it stays in the garment (detail photo at top, facing page).

I also use the clean, small, and curly wild goose feathers to knit with. I tie (with a square knot) three small feathers by the quills onto an invisible nylon host thread, about 6 in. from the end, skip a few inches, and then tie three more feathers until the string is about 18 in. long with randomly

spaced feather groups. If the string is longer, the thread becomes difficult to control. This string of feather bunches can be knit along with yarn, and the feathers can later be pulled through to the garment's right side. Yes, a feather does moult occasionally, but if you've knit enough of them, you can afford to lose a few. Feathers can be stitched in a similar way to the finished garment.

Divinity: I designed this yarn (bottom photos, facing page) for clients who are allergic to wool or who find wool too warm. I drum-card together one part each of ramie sliver and white cotton with a very small amount (about 5%) of wool for color. The wool, which I've previously dyed a brilliant red, I drum-card together with a large amount of white wool, which brings the red down to a soft, undulating pink. I then Z-spin ramie, cotton, and pink wool with a medium twist. Divinity is a bulky yarn, so I don't ply it, but I do set the twist with weights after I've washed and machine-spun it to remove excess water.

Designing a garment—My favorite yarn is usually the one I've just designed. As I knit the first swatch, I ask myself: "Would this look better with a commercial yarn knit along with it, or does it work better alone? Is it so textural that it requires rest areas of a different and more quiet yarn? What tension will allow it to breathe? Will another yarn, perhaps an inelastic silk, knit with it prevent too much stretch?"

When I design sweaters, I'm first inspired by the yarn, its texture, color, hand, and weight. I draw ideas on paper and sometimes cut and fold them as if for a paper doll. If unsure about a design, I sometimes knit a tiny garment for a wooden mannequin. Keeping the design simple, I let the exotic fibers make the statement. I don't use pattern stitches and cables, as I think they should be worked with simpler yarns than I usually spin. I design with someone in mind or perhaps an idealized body type, thinking in generous proportions. Since a heavy person looks better in a garment a size or two larger, I think loose.

For a sweater shell, I often start at one side and knit a big rectangle with a slit in the middle for the neck opening, on each side of which I knit with a separate ball, one for the front and one for the back. When the shell is wide enough, I bind off in a similar tension to the cast-on, then fold the flat piece in half and sew partway up the sides. I like to leave armholes generously large. This forms a basic sleeveless sweater, which can be the base for adding sleeves, for making a knit 1, purl 1 waistband, or for making a cowl neckline. There are many other possibilities.

If you prefer knitting from the bottom, you can make the same shape with circular needles. Cast on the number of stitches required for the bust size, join, and knit round and round to the armhole opening. Then begin knitting back and forth with two balls, one for the front and one for the back. When the garment is long enough, weave the front and back together at the shoulder, or bind off with a contrasting color or textured yarn, emphasizing the bind-off. Then use a smaller needle and pick up stitches for a knit 1, purl 1 waistband, binding off with a size larger needle in knit 1, purl 1.

If a yarn is bulky, like Divinity, and not plied but used as a singles yarn, it tends to bias. To avoid biasing, I use two balls of yarn, knitting two rows with one ball and two rows with the other. This also distributes variations of color and texture more evenly.

I like to be adventurous. If I think a yarn won't be enough for a whole sweater, I start knitting from the side, sleeve to sleeve. For one row of knitting, I allow about three times as much as the length of the row. When I'm halfway through, I can judge if there's enough yarn. If there isn't, I knit the second half with a totally different color or texture, maintaining the same gauge. If a circular-knit sweater comes out shorter than planned, I may exaggerate the knit 1, purl 1 waistband that I'll add onto the body. I'll pick up a color in the body yarn and make the cuffs and waistband prominent.

Finishing details—A crocheted edge of compatible, contrasting yarns, is a simple and beautiful way to finish the neckline, sleeves, or bottom edge of a garment. Frequently I accentuate seams with crochet, making

them part of the design. I tack down the ends of yarn inside with needle and thread.

Assuming that the gauge has been correct, washing and blocking a completed sweater aren't necessary. While I'm knitting a garment—especially when I'm traveling—I keep it wrapped in a protective cloth, and I take along towelettes in foil to keep my hands pristine. A garment of fine yarn may require a last-minute touch-up, which won't crush the yarn. A steam iron held just above a pressing cloth laid atop the sweater is usually sufficient.

Finding fibers—Acquiring exotic fibers, while serious, isn't a life-threatening disease. In fact, I find the process almost automatic—they seem simply to attach themselves to me, like passing too close to a fishhook cactus. Fiber sources keep changing, so it's helpful to belong to a guild and share information. Many stores have catalogs that they'll send you. You should keep them on file for up-to-date information.

County fairs and craft exhibits are good sources. Here, you'll deal directly with the animal breeders for raw wool, mohair, angora, and other fibers. If you really want to start at the beginning, you can buy beautiful whole fleeces, but be sure to read up on them first so you'll know what you're buying. Spinning- and weaving-supply stores have books on these specialized skills. Some of the suppliers I use are listed below. □

Helen von Ammon lives in San Francisco, CA. She has been selling her sweaters to boutiques for nine years.

Supplies

Alden Amos
11178 Upper Previtali Rd.
Jackson, CA 95642
(209) 223-4132
Spinning wheels and supplies, wool batts dyed to order.

Bonnie's Bunny Barn
Box 292
Sunol, CA 94586
(415) 862-2028
Raw angora, llama wool, mohair.

Clemes & Clemes, Inc.
650 San Pablo Ave.
Pinole, CA 94564
(415) 724-2036
Spinning and wool basics; very generous with information about finding exotic fibers.

The Llamas Loft
Box 448
Valley Ford, CA 94972
(707) 795-5726
Llama farm, raw llama wool.

Straw Into Gold
3006 San Pablo Ave.
Berkeley, CA 94702
(415) 548-5241
All kinds of fibers, retail and wholesale.

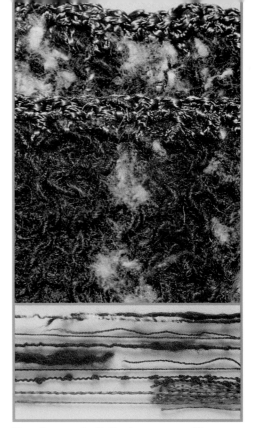

Von Ammon knit Easton, spun with goose down, together with a thin, blue commercial yarn and alternated it in random rows with a brown wool and llama handspun, knit together with a burgundy wool; it's finished with crocheted-together rayons. In the detail, Easton is on top, followed by the other yarns von Ammon combined with it.

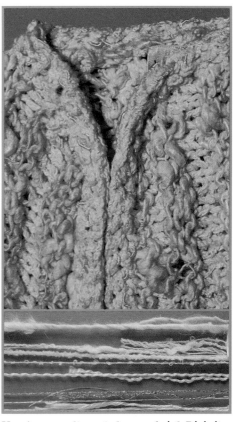

Von Ammon alternated rows of pink Divinity with random rows of knit-together commercial yarns: cotton, silk, and high-gloss rayon. In the detail, Divinity is on top, followed by the combined commercial yarns, then by yarns added only in the crocheted edging.

Six pairs of handknit gloves, representing six techniques (clockwise from top): blue houndstooth gloves (no shaping, cuff, or thumb gusset); black-and-white gloves, inspired by an embroidered sweater, with tapered fingertips and a decorated thumb gusset on the palm; oatmeal-colored gloves in Austrian cable pattern (the thumb emerges from the side, without interrupting the pattern); multicolor gauntlet gloves with double-knit hand and fingers; red gloves with a shaped cuff and thumb shaping that emphasizes the cable; ivory garter-stitch gloves worked side to side.

Handknitting Gloves

An impressive tribute to the creative hand

by Deborah Newton

though I am an avid handknitter, I have always avoided making my own gloves. I had envisioned a pincushion of double-pointed needles, stitches balancing precariously at all angles, each finger a dreaded obstacle to overcome. Even confident mitten makers stay away from the apparent complexities of fitting the hand. However, the average glove takes less time to knit than the sleeve of a child's sweater. A glove evolves in such a logical way that the creative knitter can easily develop a system and build upon it, free from dependence on printed patterns. I made many pairs last year, and they reign as my favorite knitting projects.

The handknit glove has a rich past: from a rude wool covering for a peasant's swarthy hand, to a silken casing for the hands of the most revered clergyman, to the fanciful geometrics of folkloric patterns. Knit in myriad colors and textures, the glove has been buttoned, initialed, gauntleted, tasseled, fulled, and defingered. It can be as simple as a swatch for the beginner and a miniature sculpture for the expert. Most exciting for me is the three-dimensional re-creation of the shape of the hand and the plotting of patterns on that surface.

The best way to learn to design and knit your own gloves is to start with the simplest version and then let this glove be the prototype for more complex pairs. I first mastered a basic glove in simple stockinette stitch. After learning the fundamentals of shape, I began to superimpose texture and color. Swatch in a simple pattern to get a basic gauge in the yarn of your choice. Measure the hand to be gloved so you know how many stitches to cast on and you have a record of basic lengths. Then plot out a simple hand chart to follow (see top-left drawing, page 68). Don't worry about the fingers until you get to them. And if you don't enjoy knitting fingers, you can turn your glove into a mitten. Start simple, gain confidence, and then refine the look and fit of your gloves.

You may prefer to work out your design and techniques on one glove before beginning the second, so keep records of what you have done. You can use this information later to test new yarns, patterns, and shaping techniques. I start both gloves at the same time, working up to a certain point on one, and then repeating the process on the other. This has its advantages: When one glove is done, I often lack the excitement to begin the other because the challenge of problem solving is over.

I wish I'd discovered glovemaking sooner. It suits my passion for shaping. Gloves let me play with all techniques, from colorwork and graphics to the most complex of textural patterns. Glove knitting becomes easier and more pleasurable with each new pair. My hardworking hands have finally received their most appropriate reward.

Yarns and needles

A few ounces of yarn suffice for the average glove. Wool is warm and can be blocked to even out irregularities in the knitting. The strong, smooth blends of wool and synthetics suggested for socks are good choices. Tapestry wool, split if necessary, offers an incredible range of colors for decorative embroidery or small areas of color. Inelastic cotton, rayon, or linen would create problems for the beginner, but because they are cooler, they allow the expert to extend the season designated for honoring hands.

The best glove yarns are those in the fingering category (the name says it all!). The mention of these fine yarns elicits groans even from expert knitters, but very few stitches go into the making of a glove, and these responsive yarns will surprise and delight the uninitiated. From a design point of view, yarns that range from 7 sts to 10 sts to the inch allow complex patterning in texture and color, even in small finger areas, and the ability to use large pattern repeats and combinations of patterns. They offer flexibility and great warmth when stranded colorwork is used.

Sport-weight yarns (5½ sts to 6 sts to the inch) are good for learning techniques, and unlike finer yarns, there are many textured yarns in this weight. Sport weight is suitable for small pattern repeats and colorwork in the hand area. Shetland yarns in this weight are soft and come in a wide range of colors. Heavy yarns work best in a simple pattern—not worked too tightly, or the fabric will be stiff and uncomfortable. A worsted-weight yarn (5 sts to the inch, the heaviest extreme) is fine for a large, sturdy man's glove in stockinette stitch.

Unless the glove is worked from side to side (bottom photo, page 70), double-pointed needles (dpn) are essential for seamless knitting. If casting on to three or four needles seems difficult, cast on all stitches to one needle. Then divide the stitches among the remaining ones. Five needles (two at palm, two for back, and one extra for knitting) provide symmetry, but four are easier to hold. To maintain tension, pull firmly on the yarn when changing needles.

I work test swatches back and forth on straight needles even though my circular gauge can vary slightly. It's quicker. After you've made a few gloves in a favorite yarn, let the glove be the gauge swatch. In most cases, palm width is the same as the width of the back of the hand. But for a complex pattern across the back of the hand, you may need more stitches to obtain the same width of a simpler one on the palm.

If you need more or fewer stitches for a pattern or motif, thereby making the glove width larger than the hand, change to a smaller needle size to adjust fit. If you're making gloves for someone you can't measure, carry a few rib stitches up from the cuff into the hand. This will make the width flexible enough to fit various sizes.

A glove should be tried on at all stages of knitting, even while on the dpn. Or, for greater accuracy, slip the stitches to a strand of yarn with a tapestry needle. (When you knit a glove, you'll often set aside stitches this way to work others.)

From *Threads* magazine (December 1987) 14:24-29

Recording hand measurements

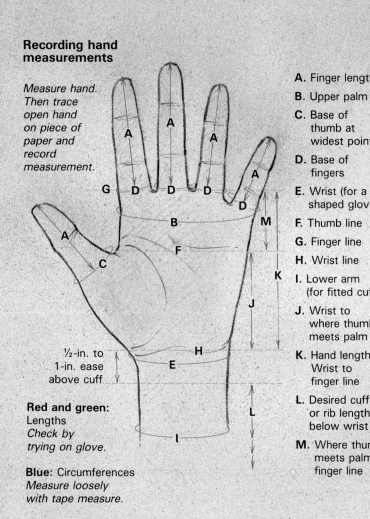

Measure hand. Then trace open hand on piece of paper and record measurement.

½-in. to 1-in. ease above cuff

Red and green: Lengths *Check by trying on glove.*

Blue: Circumferences *Measure loosely with tape measure.*

A. Finger lengths
B. Upper palm
C. Base of thumb at widest point
D. Base of fingers
E. Wrist (for a shaped glove)
F. Thumb line
G. Finger line
H. Wrist line
I. Lower arm (for fitted cuffs)
J. Wrist to where thumb meets palm
K. Hand length: Wrist to finger line
L. Desired cuff or rib length below wrist
M. Where thumb meets palm to finger line

Knitting the simplest glove
(left hand)

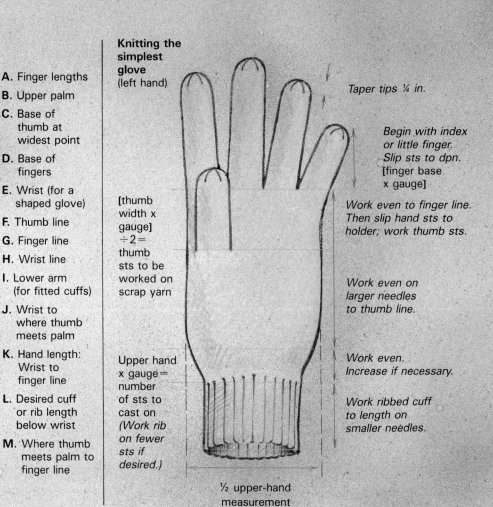

Taper tips ¼ in.

Begin with index or little finger. Slip sts to dpn. [finger base x gauge]

Work even to finger line. Then slip hand sts to holder; work thumb sts.

[thumb width x gauge] ÷ 2 = thumb sts to be worked on scrap yarn

Upper hand x gauge = number of sts to cast on (Work rib on fewer sts if desired.)

Work even on larger needles to thumb line.

Work even. Increase if necessary.

Work ribbed cuff to length on smaller needles.

½ upper-hand measurement

Dividing stitches for thumbs and fingers

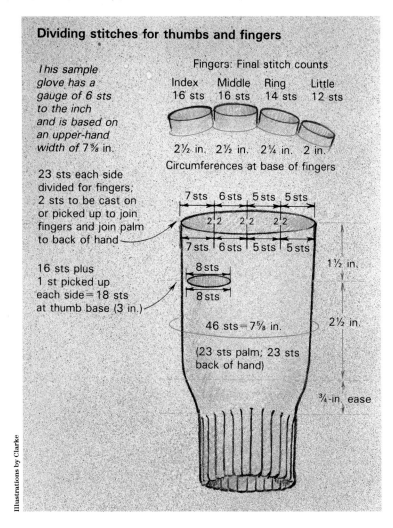

This sample glove has a gauge of 6 sts to the inch and is based on an upper-hand width of 7⅝ in.

23 sts each side divided for fingers; 2 sts to be cast on or picked up to join fingers and join palm to back of hand

16 sts plus 1 st picked up each side = 18 sts at thumb base (3 in.)

Fingers: Final stitch counts

Index	Middle	Ring	Little
16 sts	16 sts	14 sts	12 sts
2½ in.	2½ in.	2¼ in.	2 in.

Circumferences at base of fingers

7 sts 6 sts 5 sts 5 sts
2 2   2 2   2 2
7 sts 6 sts 5 sts 5 sts

8 sts
8 sts

1½ in.

46 sts = 7⅝ in.

(23 sts palm; 23 sts back of hand)

2½ in.

¾-in. ease

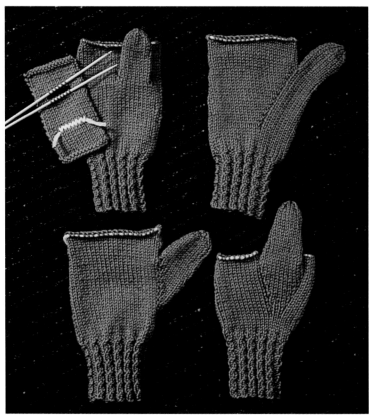

Four different types of thumb shaping (clockwise from upper left): the simplest thumb, with swatch showing how a scrap strand can be knit in and then removed so stitches on both sides of the thumb can be slipped to needles and worked; increases worked to the side of center palm to accommodate the thumb; thumb gusset formed on the palm of the glove; thumb gusset worked to the side of the glove.

Planning the simplest glove

After measuring the hand with a flexible tape measure, trace the open hand on paper and record the measurements. If you're making gloves for someone else, keep the tracing as a permanent record. Record both circumference and length measurements of the wrist, palm, and fingers. The top-left drawing on the facing page shows where to take each measurement.

The circumference of the upper palm above the thumb (B) is the most crucial measurement. The beginner can design a glove simply from this figure: *The upper-hand measurement multiplied by gauge gives the best number of stitches to begin a basic glove.* Cast on that number of stitches with smaller dpn and work edge/rib to the desired length. (Fewer stitches can be cast on for a tighter rib; increase after last rib row.) The simplest glove has no thumb shaping and is knit straight to the point where the thumb would meet the hand, as with the blue houndstooth glove and double-knit glove on page 66. (The more experienced glove knitter may opt for more shaping.)

Beginning to knit—You can begin rounds at any place on the glove; however, the best place to begin is on the outside or inside edge of the hand. This way, patterns on the front and back won't be interrupted. You can also begin the round at the center of the palm and maintain pattern symmetry. For example, in the oatmeal-colored glove on page 66 I wanted three repeats of a wide pattern to form a cuff; therefore, I began at the center palm so that the middle repeat would fall directly on the back of the hand. Let the pattern size suggest design possibilities.

A ribbed edge is a good choice for a glove intended for active use. Another option is to work a cuff or gauntlet straight from the lower edge, with or without shaping; ribbing can be inserted at the wrist line for a closer fit. After working the rib or cuff, change to larger dpn and work in pattern to where the base of the thumb meets the palm. Drop the working yarn. Then work the thumb stitches (equal to half the circumference of the thumb base) on a separate scrap strand of yarn, either on the palm or at the side of the glove, as shown in the photo on the facing page. Resume knitting with the working yarn. But in your excitement to begin shaping, don't forget (as I have) to reverse the placement for each thumb, or you will end up with two gloves for the same hand.

After the hand is complete, slip the stitches to a holding yarn. Next, remove the scrap strand; there'll be an opening in the fabric. Most variations in gloves occur in the thumb shaping. To knit the simplest thumb, pick up the top and bottom loops of this opening. It helps to pick up one or two extra stitches at each end of the thumb opening to neaten the join to the palm. (See bottom drawing, facing page.)

Shaped thumbs and gussets—The shaped-thumb gusset, which you work to the side or on the palm by increasing regularly to form a triangle, aids in creating a perfect-fitting glove. Before beginning the gusset, work even above the rib or cuff for ½ in. to 1 in. to position the wrist and prevent thumb movement from pulling up the ribbing.

There are two kinds of triangular thumb gussets: One originates at the palm of the hand and interrupts the patterns there; the other originates at the side of the hand and is worked independently of the patterns at the back and palm. To begin the thumb gusset on the palm, mark a central stitch to the right or left of center palm (depending on which glove you're knitting). The triangular gusset is best created when two increases are worked, one to each side of the central stitch, every three or four rounds until there are enough stitches to measure about ½ in. less than the measurement of the base of the thumb. (To produce a more obvious gusset for design reasons, you may wish to mark more than one central stitch as the base of the gusset.)

Work the increases to form the gusset to where the thumb meets the palm, slip the hand stitches to a holder, and work the thumb separately. If there are enough stitches to accommodate the measurement of the base of the thumb (this depends on the rate of increases in the gusset), divide the stitches over the dpn and knit the thumb. First cast on extra stitches (½ in. worth) to join the sides of the thumb together without strain. For a fine-fitting thumb, decrease 1 st every three or four rounds until the length is reached; then work the tip.

The thumb gusset can be planned as a design feature as well as for fit. I admire traditional Scandinavian gloves, which often had a thumb gusset worked in a different pattern than on the palm of the hand. I used this feature in my black-and-white glove on page 66, plotting the gusset on a piece of graph paper and accentuating it with a decorative pattern. Likewise, the thumb gusset for the oatmeal glove, originating at the side of the hand, was worked in a small textured pattern to contrast with the patterns on the front and back.

Although not technically a gusset, increases worked all to one side on the palm create extra fabric to accommodate the thumb. In this kind of glove, 1 st is marked at the center of the palm approximately 1 in. above the wrist mark. Every two or three rounds, 1 st is increased next to this, always in the same place, creating a diagonal line across the palm. For the red gloves at right, I used the increases as a design feature next to a central cable, causing the cable to move over the palm, then to the tip of the thumb.

Above the thumb—After the thumb is knit, the hand of the glove is resumed. Slip all reserved stitches back to the dpn. Before you continue knitting, pick up the same

After working the thumb, Newton resumes knitting the hand section. She has picked up three stitches (½ in. worth) in the base of this thumb to join the thumb to the hand without strain and to close the fabric.

When starting a middle finger, Newton works stitches from the back or front of the hand and picks up stitches in the completed adjacent finger, as shown here. Then she works the other side of the hand. To complete the round, she casts on the preplanned number of stitches between fingers to join the front to the back.

Newton intentionally worked increases to form the thumb shaping of these red textured gloves all to one side of the palm. This shaping is emphasized by the movement of the cable along the palm into the thumb. She shaped the wide cuffs by working gradual decreases to the wrist on either side of the tiny cable at the center front and back.

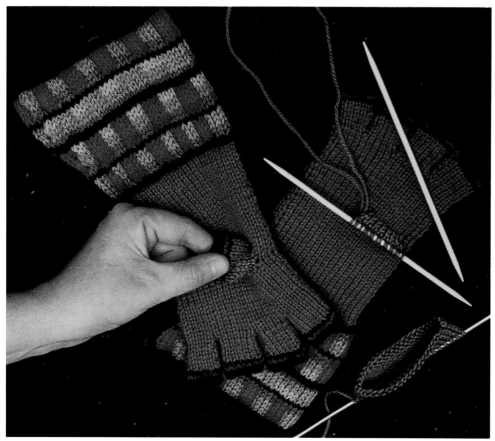

The multicolor gauntlet glove with a double-knit thumb in progress, worked back and forth on double-pointed needles. A completed thumb is held open at left. The straight needle at top right shows a single-color double-knit fabric in progress.

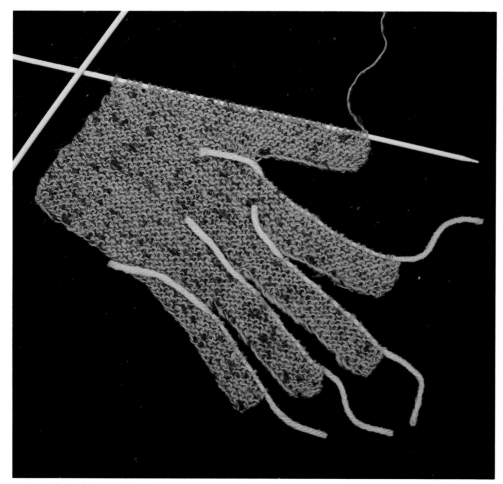

Newton is knitting this garter-stitch glove side to side; she has completed half of the hand. Instead of binding off the half fingers, she has slipped the stitches onto yarn holders. When she knits the other half of the hand, she can slip the stitches onto the needle and eliminate one seam in each finger.

number of stitches that were cast on at the base of the thumb. (See top photo, page 69.) This will join the thumb to the hand stitches without strain and will close the fabric. If the final number of stitches yield a measurement larger than the upper hand, decrease 1 st above the thumb every other round or so to reach the desired number. Fewer stitches may be started at the wrist to make up for any picked-up stitches in the thumb, forming a more shapely glove.

Work even until the finger line is reached. The stitches for the little finger may be set aside ¼ in. to ½ in. before you begin the other three fingers, but the elasticity of most knit fabrics eliminates the need for this fine tuning. Remember to try on the glove to check lengths before beginning the fingers.

Planning the fingers—Separate the front from the back stitches. For an allover pattern, just divide the stitches in half. If the patterning on the back of the hand requires more stitches to yield the same width as the palm, decrease before reaching the finger line to balance the stitch count.

For a well-fitting glove, it is necessary to cast on stitches or pick up stitches between the fingers to link the back to the palm. These stitches re-create the space between the fingers. If you were simply to divide the front and back stitches by 4 and add 2 sts between each finger, the glove would fit—knit fabric is flexible. However, decisions about where to assign extra stitches really refines the fit.

To determine the stitches required for each finger, multiply the measurement from the base of each finger by gauge. Record this figure (see bottom drawing, page 68).

Return to the glove stitch count, and assign stitches from the front and back to the little finger, planning to pick up 2 or 3 sts between the palm and back of the hand. Divide the remaining stitches by 3, assigning the same number of stitches from the front and back for the other three fingers. If it does not divide evenly, assign the extra stitch(es) to either of the first two (larger) fingers. Insert the figures in the chart, and then assign stitches between the fingers to achieve the original figure for each finger's circumference based on gauge. (Note that the index and little fingers have stitches assigned only on one side, whereas the middle two fingers need extra stitches on both sides.)

It's best to calculate stitch counts before you start the fingers to avoid ending the last finger with too few stitches. It is also then easier to concentrate just on knitting.

The base of the finger is most challenging. Begin with either the index or little finger, casting on the assigned number of stitches between fingers to join the front to the back, and begin the finger round. When starting a new finger, pick up stitches in the cast-on stitches of the adjacent completed finger, as shown in the center photo on page 69. Sometimes a small hole will occur where the front or back meets the picked-up stitches: Make a stitch here by lifting a strand from the thread below and knit into the back of it, omitting or decreasing one of the picked-up stitches. A decrease every 1 in. along the length of each finger lends an elegant tapered fit.

If you are extending an allover pattern into the fingers, consider the number of stitches that you need to complete full pattern repeats. For example, in the houndstooth glove, the pattern was a multiple of four stitches, so I picked up a number between the fingers to yield this multiple.

When beginning a middle finger, work stitches from either the back or front of the hand, and pick up stitches in the completed adjacent finger. Work stitches from the other side of the hand. Then cast on the preplanned number of stitches between fingers to join the front to the back, thereby completing the round.

Fingertips—Start to decrease rapidly about ¼ in. before the fingertip. Try on the glove, making sure the base of each finger fits the hand correctly. Divide your stitches evenly if you want symmetrical decreases. For example, 15 sts evenly divided on three needles allows two decreases each needle on one round, followed by a plain round without decreases, then one more decrease round. With some yarns it helps to change to smaller needles. With fine yarns and more stitches, decreases here can be a design feature, worked along the sides for a flattened tip (as in the black-and-white gloves on page 66) or divided evenly. Stitches can be woven, front to back, instead of gathered together at the tip. Experiment on the thumb or first finger to find the most appealing method.

An alternative knitting method and some special details

Working a glove back and forth on straight needles can be fun. It works best in garter stitch (6 sts to the inch or finer is best). Swatch to obtain a stitch and row gauge.

Begin the glove at the outer edge of the hand; a cuff can be knit in or added after completion. Starting along the outer hand, calculate how many stitches are necessary to reach from the tip of the little finger to the lower edge, according to your desired gauge. Cast on, and then work back and forth until the width of the little finger is reached; bind off to form one half of the finger. At the end of the next row, cast on enough stitches for the length of the ring finger and proceed. When you reach the thumb, work short partial rows to angle the thumb from the hand. After you reach the center of the thumb, the mirror image of the hand is worked in reverse.

To avoid seams, the experienced knitter can use the invisible cast-on method, then place stitches on holders instead of binding off so all edges can be woven. Instead, I

cast on in a traditional way but slip stitches to holders instead of binding off, as shown in the bottom photo on the facing page. On the second half of the hand, you can then slip these stitches to the needle instead of casting on new finger stitches so that one seam on each finger is eliminated.

Double-knit gloves—You can use the fascinating double-knit technique to make a seamless glove, working back and forth on straight needles to form two layers joined at the edges. It's a slow process, requiring a slipped stitch for every worked stitch, and you must be careful not to join the layers accidentally. But there is great potential here for playing with layers in different colors, and it should interest those who prefer working with just two needles. I worked the multicolor gauntlet on the double-knit glove on the facing page back and forth on straight needles, planning side closures with buttons. Then I used the stitches at the top of the gauntlet to begin the double-knit hand portion. (Those unfamiliar with the double-knit technique should scrutinize Barbara Walker's *A Treasury of Knitting Patterns* and *A Second Treasury of Knitting Patterns*.

Wrist treatment—A gauntlet or shaped cuff can be worked in place of ribbed edging and can add drama to a plain hand. If it is to cover a heavy garment, the cast-on edge should measure as much as 16 in., with decreases worked regularly to the wrist line.

Open palm—With an open palm, the hand may be temporarily freed without your having to take the glove off the wrist. You may work a wide opening above the thumb by binding off, then casting on on the next round; knitting a scrap strand to be removed later, as in the simple-thumb tech-

nique (page 69); or clipping a thread and unraveling it to either side after the glove is complete. This opening may be edged for an overlap, perhaps with a finer yarn.

Fingerless gloves—For hand warmth and finger agility, stop short of the fingertips and bind off or omit fingers. By adding a row or two of a noncurling pattern before you bind off, you'll form a neat edge.

Decorative surfaces—The hand surfaces can be divided for a variety of design treatments. Patterns can vary from front to back, horizontally or vertically, even extending into the fingers. Or the fingers can be worked in simpler patterns for ease. The wearer's initials are a traditional decoration for gloves.

Fulled gloves—Fulling will occur naturally in well-worn wool gloves when they are exposed to moisture and abrasion, but a fulled fabric can also be preplanned. The fabric is stiffer and works best for fingerless gloves; fingers require flexibility. To predict a fulled gauge, work swatches and full them by scrubbing with warm, soapy water. The knit glove will be larger than the hand, but after you've scrubbed them, you'll achieve the desired size and shape.

To keep from losing them—A handknit glove deserves this special attention! Long cords, not just for children, can go under a coat or sweater. Add a button for one glove and a buttonhole for its mate. Graceful loops will allow you to hang gloves over a belt or purse handle, and a wrist drawstring, with whimsical tassels and pompons, can be both functional and decorative. □

Deborah Newton is a knitwear designer and a frequent contributor to Threads *magazine. All photos by Cathy Carver.*

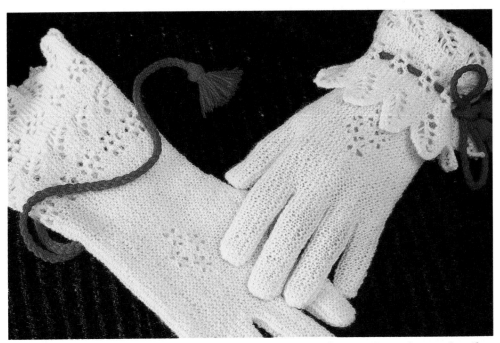

These ivory garter-stitch gloves were worked side to side on straight needles and seamed, rather than worked in the round. The lace edging, worked at the same time as the hand, forms a cuff.

The Shape of Socks

When you can turn a heel, you can knit any shape you want

by Theresa Gaffey

Socks—long or short, skinny or fat, plain or fancy—socks are ordinary things that we wear every day. But for most knitters, the way four needles unwind a ball of yarn into an article as mysteriously shaped as a sock is both amazing and intimidating.

To knit any shape that's not a square or a rectangle, you must know how to change the shape of the workpiece. There are four basic shaping methods—casting on/binding off, increasing/decreasing, working short rows, and choosing needle size/stitch pattern. Once you understand these four techniques, the prospect of "turning the heel" on a sock should not intimidate you at all. The amazement and mystery, however, will always remain.

Casting on/Binding off

The single most important element in determining the shape of your garment— sock, sweater, or hat—is one of the first techniques every beginning knitter learns: casting on. The form of the fabric is established by how it is cast on. Later in the work, casting on becomes a way to add a large number of stitches, usually abruptly and at either side of the piece. For instance, to form the cap sleeves of a sweater, you would cast on a number of stitches at the beginning of the armholes. In a sock, the picking up of stitches alongside the heel flap is a variation of casting on.

The other side of casting on is, of course, binding off. In most cases, binding off means discontinuing a part or all of the knitted fabric. The initial step in shaping the armhole for set-in sleeves usually requires binding off an inch of stitches at each edge. Similarly, most neck shaping involves binding off a number of stitches at the center of the fabric.

Increasing/Decreasing

A less abrupt way of shaping is to add or subtract—that is, to increase or decrease— one or more stitches in a row. Small, gradual increases, for example, can gently shape a sleeve. More concentrated increases will form waves of extra fabric, as in leg-of-mutton sleeves.

A series of decreases, on the other hand, will diminish the amount of fabric on which you are knitting. Therefore, if you want to taper a neckline, you work a number of decreases to eliminate fabric on the neck edge of a sweater. Decreasing occurs in socks that narrow at the calf, but the most dramatic use of the technique is in forming the gusset between heel and foot.

Short-row shaping

Short-row shaping means that instead of working an entire row, you turn the work around before you reach the end of the row. It enables you to enlarge a part of the fabric without increasing the remaining portion. On the heel of a sock, for example, you enlarge only the center part of the heel, which then creates a 90° angle, or "turns the heel."

Choosing stitch and needle size

Finally, your choice of stitch, needle size, and type or number of needles can help shape a garment. A rib stitch enables you to form the waist of a sweater and keeps the cuff of a sock snug around the leg. Changing to a larger needle will expand the fabric both horizontally and vertically, whereas changing to a smaller needle will contract it. With a circular needle or four double-pointed straight needles, you can join the beginning and end of the cast-on row and work in the round, thus forming a seamless tube, like a sock.

A demonstration sock

I think a sock is one of the most interesting shapes to knit. It involves casting on, knitting in the round, decreasing, and short-row shaping. Luckily, there is a standard method for the process, which varies little, if at all, from one sock to another. This method, along with the measurements you need to take, is summarized in the drawings on pages 73-75. To demonstrate the method, I'll discuss in detail the steps necessary to knit a knee sock for an imaginary leg. My directions for a fancy pair of bobby socks are given on page 76.

For your first experiment, I'd suggest a worsted-weight yarn; a pair of knee socks will consume about 10 oz. Fingering and sport-weight yarns make good socks (requiring about 3½ oz. per calf-length pair), but these yarns take much more time to knit. Try a lighter-weight yarn after you've had a chance to knit a few pairs of socks in worsted weight. You'll need a set of four 7-in. double-pointed needles and one tapestry needle for weaving the ends of the toes.

Before you start knitting the socks, you must measure the leg and foot, as shown in step 1 of the drawings, and determine the stitch and row gauges for the pattern you want to use. It is best to use an elastic stitch, such as a ribbing, which will conform to the shape of the leg. In fact, most of the time with an elastic stitch you won't have to decrease between calf and ankle. For the sample sock, I'll use these measurements: calf (A), 12 in.; ankle (B), 8 in.; foot (C), 9 in.; sock leg from the cuff to the ankle (D), 7 in.; heel height (E), 2 in.; decrease zone (F), 5 in.; gauge, 4 stitches per inch (sts/in.) and 6 rows per inch.

Casting on

For a short sock, multiply the ankle measurement by the stitch gauge to find the number of stitches to cast on. For a knee sock, use the calf measurement.

If you have decided to use a k1/p1 (knit one/purl one) ribbing for the cuff of the sock, you will need to round the number of stitches to the nearest multiple of two. For a k2/p2 ribbing, round to the nearest multiple of four. To start the sample sock, you could go ahead and cast on 48 sts (12 in. at calf x 4 sts/in.).

When using four needles, cast on in the same way as you would with two needles, but instead of putting all the stitches on one needle, divide them equally among three needles (step 2). For the 48 sts of the

From *Threads* magazine (December 1985) 2:28-32

sample sock, cast 16 sts on to each needle. In the case of 32 sts, you would cast 11 sts on to the first needle, 10 sts on to the second needle, and 11 sts on to the third needle. Be careful to cast on loosely. If this is hard for you, try casting on to a larger size needle or on to two needles held together.

Cuff ribbing and calf: No decreasing

Join the first stitch of the cast-on row to the last stitch, and with the fourth needle work in rounds in your ribbing pattern for 1 in. to 3½ in, according to how much cuff you want. Change to your main stitch pattern, increasing or decreasing as necessary to obtain the correct multiple of stitches. Round down when you can, or your sock might not fit.

If you are making a short sock or using a ribbing or other stretchy pattern for the main part of your sock, you simply work even in the pattern from the cuff to the top of the heel (step 3). However, if you are knitting a long sock in an inelastic stitch such as stockinette, you will need to decrease along the calf. In my opinion, decreasing the calf is a complication to be avoided whenever possible.

Decreasing the calf

When you must decrease the calf, it's best to take the decrease at the back, on either side of a seam stitch (step 4). Therefore, on the first round after the cuff, designate the last stitch as the seam stitch. Work even to the beginning of the narrowing of the calf, and make these calculations:

A. Figure out the number of rows in the decrease zone. Generally you want to complete the decrease 1 in. above the ankle, so you'd subtract 1 in. from the calf length and multiply the result by your row gauge. In the sample sock, 5 in. x 6 rows/in.=30 rows.

B. Figure out how many stitches to decrease: Subtract ankle measurement from calf measurement to get the number of inches to be decreased; multiply the result by your stitch gauge. In the sample sock, 12 in. - 8 in.=4 in. x 4 sts/in.=16 sts.

C. Find the number of decrease rows: Since you can decrease 2 sts in every decrease row, 1 st on each side of the seam stitch, you would divide the total decrease in half. In the sample sock, there'll be 8 decrease rows.

D. Finally, determine how often to decrease: Divide the total number of rows in the decrease zone by the number of decrease rows. In the sample, 30 total rows divided by 8 decrease rows means a decrease in every 4th row, starting on the 2nd row.

E. Decrease as follows: Work in pattern to within 2 sts of the seam stitch. Slip the next 2 sts separately, as if to knit; then insert the tip of the left-hand needle into the 2 sts, and knit them together—slip-slip-knit (ssk). (This is an alternative to the more frequent "k1, sl1, psso.") Work the seam stitch in knit or purl as established;

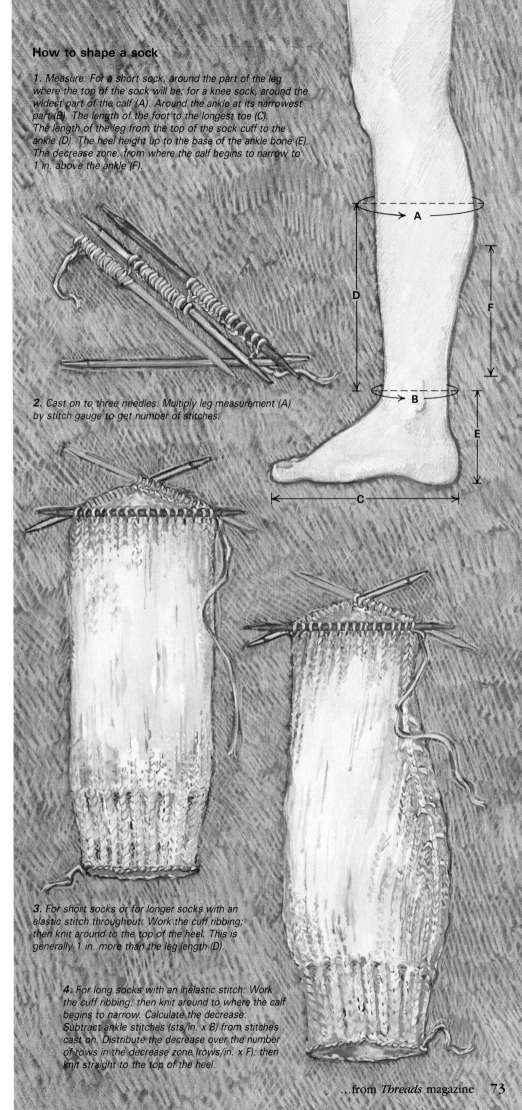

How to shape a sock

1. Measure: For a short sock, around the part of the leg where the top of the sock will be; for a knee sock, around the widest part of the calf (A). Around the ankle at its narrowest part (B). The length of the foot to the longest toe (C). The length of the leg from the top of the sock cuff to the ankle (D). The heel height up to the base of the ankle bone (E). The decrease zone, from where the calf begins to narrow to 1 in. above the ankle (F).

2. Cast on to three needles: Multiply leg measurement (A) by stitch gauge to get number of stitches.

3. For short socks or for longer socks with an elastic stitch throughout: Work the cuff ribbing; then knit around to the top of the heel. This is generally 1 in. more than the leg length (D).

4. For long socks with an inelastic stitch: Work the cuff ribbing; then knit around to where the calf begins to narrow. Calculate the decrease: Subtract ankle stitches (sts/in. x B) from stitches cast on. Distribute the decrease over the number of rows in the decrease zone (rows/in. x F); then knit straight to the top of the heel.

knit the next 2 sts together (k2tog). Work decrease rows as calculated, every 4th row or whatever, until you have completed the whole decrease—in the sample, a total decrease of 16 sts. Then work even for 1 in. This should bring you to the end of the round at the seam stitch, at the center of the top of the heel.

Heel

Whether you are knitting a knee sock or a short sock, when you reach the top of the heel, discontinue the pattern stitch and divide the stitches for working the heel flap (step 5). The heel requires one half the total number of stitches on the needles; the instep uses the rest of the stitches. Redistribute the stitches by placing the instep stitches on two needles. Do this by working to the end of the heel stitches on the first needle and placing all the heel stitches on one needle.

It is best to center the heel stitches on either side of the beginning of the round. If there are 32 sts on all three needles, you will need 16 sts for the heel. So on the sample sock, you would work across the first 8 sts on the first needle. Then you'd redistribute evenly on to two needles the remaining 3 sts, plus all 10 sts from the second needle, plus the first 3 sts of the third needle. Slip the remaining 8 sts from the third needle on to the needle with the heel stitches. If you have a seam stitch, add it to the heel stitches. Take a good look. You may want to balance the stitches to accommodate your pattern.

Now you have all the heel stitches on one needle. To add strength to the heel, you should work the heel stitches in a slip-stitch pattern, which makes a thicker fabric. Row 1 (wrong side): Purl across. Row 2: *Sl1, k1* across (the asterisks mean to repeat the stitch sequence they enclose to the end of the row). Work even in this heel stitch until the heel flap is as long as the heel height (step 6), which usually measures 2 in. to 2½ in. Mark the center of the heel flap or seam stitch, and discontinue the heel-stitch pattern.

Ready or not, it's time to turn the heel. You shape the heel by using short rows. Essentially, you work back and forth over the heel's center stitches until you've worked all stitches. To turn the heel (step 7), knit to 2 sts past the center marker (or past the seam stitch). Slip-slip-knit (ssk), k1, turn (step 7a). On the next row, purl to 2 sts past center, p2tog, p1, turn (step 7b). On the next row, knit to 3 sts past center, ssk, k1, turn. On the next row, purl to 3 sts past center, p2tog, p1, turn. Continue working out toward the edges in this manner until all stitches have been worked, and end with a purl row.

Instep

After you've turned the heel, knit to the center of the heel (step 8a) and mark the center. Now you'll need to pick up stitches

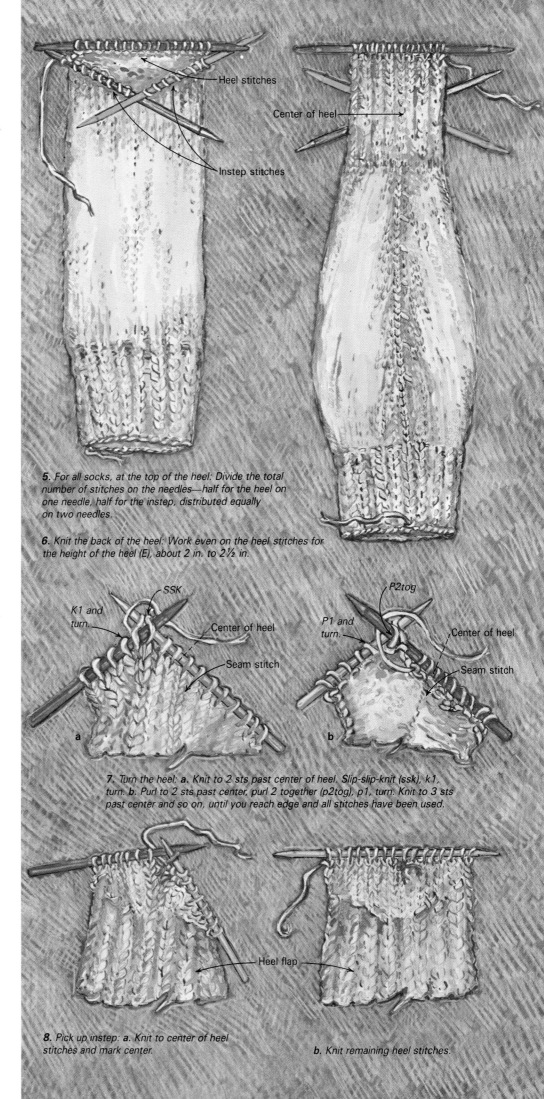

5. For all socks, at the top of the heel: Divide the total number of stitches on the needles—half for the heel on one needle, half for the instep, distributed equally on two needles.

6. Knit the back of the heel: Work even on the heel stitches for the height of the heel (E), about 2 in. to 2½ in.

7. Turn the heel: **a.** Knit to 2 sts past center of heel. Slip-slip-knit (ssk), k1, turn. **b.** Purl to 2 sts past center, purl 2 together (p2tog), p1, turn. Knit to 3 sts past center and so on, until you reach edge and all stitches have been used.

8. Pick up instep: **a.** Knit to center of heel stitches and mark center.

b. Knit remaining heel stitches.

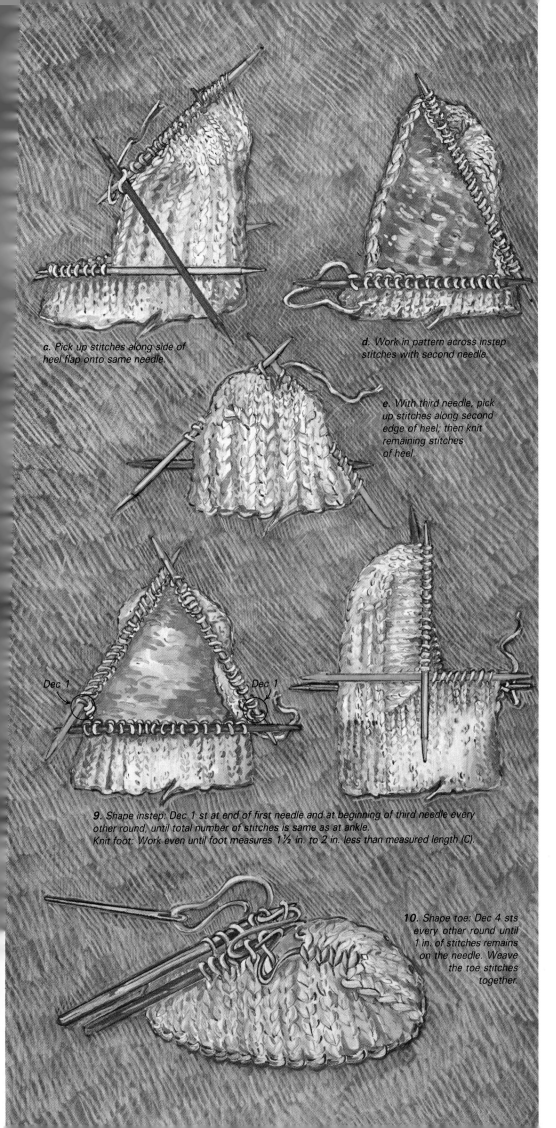

c. Pick up stitches along side of heel flap onto same needle.

d. Work in pattern across instep stitches with second needle.

e. With third needle, pick up stitches along second edge of heel; then knit remaining stitches of heel.

Dec 1   Dec 1

9. Shape instep: Dec 1 st at end of first needle and at beginning of third needle every other round, until total number of stitches is same as at ankle.
Knit foot: Work even until foot measures 1½ in. to 2 in. less than measured length (C).

10. Shape toe: Dec 4 sts every other round until 1 in. of stitches remains on the needle. Weave the toe stitches together.

along each side of the heel flap, join these stitches to the instep stitches, and resume working in rounds, decreasing to form the gusset. To do this, knit the remaining stitches of the heel (step 8b). Pick up stitches along the side of the heel on to the same needle (step 8c). You want to end up with as many stitches as the length of the heel flap times your stitch gauge. To come out even, you may at several points have to knit 2 sts into 1 st or skip 1 st.

With a second needle, work across the instep stitches (step 8d), keeping to your main pattern stitch. All instep stitches should be worked on to this second needle. With the third needle, pick up stitches along the second edge of the heel, the same number of stitches as on the first side of the heel flap. With the same needle, knit to the center of the heel stitches (step 8e). All stitches will once more be divided among three needles—the instep on one needle, the heel on the other two needles.

To form the triangular gussets that shape the instep (step 9), decrease at the end of the first needle and at the beginning of the third needle. On the first needle, knit until 3 sts remain, k2tog, k1. Work even in pattern stitch on instep stitches (second needle). On the third needle, ssk. Knit the remaining stitches on the third needle. Work one round even. Continue decreasing 2 sts every other round until the width of the foot equals the width at the ankle. Since your stitch gauge for stockinette may be different from that of your main pattern stitch, you may not end up with the same count around the foot as around the ankle. The actual measurement is what matters, so juggle the decrease accordingly.

Foot and toe

After you have achieved the same number of stitches on the foot as you have at the ankle (or the same width), work even in the established pattern until the foot measures 1½ in. to 2 in. less than the desired heel-to-toe length.

At this point (step 10), discontinue pattern on all stitches. You should have the same number of stitches on the sum of the first and third needles as you do on the second needle; if you do not, redistribute some of the stitches. Decrease row: Knit until 3 sts remain on the first needle, k2tog, knit the last stitch. On the second needle, k1, ssk, knit until 3 sts remain on the second needle and k2tog, k1. On the third needle, k1, ssk, knit even over the remaining stitches. Work one round even. Continue decreasing 4 sts every other round in this way until the opening is a slit only 1 in. to 1½ in. long. Break the yarn, leaving a 12-in. tail.

Now weave the toe stitches. First move the stitches from the first needle and the third needle on to one needle (all the stitches should now be evenly distributed over two needles). Then thread the 12-in.

How to knit eyelet–rib bobby socks

Remember bobby socks? The sock shown here is about ankle length when you've rolled the cuff down. I was ambitious—I used a fingering-weight yarn. If you are a beginner to socks, you might want to use a heavier weight.

Size: Women's medium (size 7 foot).

Materials: Two 50-gm. skeins of fingering-weight yarn; set of four 7-in. double-pointed knitting needles, #2; tapestry needle (I prefer plastic to metal needles—they tend to be blunter; if your needle's too pointed, you might split the stitches you're trying to weave).

Gauge: On pattern stitch and #2 needles—8 sts and 10 rows/1 in.

Pattern: Cloverleaf eyelet rib (multiple of 6 sts)

Rows 1, 3, and 5: *P1, k5* around.
Row 2: *P1, k1, yo, sl1-k2tog-psso, yo, k1*.
Row 4: *P1, k2, yo, ssk, k1*.
Row 6: Repeat row 1.
Repeat rows 1-6 for pattern.

Knitting the sock: I wanted the top of my sock to reach about 2 in. above my ankle. At that point, my lower calf measures 9 in. around, so I needed to cast on 72 sts. Since 72 is a multiple of 4 (I wanted to use a k2/p2 ribbing for the cuff), I cast on all 72 sts, evenly divided among the three needles, 24 sts on each. To make the row more elastic, I cast on over the width of two of the #2 needles held together.

I joined the stitches to make a circle and then worked even in k2/p2 ribbing for 3 in. I worked the next 4½ in. even in the cloverleaf eyelet pattern. Since my sock was both short and knit with an elastic stitch pattern, I didn't need to decrease along the calf.

I divided the 72 sts at the heel as follows: 35 sts for the instep; 37 sts for the heel. This adjustment from the usual 36/36 heel division allowed me to maintain the symmetry of the eyelet pattern on the instep. Since I generally prefer to work on an even number of stitches for the heel flap, I decreased 1 st to make the heel 36 sts.

I used the slip-stitch heel pattern on the flap for 2¼ in. and turned the heel according to the formula explained on page 30. For the instep, I picked up 18 sts along each side of the heel flap and distributed them among three needles: 28 sts on the first and last needles; 35 sts on the second. At this point, I wanted to ensure that the sock would hug my foot, so I adjusted my instep pattern by decreasing the purl stitch between each cloverleaf, thereby eliminating 5 sts and leaving only 30 sts on the instep needle.

I shaped the instep by decreasing 2 sts every other round until 60 sts remained. My stockinette gauge was less elastic than the gauge of my eyelet rib, so I compensated by decreasing at the instep until the width of the foot equalled the width at the ankle.

Then I worked the sock even until the foot measured 6½ in. long. I discontinued the eyelet pattern on the top of the foot and began decreasing 4 sts every other round until 24 sts remained. I moved these remaining stitches on to two needles and wove them together, making an invisible graft.

This eyelet-rib bobby sock demonstrates techniques for knitting shapes.

As you can see, I made some minor adjustments to the general method to ensure that my sock would fit my foot. As long as you follow the principles of the formula, you will be able to knit a properly fitting sock. Good luck with your project and have fun!

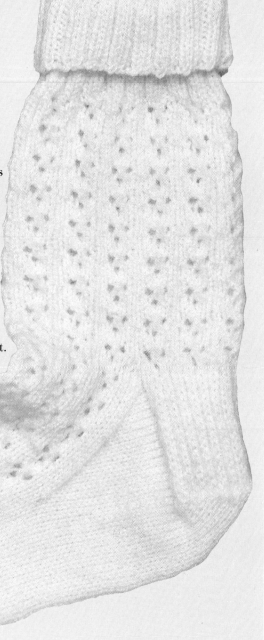

tail of yarn through your tapestry needle. Holding your two knitting needles parallel, insert the tapestry needle through the first stitch on the front knitting needle, as if to knit. Pull the yarn through, and drop this stitch from the knitting needle. Insert the needle through the second stitch of the front needle, as if to purl; pull the yarn through, but leave this stitch on the knitting needle. Insert the needle into the first stitch of the back needle, as if to purl; pull the yarn through, and drop the stitch from the knitting needle. Insert the tapestry needle into the second stitch on the back needle, as if to knit; pull the yarn through, but leave the stitch on the needle. Repeat this weaving process across the toe until all the stitches have been used.

There! You've done it! You've made a sock, or at least an imaginary one. Once you have figured out how to knit a real sock that fits your own foot, you will find that socks are excellent canvases for experimenting and perfecting techniques and patterns that you might not want to try on a larger project. □

Theresa Gaffey designs knitwear in Atlanta, GA. She was formerly an editor of Hand-made magazine.

The Oddball Sweater
Flattering chevron stripes knit in the round

by Ann Tudor

i call my favorite sweater the "unlimited-possibilities" sweater. It is a seamless neck-down design that can be made in virtually any length, any size, any color combination, any stitch combination, and with any yarn. I also call it the oddball sweater because it uses up odd balls of yarn and is a little offbeat. It requires no gauge swatch at the beginning and no seaming at the end. Start it, finish it, and wear it!

The basic sweater has a V-neck front and back, elbow-length sleeves, and a slightly blouson waist-length body, with ribbing at the neck, elbows, and waist. It's great in stripes because the design creates a striking chevron effect that looks much more complicated than it actually is.

The sweater is knit in the round, so you don't have to purl. But this is not its primary attraction. The body of the sweater (before being divided for the sleeves) is a large square; but because it is knit in the round, complicated color changes and different yarn weights can be used, and the sleeve and body "seams" will always match.

The economic advantages are obvious. The sweater uses up odd balls left over from previous projects. But once hooked on the sweater, you'll start searching sale bins for a whole collection of leftovers. Without spending a fortune, you can add two balls of an expensive, fancy yarn to the sweater to make it special.

My own introduction to the basic concept of this sweater was cryptic. Mrs. Winkler, the mother of a friend of a friend, said: "Cast on eighty-eight stitches and divide evenly into four marked sections on a circular needle. Increase one stitch each side of the marked stitch every other row until the work is twelve or thirteen inches long. Then divide for sleeves and body, and finish these off with triangles."

Originally, this was a bottom-up pattern, but 45 to 50 years ago, Mrs. Winkler, who lives in West Germany, converted it to this top-down version. Though the sweater has the simplicity of an old folk pattern, I've never seen it mentioned. It is a training ground for learning knitting principles and techniques, and each knitter who works with the pattern will come up with shortcuts and changes.

Start your sweater by collecting a pound or more of leftover yarns, even very small amounts. Choose a color range you like, and lay out the yarns on a light-colored bedspread or tablecloth, preferably in daylight. Then pick other colors, a few at a time, and put them with the chosen colors. Variegated yarns can supply wonderful "transitions" between two solids. See how black—or white—changes the effect of the

Ann Tudor made both of these oddball sweaters from her basic design. She often varies sleeve and neckline shapes and textures and pattern stitches. (Photo by John Kane)

original choices. Add a bright aqua or a purple. A dozen or two yarns will gradually emerge as the ones you want to use. You'll discard some and add others as you knit.

If a yarn is the right color but too fine, try mixing it with a thin strand of a related color (or a contrasting color, or metallic). You can even incorporate a very thick yarn without distorting the fabric. And, if you alternate rounds of the thick yarn with rounds of a very thin yarn, the thick yarn will almost look woven in. This "averaging" principle gives you a great deal of flexibility in yarn choice. There is, however, one firm rule: All the yarns must require the same washing care. Do not mix dry-clean-only yarns with hand-wash-only yarns.

You'll usually want to use medium-sized (5-7 U.S.) circular needles in two lengths (16 in. and 24 in., or longer), or check the size recommendations on a representative yarn you'll be using. In any case, use needles a size or two smaller for the ribbings. Needle kits with interchangeable points for various cable lengths (Denise or Boye) are perfect for this sweater.

Basic sweater

Cast 88 sts onto the smaller, 16-in. circular needle. Do one round of k1, p1, placing markers every 22 sts. Use three identical markers, with a different one at the end of the round. Continue in rib for about an inch.

When the ribbing is as deep as you want it, start the body of the sweater. Change to the larger needle, and begin the increase pattern. Knit every round, increasing every other round, and start playing with colors and patterns. When the stitches get too crowded, change to a longer needle.

Increase pattern—This sweater grows quickly because you increase 1 st on each side of each marked stitch (see top drawing), *not* on each side of the markers, 8 sts every other round. The marked stitch becomes a decorative "center stitch" defined by the increase pattern. I use a yarn-over increase. When you come to each marker, do a yarn over, slip the marker, knit the marked stitch, and then do another yarn over. Knit in front of the yarn overs on the alternate rounds, and you'll make eyelets; knit in the back to prevent eyelets. Be consistent.

Determining the gauge—When you have knit approximately 4 in. beyond the ribbing, you can determine your gauge. Lay enough of the sweater flat to measure the gauge. Multiply this gauge by your chest measurement plus 6 in. (e.g., 34-in. chest +6 in.=40 in. x 5 sts/in.=200 sts). Now double this number. Continue knitting until you have, in this case, 400 sts. At this point the sweater will go over your shoulders, and opposite corners will reach from elbow to elbow. It's easy to count the stitches if you count only between two markers and multiply by four. Alternatively, forget about

Oddball-sweater plan

Knit around on long circular needle, increasing both sides of marked stitches until piece is big enough to divide for sleeves. Stop halfway before last marker.

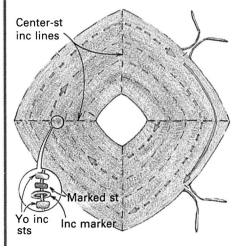

To divide for sleeves, complete round by knitting last half of last group, the marked stitch, and half of first group onto a 16-in. needle.

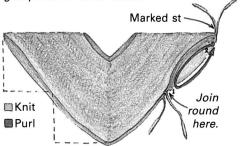

☐ Knit
■ Purl

To start sleeve, join round and knit around onto a 16 in. needle to marked stitch (1). Wrap, turn, and purl all the way back to marked stitch (2).

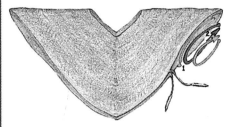

To knit sleeve, work back and forth, knitting progressively shorter rows to fill in underarm triangles.

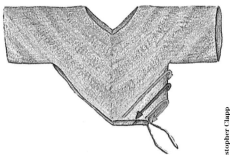

When sleeves are completed, slide lower edge around circular needle, and work each side back and forth in progressively shorter rows to fill in body triangles.

Illustrations by Christopher Clapp

gauge and stitch count, and knit until the sweater is 12 or 13 in. long. Measure from the neck ribbing to the needle halfway between two markers. This will make a size medium (10-12).

Dividing for sleeves—When you have knit to your required number of stitches, you'll have an odd-looking object. If it were laid flat, the sweater would look like a square donut (see top drawing, p. 78). If the square were folded into a point-down triangle, it would look like the drawing below it. The dotted lines on the left side indicate two of the four triangles you need to add for body and sleeves.

To begin the first sleeve, stop the last round when you are halfway to the last marker. Knit the rest of the stitches to the last marker onto the 16-in. circular needle, and continue knitting on it through the marked stitch without increasing, and through the first half of the first group of stitches. The marker will be at the center of the stitches. Leave all the other stitches on the longer needle, tied off with a rubber band, or put them on a yarn holder.

Knitting the sleeve triangles—Knit the sleeve stitches around the center stitch. Wrap the center stitch and turn to knit a short row, as shown in the "Wrapping" drawings on p. 81. Place a marker on the right-hand needle. Purl all the way around on the sleeve stitches until you reach the center stitch. Wrap it again, turn, and place another marker on the right-hand needle, as shown in the second drawing on p. 78. I call this a "double wrap." The double wrap occurs around the center stitch only, and only on the first row of each double-triangle section on each sleeve.

From now on, you'll knit progressively shorter rows back and forth in stockinette stitch (k1 row, p1 row), turning 2 sts further from the sleeve point each time, thus knitting fewer stitches in each row. The easiest way to turn at the right place is to

move the markers when you make the turn (see photo below). When you get to within 2 sts of the marker, sl2 to the right-hand needle, remove the marker, and then put one of the slipped stitches back onto the left-hand needle. Wrap the second slipped stitch, turn the work, and replace the marker. This sounds more complicated than it is. Both markers are traveling away from the center stitch and toward the underarm "seam" so that more fabric is being knit below than above the arm, as shown in the third drawing on p. 78. This creates a sleeve under the point of the center stitch.

To make sure you're forming a right triangle, do three or four turning rows. Then hold the needle so that the sleeve point and the turned rows are flat. If the edge is a straight line, you're turning at the right place. If the stitches are bunched, you need to turn a little further from the point; and if the line angles in the same direction as the chevron, you need to turn somewhat closer to the point.

At the same time you are short-rowing on the top of the sleeve, mark the underarm, and decrease 1 st each side of that marker every other row (on the knit rows). Use SSK (slip 2 sts knitwise, one at a time; then knit them together) before the marker and k2tog after it. Continue short rows and decreases to complete the triangles.

Then k1, k2tog all the way around the sleeve without turning. Finish the sleeve with k1, p1 ribbing on smaller needles.

Slide the body stitches around on the main needle (don't knit them) until you get to the other side, for the second sleeve. Divide as you did for the first sleeve; knit it to match (or not match, if you prefer).

Making the body triangles—Work these triangles just as you did the sleeve triangles, but do not join the work. Slide the stitches around on the long needle so you can begin knitting the first triangle from the left-center front to the left-center back. Decrease 2 sts at the underarm every other

row to form a "side seam." On the first row of each body triangle, pick up 4 or 5 sts along the sleeve underarm by inserting the needle into the loops of the body stitches at the underarm to close the hole that would be there otherwise. Knit progressively shorter rows back and forth, as shown in the bottom drawing on p. 78.

When the first of these two sections is even with the center-front and center-back points, stop knitting on it, break the yarn, and slide the stitches around without knitting until you get to the center front or back, to start the other side. When this triangle is complete, decrease around the whole body. The rate of decrease depends on how much you need to pull in the waist ribbing. A decrease of k1, k2tog will remove one-third of the stitches, while k8, k2tog will reduce the size by 10%. Finish with a k1, p1 ribbing on the smaller needles.

If you wove in the ends of your color changes as you knit, all that's left for you to do is trim them and weave in the neck and bind-off ends.

Variations

I suggest that you knit one sweater as described above in order to gain experience. After making this sweater, you can consider some of the following possibilities.

Neck variations—The neck offers lots of room for experimentation. For a *higher neck*, cast on fewer stitches, but always in multiples of four (i.e., instead of 88 sts, cast on 76 or 80 sts). For a *décolletage*, cast on 96 or 100 sts (again, in multiples of four).

If you don't want a V-neck in front and back, *raise the back neck* by short-rowing. After making the ribbing, do short rows for approximately 2 in., starting about 10 sts in front of the shoulder increase markers. On each row, turn about 5 sts sooner than you did the row before. On the basic sweater, any increase point can be a shoulder, but if you raise the back neck, you've changed that. You must begin the first sleeve with an increase point adjacent to the back neck. Otherwise, you could end up with a sleeve coming out of the middle of your back or front.

If you want a *cowl or a collar*, do the ribbing as usual. When the sweater is finished, pick up and work the stitches from the first row below the ribbing to make a collar that will cover the original ribbing. A k2, p2 rib about 10 in. long looks good, or you can just knit stockinette.

To make a *square neck*, use the center-stitch increase lines as raglan increases, instead of running them down the center front and back and the shoulders. Knit the sweater as usual until it's time to divide for the first sleeve. For the sleeve, take all the stitches between one center stitch and the next. In this case, there is no bias look and no chevron effect. You just knit around the sleeves and body without making triangles.

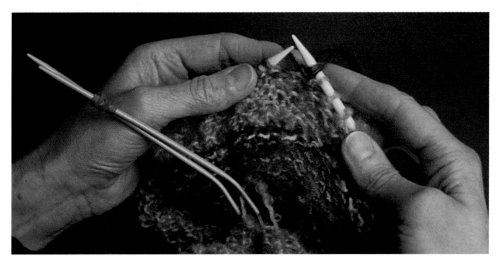

Tudor knits progressively shorter rows to fill out the sleeve's side and underarm. The original marked stitch is in front of her right thumb, and the marker has traveled 2 sts. The body and other sleeve stitches are in reserve on the long circular needle. (Photo by Brian Pickell)

Sleeve variations—For a *sleeveless sweater,* divide for the sleeve with the square-neck method. Knit a few rows of garter or seed stitch to prevent curling. Then bind off the sleeve stitches for a loose vest look.

For a *wide sleeve,* don't decrease around after completing the sleeve triangle. Instead, do a few rows of garter or seed stitch and bind off. This makes a wide elbow-length sleeve that's great over a turtleneck or blouse.

To make *long sleeves,* divide for the sleeves, and then knit around and around before starting the triangle. Keep the increases at the center stitch going as usual, but at the same time decrease 1 st each side of the underarm marker every other row. In this way, you'll always have the same number of stitches on the needle. If you want the sleeve to narrow as it moves toward the wrist, then decrease every row or three rows out of every four. When the point of the sleeve is as long as you need it (remember to figure in the length of your cuff, if desired), begin short-rowing to make the triangles.

Body variations—You can make the body as long as you like. After doing the sleeves, continue to knit around on all the body stitches, increasing at the increase points and decreasing on each side of the underarms every other row to keep the number of stitches constant, until the points are as long as you want the sweater to be (remember to allow for the ribbing). Then do the triangles as usual.

To make a *tunic or dress,* knit the long body even longer. Then do the side triangles. Or omit the triangles for a pointed front and back hem. Use the larger measurement—hip or bust, plus ease—to figure the number of stitches for a dress.

To make a *cardigan* sweater, knit the body of the sweater as usual, but create a facing in the front by using 5 or 6 stockinette stitches instead of the one center stitch. Increase as usual each side of this group of 5 or 6 sts. When the sweater is finished, cut up the middle of the "facing" and let the edges roll back. Pick up and knit or crochet edge bands, working buttonholes as desired. Or single-crochet an edge and sew in a zipper. Once you understand the basic sweater, you can make a cardigan by knitting garter stitch back and forth with a center opening. Since garter-stitch gauge is much wider than it is long, you'll have to knit twice as many rows, and your increase pattern will occur every fourth row instead of every other row.

Decorative variations—Make the center stitch into a wider, decorative band; or use no center stitch at all; or do a 4- or 6-st cable. Knit a 2- or 3-in. stripe of a lace pattern, or just a section with evenly spaced eyelets. Thread the eyelets with ribbon or feather yarn. Knit a section with colored Bohus or Fair Isle patterns. Work 2- or 3-in.-wide stripes of different pattern stitches (seed stitch, small or large cables, moss stitch) separated by garter-stitch rows. Or make the whole sweater in brioche stitch, all in one color. Use metallics, ribbon, and novelty yarns. Mix yarns and colors outrageously. Use fabric (I've knit with strips of scrap-quality kimonos that have been available lately). Make all the triangles on the sleeves and body different for a random effect.

Hints

This sweater has taught me some interesting things about knitting. The more rows you have in the triangle, the blousier the triangle will be. Blousiness also varies with the weight of the yarn. You can control it by varying the number of rows you knit as you're short-rowing. If you're knitting with heavier yarns, you'll need fewer rows than you would to knit the same length with medium-weight yarns. In order to knit fewer rows but still get the triangle effect, you must turn farther from the marker. Instead of turning 2 sts sooner each row, you must turn 3 or 4 sts sooner.

I like to use the traveling-marker approach, even though it means slipping additional stitches to reach the marker. The alternative is to keep a written record of the turnings and leave the markers where they are. Turn 4 sts before each marker, then 8, then 12, then 16, for example.

You can get good definition when changing colors by knitting one or two garter-stitch ridges, and I've found a way to work them in the round without purling. Knit one round in the color you want for the garter ridge. Instead of purling the next round, turn the work, wrapping the turning stitch, and knit around on the wrong side of the sweater. This makes a purl on the right side, or a garter-stitch ridge. When you get back to the beginning, knit the stitch you slipped before, and turn on the following stitch. The turn point would look messy in a repeated garter-stitch fabric, but it's not noticeable in one or two ridges.

Knit in your ends as you go. To make sure the new yarn is secure and the ends are woven in, I knit 1 st of the new color, then 1 st using both ends of the new color, with the old color hanging down between them (this stitch is two strands thick). The old yarn is "wrapped" by the two ends of the new color. Then I catch the tails of both colors into the back of the work for the first 8 or 10 sts knit with the new color.

The most important thing I've learned, though, is the fun of experimenting. Cast on 88 sts, and you're ready to play. □

Ann Tudor, a native of Delphi, IN, lives in Toronto, where, under her Honest Threads label, she makes sweaters, baskets, and decorative dolls. During her career in publishing, she was co-editor (as Ann Harwell) of the resource guide Crafts for Today *(Libraries Unlimited, 1974).*

Short rows: The secret is wrapping

by Meg Swansen

A short row is a row (or round in circular knitting) that's not worked all the way from one end to the other. You may stop at any point on the row, turn, and work in the opposite direction. Short rows are handy shaping techniques:
• Shape the shoulders, or raise the back of the neck of a sweater with short rows; you'll eliminate the need for "stair-step" bits of casting-off.
• Incorporate short rows across the back of the tubular body of a seamless sweater to prevent riding up. (One knitter I know makes short rows across the front of her husband's sweaters to accommodate his paunch.)
• Use short rows to form neat, mitered corners on a border worked around a square blanket (top-left drawing, p. 81).
• Make a round throw (or tam-o'-shanter) will stitches cast on from the center to the outer edges, and knit a series of pie wedges with graduating short rows to form the circle (top-right drawing, p. 81).
• Shape bust darts, elbow darts, high-fashion knit drapes, ruffles, gathers and assorted protuberances.

Short rows are best worked in stocking stitch, ribbing, or garter stitch. But, if you just turn in the middle of a round (or row) and work back, you'll get a huge hole where you turned. If you slip the first stitch after the turn, you'll get a smaller but still visible hole. Mary Thomas's method of turning in the middle of the round (*Mary Thomas's Knitting Book,* Dover, 1972) is only a partial solution. Here's where wrapping comes in.

Barbara Walker truly tamed the technique in *Knitting from the Top* (Charles Scribner's Sons, 1982). She uses no drawings, however, and many readers may have glossed over the description, needing to see what to do. The instructions that follow include a few subtle variations from Barbara's original method. The technique was named wrapping by weaver and publisher David Xenakis.

The turning stitch is wrapped when you begin the short row, and it must be dealt with later when you meet it again. The instructions for the wrap itself are always the same, whether you are on the knit or purl side. There are three instances in which you meet the wrap again; each is handled slightly differently.

Wrapping—When you get to the turning place, leave the working wool where it is—in back if you're knitting, in front if you're purling. Slip the next stitch onto the right needle, and carry the working wool to the other side of the knitting, as shown in "Wrapping" drawing 1. Replace the slipped stitch onto the left needle, turn, and you're ready to work the short row. Now you can see how the name came about; the working wool has been wrapped around the base of the unworked stitch, as shown in "Wrapping" drawing 2. You perform this process exactly the same way for knit or purl, but always keep the wrap fairly loose.

Meeting a wrap—There are three ways you can meet the wrap again. Here's what you do in each case.

When you meet a wrap on the knit side that you made on the knit side, you can dig the right-hand needle into the wrap and the stitch and knit them together, as shown in "Meeting the wrap" drawing 1, or place the slipped stitch onto the right needle, pick up the wrap on the left needle, replace the slipped stitch, and then knit the two together.

There are three ways in which you can deal with a wrap on the knit side that you made on the purl side—as when you are inserting a short row across the back of a circular sweater: (a) knit into the stitch and wrap together, (b) slip the wrap, knit the stitch, pass the slipped wrap over (psso), or (c) slip the wrap, slip the stitch, insert the tip of the left needle into these 2 sts and knit them together (SSK), as shown in "Meeting the wrap" drawing 2. My favorite method is SSK, but you should choose the one that suits you best.

When you meet the wrap on the purl side that you made on the purl side—as when you're working ever-lengthening short rows back and forth for shoulder or neck shaping—lift the back of the wrap (which is actually on the knit side of the work) and put it on the left needle, as shown in "Meeting the wrap" drawing 3. Then purl the two together.

Short rows in garter stitch are even easier to make. It is impossible to make the wraps invisible, since two ridges will suddenly become one, but it will be least noticeable if you perform the wrap. Then ignore it. The spot where the wrap strangles the slipped stitch makes a little horizontal bump that looks like a purl.

Once you've mastered short rows and wrapping, you may be surprised at the number of new shaping options that present themselves.

That's a wrap.

Meg Swansen, the daughter of Elizabeth Zimmermann, is an author, a video producer, and a businesswoman, as well as a skilled knitter and designer.

Short-row applications

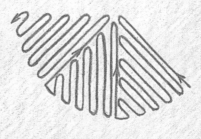
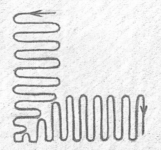

Knit a border with mitered corners, using short rows, or make a circle with short-row wedges.

Wrapping

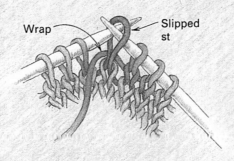
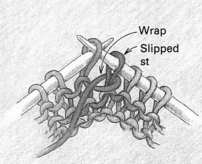

Wrap — Slipped st

Wrap — Slipped st

1. Carry working yarn to opposite side before replacing slipped stitch on left needle.

2. Wrapping prevents a large space from developing between worked and unworked stitches.

Meeting the wrap

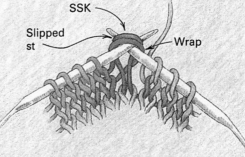

Slipped st — Wrap

SSK — Slipped st — Wrap

1. On knit side, work wrap that was made on knit side by knitting wrap and slipped stitch together.

2. For a knit-side wrap that was made on purl side, Meg Swansen's favorite method is ssk (slip, slip, knit).

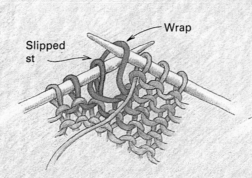
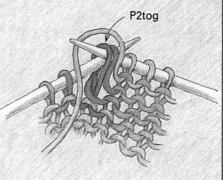

Wrap — Slipped st

P2tog

3. When meeting purled wrap on purl side, lift back of wrap and place on left needle.

Slip right-hand needle into wrap and slipped stitch, and purl both together.

Easy Striped Knits
Bias stripes in a basic garter stitch

by Barbara G. Walker

bias stripes are hard to achieve in almost all types of knitting. However, for the design shown here, very neat bias stripes have been made with the simplest kind of knitting: a plain garter stitch (knitted on both sides of the fabric). The piece is ingeniously worked across the diagonal from one corner to the opposite corner and is designed so that the knitter never has to do any purling, counting, or measuring of gauge. Stitch gauge does not matter very much, because the knitter works only from measurements.

Technique

I'll use a place mat (detail shown above) to illustrate bias-knitting techniques. This place mat was made with four 100-yd. balls of Coats & Clark's Speed-Cro-Sheen cotton, two of each color. Metallic blends, plastic ribbon yarns, rug yarn, knitting cotton, or ordinary heavy string are also suitable for place mats. It is best to use materials that can be easily washed. I used a 30-in. circular needle, size 1, but you can also use straight needles. A circular needle allows the work to spread out more, but the knitting still goes back and forth in rows, as if on a pair of straight needles.

Increasing—To begin, cast on 2 stitches (sts) of the first color (Color A). Tie on a strand of the second color (Color B).

Row 1 (right side): With Color B, k1, yo (yarn over), k1, making 3 sts. To work a yo, simply carry the yarn over the right needle once, thus placing an extra loop on the needle before knitting the next stitch (drawing 1, facing page).

Row 2 (wrong side): With Color B, k1, knit into the back of the yo loop, k1. As you face the wrong side of the fabric, observe that the yo loop comes toward you over the top of the needle from your left to your right. To knit into the back of this loop, insert the right-needle point behind the right side of the loop, under the left needle, and in front of the left side of the loop (drawing 2, facing page). Knit the stitch in the usual way and draw through. This twists the yo of the previous row, so it won't make a hole.

Row 3: Drop Color B strand in front of the work, toward you; pick up Color A strand behind it. With Color A, k1, yo, k1, yo, k1 (5 sts).

Row 4: With Color A, k1, knit yo loop in back as before, k1, knit yo loop in back, k1.

Row 5: Drop Color A strand in front of the work, as before; pick up Color B strand behind it. With B, k1, yo, k3, yo, k1 (7 sts).

Row 6: With Color B, k1, knit yo loop in back, k3, knit yo loop in back, k1.

Row 7: Drop Color B strand, pick up Color A; with Color A, k1, yo, k5, yo, k1 (9 sts).

Row 8: With Color A, k1, knit yo loop in back, k5, knit yo loop in back, k1.

Row 9, etc.: Continue as established, changing colors at the beginning of every right-side (odd-numbered) row. Always work a yo after the first and before the last stitch of every right-side row, and knit into the backs of these loops on the returning wrong-side rows.

It is not always easy to tell the right side from the wrong side when garter stitch is worked in one color, since both sides of the fabric look the same; however, it's easy to tell with two-color stripes. The stripes are sharply defined on the right side and blended together on the wrong side. The latter effect is attractive too, and garter-stitch table mats can be considered reversible. Some knitters may prefer to show the wrong side.

Working even—Increasing the first half of a garter-stitch piece and decreasing the second half will always create a square no matter what the yarn type, needle size, or stitch count. Measuring one side will give the finished proportions of the square, since all four sides will be the same. As soon as one side is the desired length, you begin decreasing.

For this place mat, however, a rectangle is needed. That means you must work some length without adding stitches, although you'll increase and decrease to continue the long side of the rectangle.

Without purling, counting, or measuring gauge, you can knit striped fabric. This place mat (detail of right side above) was worked entirely in garter stitch and knit diagonally from one corner to the other, as shown below.

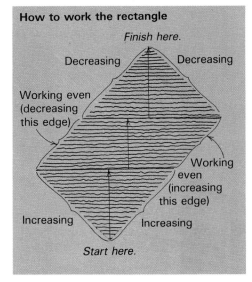

How to work the rectangle

Finish here.

Decreasing · Decreasing

Working even (decreasing this edge)

Working even (increasing this edge)

Increasing · Increasing

Start here.

When one side is the desired length for the short side of the rectangle (12 in. for an average-sized place mat), start on any right-side row: k1, yo, knit across to the last 2 sts, k2tog through back of loops. On the wrong side, knit across, working into the back of the yo loop as usual. Thus the right-side edge continues to increase, while the left-side edge begins to decrease. Work every right-side row the same, until the right-side (increasing) edge is the desired length for the long side of the rectangle (18 in. for an average-sized place mat).

Decreasing—Begin decreasing on a right-side row. At the right-hand edge, k2tog. Knit across to the last 2 sts, k2tog through back loops (or sl1, k1, psso; or ssk). On wrong-side rows, just knit. Continue removing 1 st from each side edge in this manner every right-side row, until 3 sts remain at the final corner. Break the yarns and draw a strand through the last 3 sts (drawing 3 below). To fasten off, run the yarn ends about 2 in. along the edges of the piece with a yarn needle to hold them secure.

If you are working one of a set of identical items, like matching place mats, be sure to mark the stripe where you begin working even, and also the stripe where you begin decreasing both sides. Then, by counting stripes, you can work all matching pieces the same.

To make wider stripes, work four or perhaps six rows of each color. To use more than two colors, simply tie in a new color at the beginning of a right-side row.

A scrap-yarn afghan

Nearly every knitter has scraps left over from previous projects: too much yarn to throw away, but not enough of any one color to finish a new item. Striped bias afghan squares offer a perfect solution to the problem of how to use up scraps. The more colors, the better. A hundred different stripe combinations will make a brilliant afghan.

If you have small quantities of many different colors of yarn, make your afghan of 4-in. to 8-in. squares. If you don't have enough scraps for a whole afghan, make a baby blanket, pillow cover, bag, or patchwork sweater out of multicolored squares.

Afghan squares are quick to work, portable, and good for making productive use of waiting time anywhere. For bias-knit garter-stitch squares, you don't have to carry directions. As long as you use the same needle size and yarn weight (knitting worsted is preferable) for every square and always increase to the same number of stitches or stripes before starting to decrease, all squares will be the same size and will fit together when they are sewn. Then, with every color of the spectrum and bias stripes running in all directions, you'll have a dazzling afghan indeed.

More uses for bias-striped knitting

Now that you know how to make bias garter-stitch stripes, you can try some of these other items. Here are some hints for working them.

Coaster: Increase as described for the place mat until the piece measures 4 in. to 4½ in. on one side. Decrease as above.

Side-dish mat: Increase as described for the place mat until the piece measures 6 in. on one side. Then decrease as above.

Facecloth: Select a soft knitting cotton, and use size 3 or 4 needles. Work a 10-in. to 12-in. square.

Potholder or hot-dish mat: With heavy cotton rug yarn or two strands of knitting cotton held together and small needles (for thickness), make a 6-in. or 7-in. square.

Dollhouse rug: With fingering yarn and size 1 or 2 needles, make a 3-in. to 4-in. square or rectangle, or work to the desired proportions for the dollhouse room.

Bath mat: Select a heavy cotton rug yarn, and use large knitting needles. Work a 20-in. by 30-in. rectangle.

Baby blanket: Use baby yarn and size 4 or 5 needles. Make a 25-in. by 40-in. rectangle (or work to the desired proportions).

Scarf: With sport yarn and size 5 needles, make a skinny rectangle about 6 in. wide by 3 ft. or 4 ft. long. Add fringe to the ends if desired.

Shawl: With fingering yarn or baby wool and size 5 or 6 needles, make a 4-ft. to 6-ft. square. Use a long circular needle (36 in. or 42 in.) to accommodate the width of the piece, or if you prefer, work back and forth across 2 or 3 long circular needles as if they were straight needles. Fringe the edges.

Pillow cover or bag: With any desired yarns, make two identical squares or rectangles in the necessary proportions. Sew pieces together back to back, leaving one side open to insert zipper. For a handbag, add loop handles of cord or knitted or crocheted straps. Add lining if desired.

Bureau scarf or coffee-table runner: With cotton or metallic yarn, make a long rectangle in whatever proportion your furniture requires.

Tablecloth: With washable knitting cotton, make a square or rectangle according to the shape of the table, using long needles, as for the shawl. A square of bridge-table size is a good project for a beginner.

Reversible tunic or sweater: With any desired yarn or combination of yarns, make two identical rectangles, each wide enough to reach halfway around the body at hip level and long enough to reach from the hip to the top of the shoulder. Sew the two pieces together at the sides and shoulder edges, leaving slots for armholes and a center neck opening. This will make a simple pullover. To add ribbing or a border pattern, pick up stitches around the lower edge and/or neck opening. To add sleeves, pick up stitches around the armhole edges and work down in straight knitting to the wrist, decreasing as necessary. □

Barbara G. Walker has written ten knitting books, including A Treasury of Knitting Patterns, Charted Knitting Designs, Knitting from the Top, *and* Mosaic Knitting, *all published by Charles Scribner's Sons. She has also written three nonknitting books, published by Harper & Row* (The Woman's Encyclopedia of Myths and Secrets; The Secrets of the Tarot: Origins, History, and Symbolism; The Crone: Woman of Age, Wisdom, and Power).

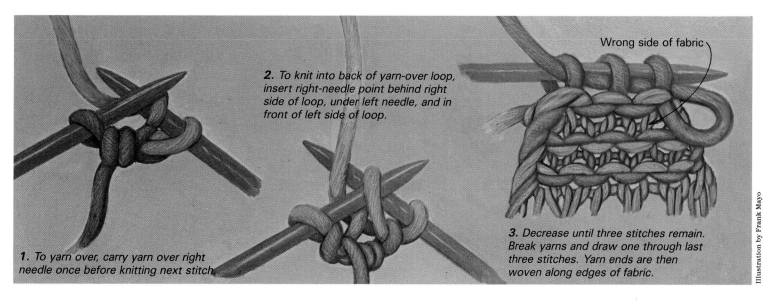

1. To yarn over, carry yarn over right needle once before knitting next stitch.

2. To knit into back of yarn-over loop, insert right-needle point behind right side of loop, under left needle, and in front of left side of loop.

Wrong side of fabric

3. Decrease until three stitches remain. Break yarns and draw one through last three stitches. Yarn ends are then woven along edges of fabric.

Illustration by Frank Mayo

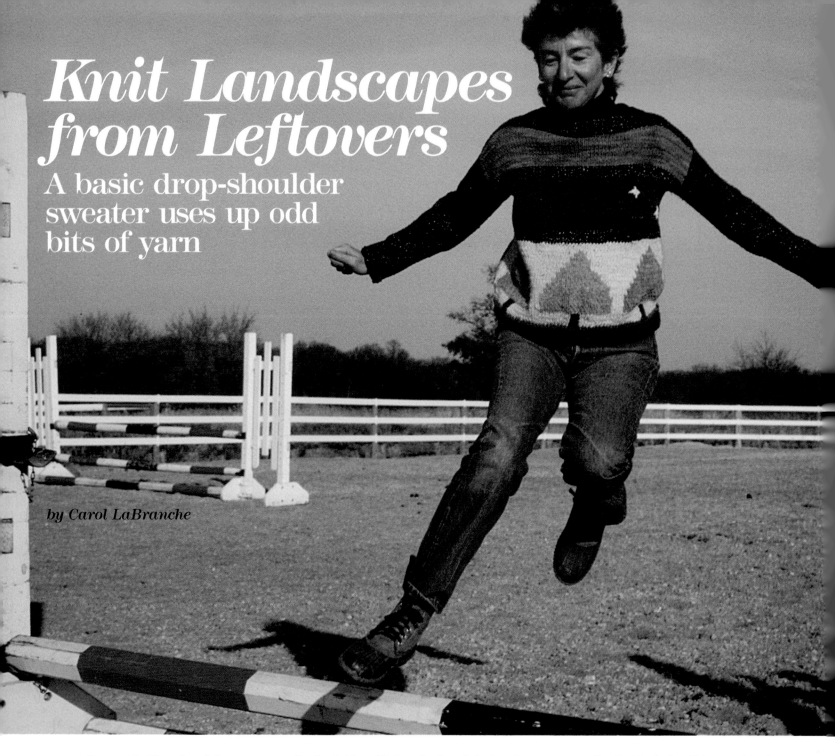

Knit Landscapes from Leftovers

A basic drop-shoulder sweater uses up odd bits of yarn

by Carol LaBranche

like most knitters, I can't throw away even the oddest ball of yarn. I also add to my collection by buying irresistibly luscious skeins of sale yarn at the local store. The result? Boxes overflowing with yarn in small lots, all of different weights and colors.

One day, I decided to face my closet collection and make something from all those mismatched yarns. It seemed logical that my design should echo the basic structure of the knitting without falling into unflattering stripes. I asked myself, "What else is structurally horizontal?" And the first answer I came up with was, "The world, the sky above, and the earth below." That's how I started knitting landscape sweaters.

Besides leftovers, all I needed for the sweaters were the measurements for the length and width of the sweater body, sleeve length, and armhole depth. To illustrate the basic idea, I'll describe how I designed two of my sweaters (I made four) as I knit. I'll also explain how to adapt leftover yarns and individual ideas for a landscape. My woods may be your seashore. Let your imagination and leftovers be your guides. Don't worry if you don't have a fully realized plan. One thing will lead to another.

Blending yarns in a basic shape—My first sweater was a rendition of the woods where I walk my dogs. I began by deciding which yarns I wanted to get rid of the most. The winner was some gold metallic stuff. Since it was too thin and scratchy to knit alone, I teamed it up with some soft blue wool. With that color selected for the sky, I knew the sweater was going to depict a night scene (photo above); hence I call it "Starry Night." But I had to start with the earth, so I dug out some brown handspun, grabbed some needles that looked as if they matched the weight of the brown wool, and cast on.

Here is where the beauty of the landscape sweater idea is revealed. No planning is required, and there are no special materials, no exact sizes, no knitting gauges, and no swatches. The front and back of each sweater are rectangles. There are no set-in sleeves, because that might ruin whatever is going on in the landscape at the underarm. This means the sleeves will have no cap shaping. The drop, or sloping, shoulders are easy to fit.

I knew how wide I wanted my rectangle, so I cast on enough stitches with brown wool to make that measurement. A few rows in, I measured the width to be sure it was generally right. Sweaters are usually loose-fitting, so a small variation either way doesn't matter. I had very little of the brown handspun, so I divided it roughly into thirds

Combine different weights of yarn and different fibers in one sweater? Why not! Carol LaBranche knit "Starry Night," the landscape sweater at left, from odds and ends of yarns, with basic measurements and a minimum of planning.

and used one-third for the front, saving the rest for the back and sleeves.

For a hem, I knit ten rows of garter stitch (knit every row), which makes a nice, but unobtrusive, edge. I seldom use ribbing at the base of my sweaters because I don't like to waste 3 in. of knitting that doesn't add to the design or overall feeling of the sweater, and ribbing seldom does.

After the brown yarn ran out, I found some mottled green and knit two rows of garter stitch for grass. Then I planned the trees by counting the stitches and dividing the number by three. I made the trunks with another bit of brown yarn, knitting in garter stitch for textured bark. The trees are intarsia-knit with yarn on a separate bobbin for each tree; I just eyeballed the diagonal sides as I knit. The background used up some rough white handspun, and the trees are a wonderful green cotton chenille. Can you mix cotton and wool? Of course! Don't worry about mixing different types of yarn. They can usually be hand-washed or dry-cleaned together.

At this point I had used five different yarns, all of different weights. There is no problem with this as long as the yarns are approximately the same in diameter. If they aren't, you can do several things. The green I used for the grass was much thinner than the brown earth yarn, so I doubled it and knit with two strands. The thicker white handspun was offset by the thinner green chenille, but together they were roughly the same as the yarn combinations in the rest of the sweater. I knew my balancing act was working because the rectangle had straight sides, a good test and guide. If the sides start to bulge or pinch, increase or decrease stitches only as a last-ditch solution. A better way is to balance the yarns by combining threads, or use yarns that are all about the same diameter.

When I got to the treetops, I had 8 in. of knitting. I like my sweaters about 22 in. long, so it seemed as if I'd have lots of sky and not enough blue wool and metallic. By that time it was evening, so I went outside for inspiration and noticed that the night sky was not all one color but was much lighter and hazier nearer to the earth. Back at the yarn box, I found some turquoise wool waiting. When that was used up, I added some lavender wool and finished with more blue and metallic. I made a straight-across neckline because that's the easiest, and it doesn't mess up the rectangular landscape. I finished with a few ridges of garter stitch for a nonroll top edge.

I knit the back to match the front and started on the sleeves. Again, I just cast on

what seemed to be plenty of stitches to get my hand through, and I increased at even intervals to match the size of my arms. I checked the sleeve as I knit by folding the knitting over my arm. This is knitting by common sense rather than by formula. Count how many stitches you cast on and how many you increase, however, because you'll have to do it again for the other sleeve.

After knitting a few rows of garter stitch for a hem, I switched to stockinette stitch and knit away until I ran out of deep blue. I found some other blue, fairly close but with more purple, and kept knitting. The metallic makes the two colors seem closer than they are, which is an old Persian-rug trick. The wool for Oriental rugs is dyed in small batches. The result is that the background, which takes the most wool, has a fair number of slightly different color values. Rather than looking odd, the colors add richness and subtlety to the rugs. I think the occasional color switches in my sweaters are part of their charm.

Then I sewed the sweater together. When I tried on "Starry Night," it had too much sky and too many broad stripes, just what I was trying to avoid. To break up the bands, I embroidered a few off-center stars in the sky. The stars insist that the top be seen as sky and not stripes, and being somewhat random, they take the focus away from the dreaded horizontal.

After knitting a second sweater, I had substantially cut into my leftover pile. That was good, but it caused a new problem. What I had left over from the leftovers was very motley indeed. There were not three skeins of any one color. The next sweater was going to be more of a challenge.

Texture and reversibility—"Day and Night in the Forest" (photos below) is a basic rectangular sweater with a few new twists. This time I knit 1 in. of stockinette stitch and then did a row of picot edging (k1, yo,

k2tog). The picot row becomes a pretty scalloped edge when the first inch is folded to the back. Bored with my literal idea of the landscape, I started looking for other parts of the outdoors to add interest. I turned to Barbara Walker, whose three treasuries of knitting patterns (Charles Scribner's Sons, 1968, 1970, 1972) I recommend for patterns that resemble landscape features. There are cable patterns that look like vines and lace patterns that depict windmills. I chose a three-dimensional pattern of three flower buds with leaves. After knitting 1 in. of black earth, I changed to pink for the background and knit the flower pattern, which requires only one color per row.

I didn't want to crush the flowers with trees, so I just knit colors that reminded me of flower borders seen from a distance. Then came ribbed triangular trees in variegated blue-green wool to add texture to balance the three-dimensional flowers.

The sky problem remained because of the shortage of blue, but Barbara Walker rescued me again with her String of Pearls bobble pattern, which I used for white clouds. Next came a rainbow, and then some shaded purple.

For the second rectangle, I reversed the colors of the trees and their background. On one side, the trees are mottled blue-green against a pale green (Day); on the other side, they're pale green against the darker color (Night). Which is the front? Both sides are. Rectangular sweaters are reversible since they have no shaping. No one can see both your front and back at the same time, so there's no visual disjunction when the front and back are different. Sometimes I wear the Day side in front, and sometimes I wear the Night side in front. It depends on how I feel. □

Carol LaBranche, the former editor of Needlepoint News, *lives in Chicago, IL. Photos by Art Tursh.*

"Day and Night" is reversible back to front because the body is made of identical rectangles. LaBranche added texture by knitting bobble-patterned clouds, three-dimensional flowers, and ribbed trees. Picot stitches form a scalloped hem.

Designing with Cables

Chart textured designs drawn from nature on your own proportional graph paper

by Kathy Brunner with Sue M. Parker

started knitting when I was about four years old. After I became skilled enough to handle a spoon and fork, my mother decided that I was ready for another type of utensil and gave me a pair of knitting needles to play with. Like most beginning knitters, I found my first rows very frustrating. To make knitting more fun for me and to help ease the frustration, my mom tied a piece of candy to the yarn every few yards and wound the ball with a small gift in the center. Although most of the time I unwrapped the entire ball of yarn to find the candy and gifts, I continued to knit.

Cables, with their three-dimensional look, have always fascinated me. I've devoted a lot of time to cable designs and how they can be manipulated. Nature is one of my best sources of inspiration. Growing up in Switzerland, I was exposed to beautiful scenery and was especially attracted to trees and plants. Experimenting with cables, I found that trees and other plants lend themselves well to textured knitting.

Abstracting a design—After you decide on the design you plan to use on the front, back, and sleeves of the textured sweater, you must design a simple abstraction for each piece. My sweater design (facing page) was inspired by a straight, bare tree on campus. My first step in abstracting its shape to make it suitable for knitting was to draw a simplified version of it that included only the trunk, two or three main branches, and a few of the smaller branches to fill out the shape, as shown at left, below. You can model your abstract on evergreen trees, bushes, or vines just as easily. You don't need talent to draw such simple trees or plants. Just don't let yourself be distracted by the little branches. Focus on the trunk and the shape of the main branches, and remember that vertically flowing cables work best, so start with an upright plant.

Next, translate your first abstract into cable shapes of different relative widths for the trunk and main branches. The trunk will have the heaviest cables. Mine is a pair

of 4x4 knit cables right next to each other in mirror image. Main branches are likely to be 2x2s, 3x3s, or 2x3s. I think the slight asymmetry of the 2x3 gives a very natural look. Leave lines for some of the small branches. These will be 1x1s, with a knit stitch crossing over the purl background; or they may be 1x2s with a single knit stitch crossing over two purl background stitches. Such narrow cables can be moved diagonally in this way, but they can't go horizontally. Be sure to keep the cables the same proportional width as the branches of the original abstract so that the tree remains representational. Finally, you simplify the cables even more when you sketch their shapes on the scale drawings of your sweater pieces, as shown at right, below.

Planning the sweater—The style and shape of your sweater should be as simple as possible because a lot of shaping is likely to distort the appearance of the cables. The simpler the basic shape, the better the cables will look. Accordingly, my sweater has

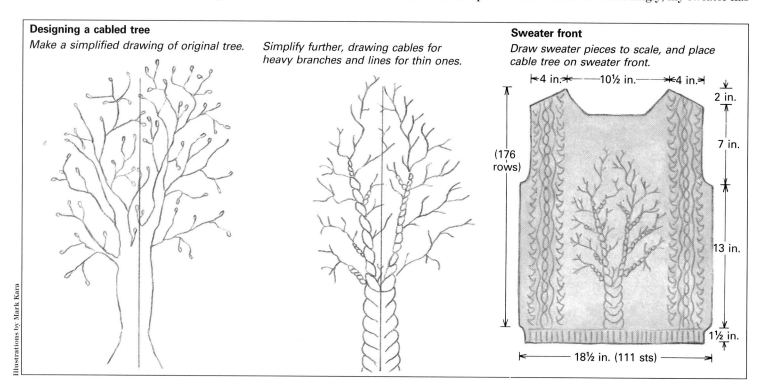

Designing a cabled tree
Make a simplified drawing of original tree.

Simplify further, drawing cables for heavy branches and lines for thin ones.

Sweater front
Draw sweater pieces to scale, and place cable tree on sweater front.

|←4 in.→|←——10½ in.——→|←4 in.→|
2 in.
7 in.
(176 rows)
13 in.
1½ in.
|←———— 18½ in. (111 sts) ————→|

From *Threads* magazine (October 1988) 19:48-51

In this tree sweater, Kathy Brunner combines her love of textured knitting with her fondness for nature. She puts smaller trees on the sleeves and related cables on the sides of the front and back.

Making proportional graph paper

Mark horizontal and vertical lines on square graph paper at ratio calculated for gauge swatch: 16 rows to 12 sts = 4-unit-wide sts x 3-unit-high sts.

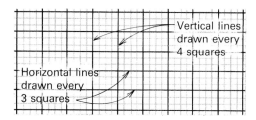

Vertical lines drawn every 4 squares

Horizontal lines drawn every 3 squares

Knitting symbols

▨	Knit
▨	Purl
▨	*Purl recessed or last stitch of cable when turning.*
◩	1x1 cable (front cross, recessed stitch purled)
◪	1x1 cable (back cross, recessed stitch purled)
◱	2x2, 3x3, etc., cable (back cross)
◲	2x2, 3x3, etc., cable (front cross)

Graphing the tree

Draw your cable design on the graph paper you've made. Then translate each line to knitting symbols. Knit pattern in round, turning on every row.

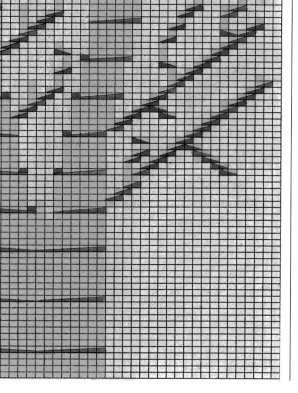

straight front and back panels, and the set-in sleeves have minimal shaping at the underarm and straight line decreases to the top of the cap to keep the armhole line straight and simple.

After I determined the exact measurements for the sweater (including ease), I drew the shapes of front, back, and sleeves to scale on 10-to-the-inch graph paper. The front is shown in the scale drawing on p. 86. Then I calculated the number of stitches and rows the sweater parts required by knitting a stockinette gauge swatch with the yarn and needles I planned to use. My gauge for a 2-in. square was 16 rows x 12 sts. So I multiplied the desired widths and lengths to arrive at the numbers of stitches and rows for the sweater parts, as shown in red on the scale drawing on p. 86. Although I drew and calculated the front and back as separate, flat pieces, I planned to add their totals together and knit the body of the sweater on circular needles after I had worked out all the calculations and charts.

According to my stockinette gauge, the front required 111 sts and 176 rows. But since cables pull in, they decrease the width of the knitting. To compensate for this draw-in, you must add stitches unevenly across, in the areas of the cables above the ribbing, according to the number and type of cables in the design. I have developed a formula for how many stitches to add for different cable types to compensate for their different draw-ins:

Cable type	Sts to add per cable
1x1	½
2x2	1
3x3	1½
4x4	2
5x5	2½

My general rule of thumb is to add about 25% of the number of stitches in a given cable to compensate for its draw-in. In the case of a 2x1 cable, I round up the next ¼ of a stitch and add 1 st. It's better to err on the side of too much ease rather than too little.

On my sweater I used five different cable types on front, back, and sleeves. While I put modified trees on the sleeves, the back was somewhat plainer—having only vertical cables that recalled those on the front. To figure out how many stitches to add around the body and sleeves, I figured out the stitches needed for the back and sleeves the same way I figured out the front, which I calculated as follows:

Cable type	No. of cables	Sts to add per cable	Total sts to add per cable type
1x1	4	½	2
2x1	4	1	4
3x3	2	1½	3
4x4	2	2	4

The front therefore grew from 111 sts to 124 sts (+13). The back had more cables, so it needed 20 more sts, and the body total above the rib was 255 sts—unevenly dis-

Wrapped satin stitch embroidered along each side of a temporary basting thread above the knit-stitch stalk looks like grains of wheat.

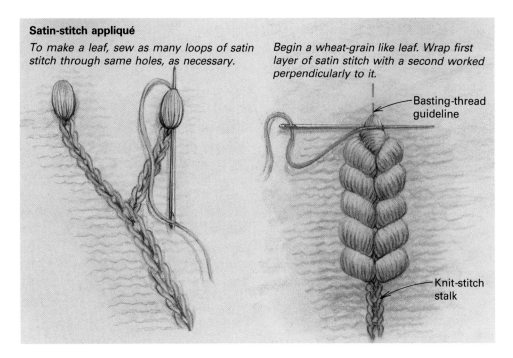

Satin-stitch appliqué

To make a leaf, sew as many loops of satin stitch through same holes, as necessary.

Begin a wheat-grain like leaf. Wrap first layer of satin stitch with a second worked perpendicularly to it.

Basting-thread guideline

Knit-stitch stalk

tributed on the front and back. In addition to the 7 sts I needed to add for draw-in on the sleeves, I added 5 sts for ease above the cuff. I also increased 1 st on each side every inch up to the armhole, as usual.

Making your knitting graph paper—There are several knitting graph papers on the market, but I prefer to make my own. The rectangular, proportional relationship of knit stitches varies with almost every sweater, depending on the size and type of yarn used, the size of the needles, the looseness or tightness of the stitches, and the stitch pattern. Therefore, the 5x7 relationship of the rectangles on most commercial knitting graph paper is not always appropriate.

The ratio for the relationship between your stitches and rows is easy to calculate from the gauge swatch. Divide the rows and stitches (16 rows and 12 sts) by their largest common denominator: 16 to 12 becomes 4 to 3. This means that 4 rows x 3 sts is the smallest square unit of knitting. Since the stitches are wider than they are tall, each stitch will fit on a rectanuglar grid that's 3 units high and 4 units wide.

Purchase commercial graph paper with light blue lines and small squares. I start with 10-to-the-inch paper. Use a ruler to draw new lines for the rows and stitches on the graph paper. In this case you would draw horizontal lines every 3 squares for the rows, and vertical lines every 4 squares for the stitches, as shown at top left, facing page. Then photocopy the sheet, and the blue lines will disappear. Next, reduce the photocopy about 65% to get a more manageable size grid, make several copies, and tape them together into an 8½-in. x 11-in. page. Reduce this sheet another 65%, and make at least 20 copies. You'll now have an accurate grid with reasonable-sized rectangles on which to plot your sweater design. Finally, tape enough of the copies together

to make a sheet with the necessary rows and stitches for each sweater piece. My sweater front required a sheet of graph paper 124 blocks wide x 176 blocks long.

Although this process takes time, it's worth the effort when you want to create an accurate proportional design. Even so, if you're working with cables and other stitches that draw in to varying degrees, the design you draw on the graph paper won't look exactly like the final version on the sweater.

Recording the design on graph paper— Transfer your abstract cable drawing to the graph paper with a pencil. If necessary, adjust the design until you have just the look you want. When you're happy with the design, translate the drawing into knitting symbols, as shown in the chart on the facing page. Erase the pencil lines of the cable abstract one row at a time, and fill in the rectangles with knitting symbols as you go.

Knitting the sweater—Before you start knitting, you must consider several factors: A cable looks best with the same number of rows as its width. Thus, a 1x1 cable should turn every second row; a 2x2, every fourth row; a 3x3, every sixth row; and so on. Of course, you can always knit more rows between cable turnings, but too few rows ruins the cable shape.

You can avoid the excessive tightness that often occurs when a 3x3 (or wider) cable is turned by working a yarnover in the middle of the cable the row before you turn the stitches for the cable. On the turning row, drop the yarnover to open up a little more room for the turning stitches.

To produce a bulky or more textured look in a 1x1 or 2x1 cable than you can get by knitting and purling as expected, knit the stitch that crosses in front, and purl the single stitch or stitches that cross behind. You should repeat this technique at

least every other row to make it look uniform. I did the thin branches on the tree this way to achieve flowing lines that look three-dimensional.

I knit all my sweaters, particularly complex, textured ones, on circular needles. I like to have the right side facing me so that I can see what I'm doing at all times. I also try to omit as many seams as possible, and since I knit much faster than I purl, knitting in the round enables me to make the sweater much more quickly.

Adding finishing touches—I like to use appliqué to add special touches. I appliquéd the leaves on my tree design after I finished the sweater. I worked satin stitch with a blunt tapestry needle and produced a padded effect by going into the same place several times, as shown in the drawing at left, above, until the leaf was as wide and heavy as I wanted it. For my wheat sweater (detail in above photo), I used my leaf technique to form the basis of each wheat grain. But after stitching five or six diagonal satin stitches, all originating in the same spaces, I wrapped them with horizontal satin stitch, as shown in the drawing at right, above. I used a basting thread to align the pairs of grains and set a vertical grain on the top of each shaft. The stalk is a plain knit stitch on a purl ground.

Instead of embellishing with yarn appliqués, you might apply other things, like beads. With a little ingenuity and these basic techniques, you can come up with many ways to create a unique textured sweater.□

Kathy Brunner is a student from Switzerland who is studying apparel design at The University of Alabama. She is also an Olympic diver. Sue M. Parker, Assistant Professor in Clothing, Textiles, and Interior Design, helped with technical clarifications of the knitting processes.

Knitting from Sewing Patterns

Both hand- and machine-knitters can find inspiration at the sewing shop

by Pat Morse

Sweater patterns these days are beautiful—but there are probably 20 sewing patterns produced for every new knitting pattern. I've been taking full advantage of sewers' vast resources by knitting sweaters directly based on commercial sewing patterns and have found them to be a terrific source of inspiration for knit garments. Both hand- and machine-knitters can just as easily use the shapes and styles of sewn garments to expand their pattern choices.

Evaluating patterns—Sewing patterns can be divided into two broad categories: those designed for woven fabrics and those designed for knits. Either type of pattern can be used as a knitting pattern, but you'll have to think about how the fabrics in each category drape and stretch and try to design knit fabrics with similar qualities. Many of the knit patterns on the market are very similar to sweater patterns; they are boxy shapes, sometimes loose-fitting, sometimes tight, with no darts and few fitting lines. Since they're designed to be used with stretch fabrics, the amount of ease usually isn't excessive, and these patterns can often be used as knitting guides just as they are.

Patterns for woven fabrics offer the knitter more variety and more new possibili-

ties. They usually have more pieces and, as a result, they have more seams than patterns for knits. Fortunately, darts, which don't translate well into knitwear, are rare these days; shaping has been moved to the seamlines. The amount of ease in these patterns can vary considerably, depending on both the style of the garment and the designer, but when you convert them to knit fabrics, there's frequently more ease than you need; buying woven patterns a size smaller than usual is often wise. Look carefully at the photo, if there is one (fashion drawings are harder to judge for fit), to get a sense of the ease, and also read the description on the back of the envelope. If it says "loose-fitting," there's about 8 in. of design ease. "Very loose-fitting" means 10 in. or more; either case would be a good candidate for a smaller size.

Once I'm attracted to a pattern, I look at the suggested fabrics on the back of the envelope. If the garment is designed for firmly woven fabrics, then my knit fabric should also be firm with a tight gauge. Otherwise, my finished sweater won't have the look that attracted me to the design in the first place. If the garment is designed for softer fabrics that drape, then the yarns I knit with can be softer, and the gauge looser.

Besides knitting tighter and with firmer yarns to stabilize hand- and machine-knit

fabrics, you can felt them; layer or face them; add elasticizing textures, like cables and ribs; or interface them with fusible knits if the yarn can take the heat and pressure of fusing without flattening out. All these stabilizing techniques, especially fusing and felting, must be tested on substantial swatches, but the results, and your increased confidence, are worth the effort. There are, of course, limits to these strategies. Patterns requiring very crisp and stable, even starched, fabrics, and very tailored styles are probably the only really unsuitable patterns for converting to knitwear.

Don't be put off by unusual or complex shapes among the individual pattern pieces or by a lot of seams. If you know how to increase and decrease, you can knit almost any flat shape. You may also be able to eliminate some of the seams. Don't worry at this stage about construction steps. If you're attracted to a pattern and can see it as a sweater, just try to buy a size you can work with.

Taking measurements—When you're planning a new garment, the first place to start is with body measurements. The most important measurements for a sweater are the circumferences at the bust (or chest) and the hips, the shoulder width, and the body and sleeve lengths. The type of gar-

There are many sewing patterns that are appropriate for conversion to knitting patterns, whether they were originally intended for knit fabrics or for woven fabrics. Pat Morse selected each of the patterns on these two pages as good candidates for conversion to knitting guides; her sweater from Vogue's Basic Design jacket is shown on p. 93.

Adjusting the pattern—After taking the necessary body measurements, measure the pattern in the corresponding places. Don't include the seam allowances. In fact, if I'm not planning to use this pattern to sew a garment, I cut off the seam allowances, since I'll be hand-stitching the pieces together, catching just the selvages, as in ordinary knitting. Determine how much ease is built into the pattern by subtracting the body chest measurement from the pattern chest measurement. Measure the pattern—don't rely on the measurements on the pattern envelope. If the difference is more or less than you want, adjust the pattern, or use a different size.

If I've chosen a pattern with many pieces or that's a style I've never used, I make a muslin—a simplified garment, using just the major pattern pieces. It lets me see the style and fit on my body before I've committed my time or yarn. It's an extra step, but the time spent is worth it.

Muslins for knit garments can be made out of inexpensive stretch fabrics or wovens like muslin fabric. If I've chosen a substantial garment—a jacket, for example—I use a woven fabric. I'll be knitting a fabric that's tighter and more firmly knit than usual for this garment, and a woven muslin will show me how it will hang. If I'm making a lightweight blouse or skirt, I use a soft stretch fabric; it will have many of the same properties of my regular knit fabric.

While you're adjusting the pattern pieces to suit your body measurements, take a close look at them to see if you can also simplify any of the shapes for easier knitting. For example, sleeve and side-panel pieces that are slightly curved can probably be straightened out, since the effect of the curve is likely to be lost in knit fabric.

This is also the time to look at construction details in the pattern. Since you're making a sweater and not a woven garment, many of the construction techniques will be changed to suit the simpler methods used in a sweater. Some pattern pieces, like facings, might be eliminated. Lay out all the pattern pieces for your garment and evaluate each piece. Is it a major part of the garment? Could it be knit together with another piece and retain the look of the original? Could it be eliminated? See "Blue Jeans Jacket," p. 93, for a step-by-step run-through of one of my recent projects.

Think about changing pattern pieces by converting sewn details to knit details. Hems, collars, and cuffs could be ribbings

ment you're making may call for other measurements, like cuff, waist, or neckline; and if the garment is a skirt, you'll need to measure the waist, the hip at the widest part, and the overall length.

Take the bust measurement around the fullest part of the chest. Be careful not to let the tape measure droop in back. If you're making a sweater that will be worn over another garment, take the chest measurement while the other garment is being worn.

If the garment has sleeves that fit at the shoulder point, the shoulder measurement is critical. If the shoulders are too wide or too narrow, the whole sweater will look wrong. If the shoulders are too narrow, the sleeves will look as if they're riding too far up on the shoulder and will stretch or have pull lines across the cap. I use an unusual method to find the correct shoulder measurement; it builds in a bit of precaution against the natural stretch of knits. If you're making the sweater for yourself, have someone measure you about 4 in. down from the center-back neckline, and at that point have him or her measure across the back of your shoulders between the points where your arm joins the body. Find the same locations on the pattern back, and make any adjustments in the shoulder-blade area, not the center back, so that you don't inadvertently alter the neckline.

You can sometimes draw in slightly too-wide shoulders, and keep correct ones in place, with a stay tape applied to the seams from one shoulder point across the back neck and over to the other shoulder point. If you skip the back neck and stay only the shoulders, the stitches at the neck can stretch out of shape. Twill tape or woven seam binding works well.

I measure sleeve length in different ways, depending on the style of the garment. If the garment is a drop-shoulder style, I have someone measure me from the center-back neck down to my wrist with my arm straight out at the side. From this measurement, I subtract half the width of the back of the sweater, add 1 in. of ease, and the remainder is the sleeve length. If the garment has a set-in sleeve, I place a thin book under my arm up next to my body and have my helper measure from the top of the book to my wrist. This provides 1 in. of ease in the sleeve length, since the armhole will fall about 1 in. below the armpit.

The finished length that you want for your sweater determines where you need to take the hip measurement. If the sweater is designed to fall approximately 3 in. below the waist, then measure the hips at this point. If the garment is to be either tunic or coat length, measure the hips at the widest part.

Converting sewing pattern pieces to knitting shapes

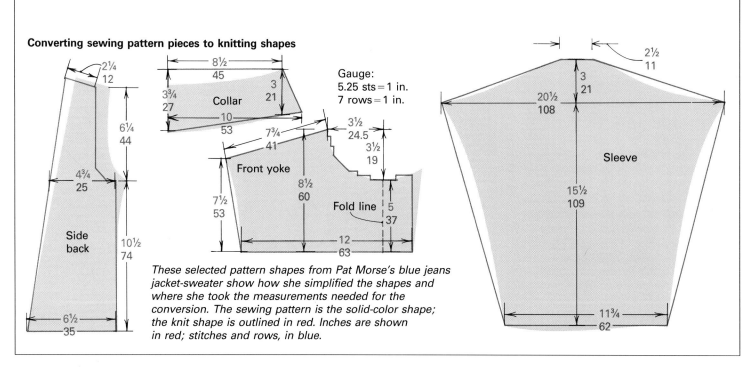

These selected pattern shapes from Pat Morse's blue jeans jacket-sweater show how she simplified the shapes and where she took the measurements needed for the conversion. The sewing pattern is the solid-color shape; the knit shape is outlined in red. Inches are shown in red; stitches and rows, in blue.

Morse sometimes finishes raw edges with a machine-knit bias strip. For added definition, she tacks a twist of contrast yarn over the seam.

Using a grid

Lay a knitter's grid that matches your stitch and row counts over pattern shape and outline grids that are just outside pattern.

and treated as single layers, knit together with the body or sleeve. Seams that are also prominent design lines could be emphasized with a carefully placed cable, a decorative decrease, or a crocheted join (see jacket, facing page). If a seamline provides design interest only, perhaps it could be simulated with a row of purl stitches on a knit ground, with duplicate stitch embroidery, or by a change in the knit texture.

Converting the pattern—Once you've adjusted the pattern pieces and edited out those you don't need, measure them again so you'll be able to convert them from inches to stitches and rows, but first examine them for slight curves that you could straighten out so that knitting them will be easier. The top drawing above shows the original shape of several pattern pieces and how I simplified them without losing the character of the original. Mark and measure horizontal and vertical width and length lines on all pattern pieces. Don't measure along diagonal seamlines, except at the shoulder seams. Include the width and depth of armholes and neck shapings. If a pattern piece includes unusual shaping that you can't simplify without spoiling the pattern, measure the piece also along the shaped edges.

To get accurate stitch and row counts for your fabric, you need an ample gauge swatch. I work a large swatch—at least 6 in. x 6 in. (8 in. x 8 in. if I'm using a textural stitch). I measure it in the middle over at least 4 in. to determine my gauge; anything less isn't accurate enough. At this point, you can go back to your pattern and change all the inches previously marked to stitches or rows.

To determine when and where to decrease or increase for slopes and curves, you have to compare the number of stitches you need at the beginning of a shape with the number you need at the end and then divide the difference into the number of rows you have in which to make the change. For example, for the side-back panel in the top drawing, above, I had 35 sts at the start and 74 rows in which to get down to 25 sts at the underarm. I took 25 from 35 to get 10 decreases needed and divided 74 by 10 to get 7 and 4 left over—in other words, I needed 1 decrease every 7 rows 10 times, with 4 rows even. If you convert curves, like the armhole on this side piece, to a series of straight lines, you can calculate them the same way as simple slopes.

If you're machine-knitting, you can use a pattern-charting device, like a knit leader, and trace the outline of the pattern piece so the machine will show you where to in-

crease or decrease. If your machine takes half-scale patterns, you can have a copy shop reduce your pattern pieces by 50%.

Hand knitters with access to copiers could copy knitters' graph paper onto clear plastic, which they could lay over a pattern, and Xerox the two together. This would show decreases and increases right on the pattern, as in the drawing at right, above. The only problem is to find, or make, graphs that accurately reflect your gauge. (A variety of knitters' grids are available from Hallandall, Box 91, Rembrandt, IA 50576; 712-286-KNIT.) Any of these methods will work, but the math-and-measure method is easy, and the fastest in the long run.

Cut and sew—Machine knitters can use sewing patterns very much as they were intended: The speed of our machines means that knitting flat yardage and simply cutting out the pattern shapes is an efficient possibility. The technique is known in the garment industry as cut and sew. This method wastes some yarn but saves a lot of knitting time because you can knit plain rectangles instead of complex shapes. You can even start with a few inches of ribbing and make what the industry calls a "sweater blank." Just position the body pattern with the hem on top of the ribbing and cut to shape.

Knit fabric won't suddenly fall apart or ravel when you cut into it. You must treat it gently and not pick it up by the cut edges, but otherwise it can be treated like any other fabric. So long as you plan ahead for shrinkage, you can also felt it before cutting it to give it a different texture.

Cut-and-sewn garments are naturals for sewing together by machine because they don't have selvages like hand- or machine-knit shapes; in this case you do need a seam allowance. Allow at least ⅝ in.; you can always trim it later. You can sew stretch-stitch seams on the sewing machine, then finish the edges with a lightweight bound overlay, or you can use an overcast stitch, or a serger, for a seam and a finish at the same time. You can face raw garment edges or cover them with machine-knit bias bindings, as in the photo on the facing page.

Sewing knits with a machine occasionally calls for some ingenuity. The stitches may catch on the presser foot, or the garment may not feed smoothly through the machine. Try using a layer of tissue paper between the feed dog and the sweater and between the presser foot and the sweater. The sweater will go through easily, and the tissue paper tears away after sewing

Interfacing—You may also find that the knit fabric needs some temporary or permanent stability to handle well in the sewing machine. I've fused shaped strips of knit interfacing lightly along curved seamlines to simplify the stitching of a complex seam, then pulled the interfacing away and trimmed it off, leaving just what was caught in the seam to provide permanent support. When I want to permanently stabilize an entire piece, I cut the interfacing larger than the blocked-to-shape knit and spot-fuse them together in the middle of the piece. Then I trim the fusible to fit the knitting and fuse permanently, just as I'd do to a purchased fabric, using steam and a press cloth. Cotton, wool, linen, and blends containing these fibers can usually take the heat, but don't take anybody's word for it—test!

Other possibilities—You needn't knit all the pieces in a sewing pattern. Combining knits and wovens can be very effective. Knit sleeves for woven tops are common and work well, but you could knit the body and add sheer fabric sleeves for a dressy sweater. Try adding lace insets, or alternate fabric and knit panels. Once you've used a sewing pattern for a knit garment, you'll begin to look at all patterns with an eye toward their use as knitting patterns. Skirts, dresses, and children's and men's patterns all become possibilities. Spend some time looking through a pattern catalog, and experiment! □

Pat Morse teaches regularly at The Knitting Guild of America's national seminars. She also teaches apparel design at California State University in Sacramento.

Blue jeans jacket

I recently made a sweater from a jacket pattern, Vogue 1968, view B, a variation of the popular and timeless blue jeans jacket. It's a good example of how I convert sewing patterns to knitting projects (top photo). Here's what I did.

This jacket is designed to stand away from the body, so it needs firm, denimlike fabric. The long, straight lines of the front, back, and yoke seams are all important design lines. I chose a firm cotton/acrylic yarn with a recommended gauge of 4½ sts/in. to 5 sts/in. and found a workable fabric at a final tension of 5¼ sts/in. in plain stockinette. The fabric had lots of body, but it wasn't boardy.

I laid out and examined the pattern pieces for view B and decided to use a fold-over band for the cuffs and hem, with a soft sewn-in interfacing, which I could also use behind the center-front fold-over facings. These areas would have to support snaps, and the interfacing would help. The fold lines on the bands and facings would be a line of slipstitch to provide a crisp, easy fold. I decided to keep the collar a single, soft layer; but it would have also worked well as a double, interfaced detail. The two pieces for the sleeve would easily combine into one piece. I'd eliminate the pockets.

This left me with 10 pattern pieces, which would make up into a total of 16 garment pieces. I measured all the lengths and widths, and along each curve. I converted the measurements to stitches, rows, and decrease rates, and began knitting. As each piece came off the machine, I blocked it and checked it for accuracy against the simplified pattern shape.

To emphasize the lower edges of the front- and back-yoke seams, I worked a single-crochet edging along them (bottom photo), then lapped them over the front and back sections and hand-sewed them down. I tacked interfacing to the front facings along the slipstitch line, then folded the extended facings to the inside and slipstitched them in place. After joining the shoulders and side seams, I interfaced the lower band and worked another single-crochet edging along one long side. I pinned the band in place along the lower edge of the garment with the crochet edge overlapping the lower edge of the garment, sewed it in place, folded the back up, and stitched that in place. I did the cuffs the same way, then set the sleeves with a backstitch, sewed on the collar, hammered on the snaps, and it was done. —P.M.

Morse based this sweater on Vogue pattern 1968, an oversized blue jeans jacket style.

To emphasize the seams on the blue jeans jacket, Morse crocheted one edge and over-lapped it, sewing the edges together by hand, all in matching yarn.

Knit One, Sew One
Combine wovens and knits in a single garment

by Deborah Abbott

i often find myself wanting to sew with a piece of beautiful fabric that isn't quite big enough for the project at hand. Even though I'm a weaver and may have woven the fabric myself, weaving more fabric is likely to be as out of the question as buying more. But knitting additional fabric is a wonderfully flexible option. The process that I've found most useful is to start with a commercial dress pattern and then to knit carefully chosen pieces to complement the remaining pieces that I cut from the woven fabric, using the appropriate pattern pieces as knitting patterns.

Just about any woven fabric can be combined with knitting as long as the scale of the knitting harmonizes with the woven piece. Since I usually prefer to knit with larger needles (sizes 5 to 8), I gravitate toward more coarsely woven fabric. A rough rule of thumb is: The number of ends per inch in a fabric is about twice the number of stitches per inch in a comparable knit section; e.g., if a fabric is woven at 12 epi, the knit section is knit at 6 sts/in. Your choice of pattern stitch, combination of yarns, and the hand of your gauge swatch will affect the number of stitches per inch.

If you're planning to knit directly from the woven piece or crochet along its edge, you must consider whether your needle or crochet hook can pierce the fabric without splitting ends if it's too closely woven or fray the edge so it falls apart if it's too loosely woven. This wouldn't mean that the fabric was inappropriate, but you'd need a different method of attaching the knitting to it.

The knit and woven fabrics should also coordinate in style. The knit and woven sections must relate to each other visually and functionally. For sources of handwoven fabrics and coordinated yarns, see the supplies list on p. 96.

I use commercial patterns extensively. Because they're already sized, and most of the quirks have been worked out, I can save time. And, if I'm working with a client, the pattern catalog can help us communicate. I can draw over the image as we discuss a commercial design she chooses and use the pattern as the starting point. I often use the same process when planning clothes for myself, but designing one's own suitable patterns for woven/knit combinations can also work well, as they're usually made from simple shapes. In many cases you don't need a pattern to knit from, especially if you're adding knit waistbands, cuffs, and neckbands to woven garments.

Selecting patterns—When going through a pattern catalog, I isolate the essential lines of a pattern. It's helpful to look at the small line drawings at the bottom or side of the catalog page; they're usually on the back of the pattern envelope. These show the seamlines and garment proportions stripped of the glamour of the fashion illustration. Because I'm designing the fabric, and it will be the focus of the garment, I look for patterns with simple seamlines, where blocks of cloth can be admired without the distraction of complex construction. The illustration on the facing page shows patterns that could easily have knit sections.

I avoid curved seams because it's difficult to knit a curve unless you're using very fine yarn. I find the stepped gradations of decreases awkward, and if left in the seam allowance, they're bulky. I look for seamlines that can be eliminated, like a straight center-back seam. Two adjacent pattern pieces can often be pinned together and knit as one; e.g., the front band or lapel of a jacket and the jacket body. With woven fabric, these pieces are cut separately to create a bias area to facilitate folding the lapel. If they're knit, the natural elasticity of knit permits them to be knit as one piece.

Short-rowing (turning and knitting back before the end of a row) can be done to internally shape a single piece of knitting to replace shaping seams and darts in wovens, but it can't be done with many pattern stitches. A godet can be inserted into a skirt with short rows instead of seamed in place, and in the same manner, extra fullness can be added to the bust area, serving the same purpose as a stitched bust dart.

One of the pleasures of knitting from a sewing pattern is translating the sewing details into knit ones. Small fabric tucks can become knit tucks. Applied trim can be replaced with a fancy textural stitch; prints or patterned fabrics can be mimicked with brocade or lace knitting. Fabric piping can give knit seams emphasis and stability and can visually tie the woven and knit pieces together. Knit piping, edging, or cording can do the same thing against woven pieces. Any pattern that calls for commercially knit ribbing bands can use a handknit or machine-knit substitute. Knit stripes can replace woven ones; popcorn stitch can echo polka dots. Bias bands, contrast bands, collars, cuffs, godets, lapels, yokes, belts—all these can be replaced by knit shapes.

Once I've chosen the pattern and altered it to fit, I pin the pieces together on the seamlines as if I were sewing them up to wear. I put this paper garment on my dress form or try it on in front of a mirror. Even though it's flimsy, this three-dimensional mock-up gives me a good idea of the garment's construction and helps me decide which pieces I'll knit and which I'll cut from woven cloth. Then I choose a knitting stitch and knit my first gauge swatch.

Planning the knit fabric—Since I usually start with a piece of fairly complex handwoven fabric and then try to find a yarn that will complement it, I often need to mix several fine yarns of different colors and textures to make a suitable yarn of the right gauge. If possible, I use some of the same yarn that I used in the weaving. Sometimes the yarn I want to use will dictate what pattern piece I knit (a fine yarn in the right color might suggest sleeves), but more often the pattern piece is what dictates the weight and selection of the yarn and the stitches I use.

A balanced combination of knit and purl stitches (e.g., in a seed or basket stitch) creates a fabric that will lie flat and have less tendency to stretch, appropriate for a yoke, or a section with a pocket. For a gathered or draped effect, a loosely knit stockinette or lace stitch would be a good choice.

Because the selvages become part of the piece, selvages chosen beforehand produce the best results. For enclosed edges, I make a simple selvage by knitting the first and last stitches of every row. This makes a vertical row of loops, which I pick up when seaming, pulling the sewing yarn as lightly as possible to allow for an elastic edge.

From *Threads* magazine (December 1989) 26:64-67

Deborah Abbott plans her knit/woven garments around commercial patterns, often knitting and weaving with the same yarn.

A chain selvage is a neat edge. I use it when there will be stitches picked up and knit and when the selvage will show:
Row 1 (right side of work): Slip 1st st (k-wise), work to last stitch, knit this stitch.
Row 2 (wrong side of work): Slip 1st st (p-wise), work to last stitch, purl this stitch.

A picot selvage is fancier and is a good choice with lace patterns or when the knit piece is being appliquéd on top of wovens:
Row 1 (right side of work): Yarn forward to make 1 inc, k2tog.
Row 2 (wrong side): Yarn to back of needle to make 1 inc, p2tog.

Once I've picked a knit fabric that I think will work, I knit a 6-in.-sq. swatch, wash it, and measure it. Then I scrutinize it. Will it do what I want it to do? Does it have body? Does it feel scratchy or limp? I continue making swatches, judging them after washing, until I've designed a fabric that seems right for the pattern. From the final swatch I determine the gauge.

Knitting from a paper pattern Having determined the gauge, I go back to the sewing pattern and examine the pieces. Do any need lengthening or shortening because I'm going to knit them or attach knitting to them? For example, when I added a knit cuff to the sleeve in the jacket in the photo on p. 97, which was originally designed to be rolled up, I shortened the sleeve piece a lot because I was adding a cuff and taking away the roll-up allowance.

Next, I review the construction steps and the seam allowances I'll need. Which piece will be sewn to what, and in what order? Will the knit pieces be sewn to the woven pieces, or will they be crocheted together? If they're crocheted, I won't need seam allowances, but if I'm going to sew them I will. For a related discussion of knitting from sewing patterns, see pp. 90-93.

For my jacket, I knit the upper front and back. I eliminated the shoulder seam allowances because I knit the shoulders together, but I left the side seam and armscye allowances intact for the traditional ⅝ in. Since the shoulders support the weight of the garment, I inserted twill tape in the seam, and along the shoulder line, to prevent the knit piece from stretching.

I decided to lap the upper front and back over the lower, woven parts and appliqué them down. Therefore, I needed the lower body's seam allowance but not the upper body's. I eliminated the seam allowance around the neck because I picked up and knit the collar instead of sewing it on.

Once I've made these decisions, I put the original pattern piece under a piece of tracing paper and trace a new pattern that's exactly the shape I plan to knit. I use a solid line for the outside edge, but when I'm in-

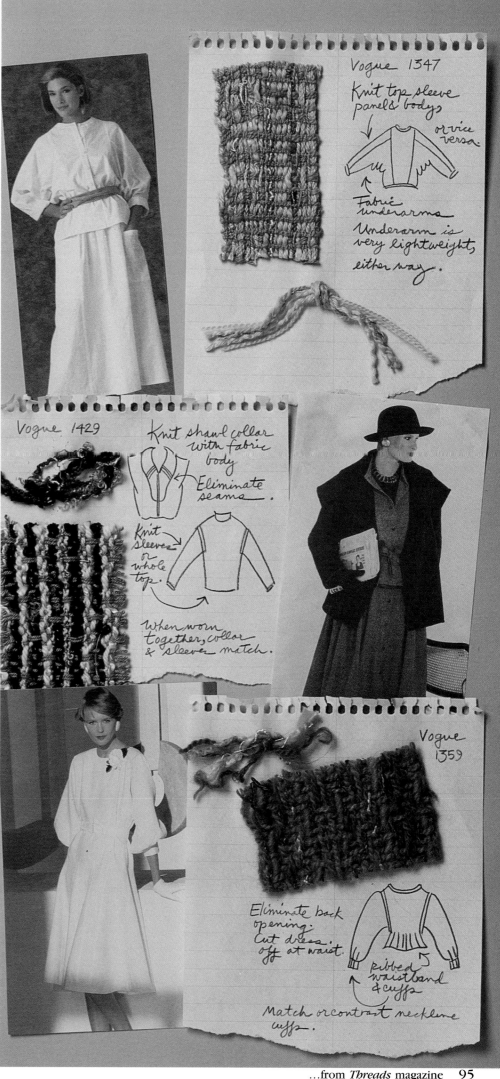

Finishing techniques for combined wovens and knits

by Julie Cherry

I weave yardage and then cut it to sew into garments with knit waistbands, necklines, and cuffs, like those in the photo on the facing page. I call them sweaters, and I put them together with a few tried-and-true techniques that give me a finish I like. I spend a long time on finishing; I like to cover any edge that might be seen. I serge all the woven cut edges and add a few rows of tight straight stitch, ⅛ in. to ¼ in. inside the serging.

When I'm handknitting into a woven edge, I start by pulling a row of yarn loops through to the right side of the fabric on the seamline with a crochet hook, counting and measuring the loops very carefully to match my knitting gauge. Then I pick the loops up on circular needles and knit away. I do the same thing for knit neckbands, but for neckbands I fold back the woven seam allowance and hand-stitch it with doubled thread to hold it against the garment body. This works well when I'm handknitting, but I prefer to do as much as possible on my bulky knitting machine. I learned to machine-knit in order to add shape to my garments, and I'm by no means an expert, but there's no doubt that machine knitting is a far more efficient method for many knitting tasks. People have suggested that I hang the woven pieces on the machine and knit directly, but

when I've tried that, it has caused me many more headaches than hand-finishing.

I knit the ribbing for the cuffs and the waist on my machine in one or two parts (a waistband may be too wide for the machine) and take it off on waste yarn. I unravel and discard the waste yarn and sew the knitting to the fabric as follows: Laying the raw knit edge along the ⅝-in. seam allowance of the fabric and using a needle threaded with the yarn I knit with, I stitch up through the fabric and back down into a knit loop. I take a small stitch in the fabric and come back through the same loop; then I go down into the next loop, and so forth, around the ribbing. This keeps the knitting flat against the woven fabric, and it stays stretchy. To prevent the stitches from gathering the woven fabric, about every 4 in. I make a backstitch with the yarn that I'm stitching with. After catching six or eight loops, I hold the yarn tightly with my right hand at the first loop and pull the end threaded through the needle taut, then backstitch and continue.

Whether I'm attaching hand or machine knits to garments, I usually mark both the woven edge and the knit piece in fourths to help get the stitches distributed evenly. I try to keep the ribbing approximately 4 in. shorter than the garment edge, like a ribbing is on a knit sweater.

When I'm sewing a machine-knit band of vertical ribbing onto the front of a cardigan and around the neckband, as in the photo on the facing page, I use the following method to hide the serged edge (see top drawing at right): I pin the band to the garment edge, wrong sides together. Then, with the same yarn that I'm using for the knitting, I sew the pieces together, using a running stitch. I usually hide this seam in a purl row. Then I turn the ribbing out and go back along the edge of the knitting with a whipstitch, catching the knit edge to the main body of the garment on the right side and hiding the serged edge inside the seam.

I've been using bands of vertical ribbing a lot. I take them off the machine with a few rows of waste yarn and pull out the waste yarn as I slip the stitches onto a knitting needle. I graft the two opposing rows of stitches (one from each bed) together with the bind-off shown in the lower drawings at right. This way, both cast-on ends look the same, and it's an especially useful trick if I'm doing a long band. I knit the band a few rows longer than I need, apply the band, and adjust the length by pulling out any unneeded length. Then I bind off the end just where I need to.

Julie Cherry is a production handweaver in Eugene, OR.

Stitching vertical ribbing bands to wovens

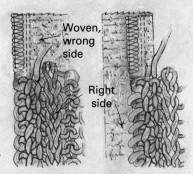

Woven, wrong side

Right side

With woven fabric and ribbing wrong sides together, attach with running stitch along seamline and in first purl rib. Open seam and whipstitch rib selvage to cover woven seam.

K1, p1 rib bind-off

Go p-wise into 1st knit st and k-wise from behind into 1st purl st. Leave both stitches on knitting needle.

Insert tapestry needle k-wise into 1st knit st, and drop it. Then go p-wise into 2nd knit st.

Go p-wise into 1st purl st, and drop it. Loop yarn to right under knitting needle, and insert tapestry needle k-wise from behind into 2nd purl st.

Illustration by Victoria Vebell

---

cluding a seam allowance, I mark it in with a dotted line, as a reminder that this edge will be hidden in a seam.

Next, I measure the width at the starting edge of the pattern piece, multiply that by the number of stitches per inch from my swatch, and cast on the appropriate number of stitches. I don't calculate increases beforehand. As I knit, I follow the pattern piece, matching my knitting to large curves in the pattern with increases and decreases and ignoring slight curves because of the knit's ability to stretch.

As I work, I always write down what I do. I may want to change something later and

not remember what I did. I may want to repeat the directions for the other side but reverse the shaping. I may want to make the garment again but in another size: I can grade up or down one or two sizes from my own directions instead of buying another pattern and figuring it out all over again. And, if I can't finish the garment in one sitting, I can easily discover where I left off when I pick up my work again. □

Deborah Abbott is a frequent contributor to Threads. *She is currently marketing a line of yarns to knitting and needlework stores under the name Aurora Designs.*

Sources for handwovens & yarn

R. Brown Textiles: (602) 837-9227
Box 17360, Fountain Hills, AZ
See "Notes," p. 24, for report on R. Brown.

Connected Threads: (919) 852-4560
Box 19101, Greensboro, NC 27419-9101

Patrice Designs: (505) 835-1304
Box 331, Socorro, NM 87801

Picks: (703) 548-0573
3316 Circle Hill, Alexandria, VA 22305

Jennifer Pixley: (207) 866-3783
175 Main St., Orono, ME 04473

When chosen carefully, knit and woven fabrics combine in garments marvelously. In Abbott's jacket, handknitting fills in for insufficient fabric at shoulder and cuffs and adds interesting detail. Machine-knit cuffs, waistbands, and necklines convert Julie Cherry's woven tops into sweaters.

Knit to Fit

Accurate measurements and common sense make an attractive handknit sweater

by Mary Studeny

Working with the basic pattern that she explains here, Mary Studeny knit these custom-fitted sweaters, using stockinette for the body and a rib variation for the yoke. With her method, any stitch can be used to fit any body.

*i*f you know basic knitting techniques, then with the method I'm going to explain and a little self-confidence, you'll soon be able to handknit any sweater you can dream up in any size or fit you want. All you need to do is observe what is happening as you work and see cause and effect.

My method for design and construction is the same whether I'm making a plain stockinette or an intricately patterned sweater. The basic set-in-sleeve sweater offers the simplest structure to design when you're translating body measurements into a custom fitted garment, so I'll explain how I planned and knit a crewneck sweater with folded-over ribbing at the neck—like the sweaters at left—to fit my friend Stewart. Once you understand the elementary design process, you can adapt the method for variations in necklines, sleeves, and patterns.

Choosing the style—The first step in designing your sweater is to select a style. I keep a notebook with several sections. One section is just for design ideas, ranging from catalog pictures to my own sketches. Most important to compile for ideas are overall styles and pattern designs, types of yarn, individual stitch patterns, and occasional photos of patterns.

From this body of ideas, I select a style and stitch patterns. I consider the intended use of the sweater. Will it need to be large enough to be worn over clothing or closely fitting and dressy? The ultimate goal in designing your own sweater is to achieve a perfect fit. But what does this mean? A sweater that's to be worn over a blouse or a shirt requires a relatively close fit, while one that's to be worn over layered clothing needs to be larger throughout.

Checking the gauge—Once you've decided on a sweater style, you must select your yarn and needle size. Keep in mind the finished look you want, and choose a yarn that will accommodate your needs. Test the yarn on the needle size recommended on the label, as well as on larger and smaller needles. Look for the best overall appearance of the yarn no matter what size needle it takes to achieve that look.

You'll need to make a test swatch for every pattern in your sweater and to calculate the width gauge (stitches per inch). An important difference between my method and other methods is that I measure the length of each sweater part as I proceed, so I don't calculate a length gauge (rows per inch).

Make the test swatch large—at least half the width of the sweater back and 4 to 5 in. deep—to get the most accurate gauge. A gauge error of $\frac{1}{10}$ in. in a swatch that's only 1 to 3 in. wide can increase to several inches across the sweater width. Lay the test swatch flat and take gauge measurements from at least three areas in the center of the swatch; then average them.

Although gauging is time-consuming, it will eliminate the need to rip out a piece that's too big or too small. For yarns I routinely use, I keep a chart in my notebook in which I list gauges for different needle sizes with a given yarn. This way, I don't have to do a test gauge for every project.

Measuring—Now you'll need to get some measurements. For measurements, I use and evaluate three sources: the actual body, a set-in-sleeve sweater, and a fitted shirt or blouse with set-in sleeves. I suggest that you enter your measurements, with comments, in a chart like the one below.

First take body measurements with the person wearing either a shirt or layered clothing according to your original decision. Also measure a sweater that fits that person well; evaluate how its measurements correspond to what you'd like to see in the sweater you'll make. Note on your chart how the sweater fits, especially the total length (distance from shoulder seam to sweater bottom). Lay the sweater flat and record its measurements. Perhaps the best source for measurements will come from a blouse or shirt that fits closely, since its seam construction gives an accurate measurement on critical dimensions of armhole depth, yoke width, and sleeve length. Are there areas where the fabric pulls, indicating a need for more ease? Are

there dimensions that are too large? Remove the shirt, button it, lay it flat, and take measurements.

Use your comments on fit to choose final sweater dimensions and make adjustments. Your goal is to combine the accurate shirt measurements with the amount of ease you think the sweater will need. If you're making a sweater as a surprise and can't take body measurements, you can still get it to fit will by using the guidelines I've given in the chart on p. 101.

Creating the pattern—For Stewart's sweater I was able to get very accurate measurements. I multiplied my gauge for the stockinette pattern (4¼ st/in.) by each measurement and then drew up my plan, as shown below. I knit all but the yoke in stockinette. I made two changes to the yoke. First, although Stewart's yoke width was 17 in., I based my calculations on 16¾ in. By working the yoke width between ½ and ¾ in. less than the actual measurement, I compensated for the sleeve weight and yarn

Combining measurements for a custom fit

Measurements for Stewart's sweater (in inches)	Actual body	From shirt	From sweater	To make
Chest circumference (under armpit)	40	42	42	42
Yoke-back width (sleeve seam to sleeve seam)	17	19	18	16¾
Shoulder width (sleeve seam to collar seam)	4½	5½	5	4½
Armhole length (shoulder seam to 1 to 2 in. below armpit)	10½	10½	11	11
Total length (shoulder seam to sweater bottom)	27½	–	26	27½
Bottom-to-armhole length (total minus armhole length)	17	–	15	16½
Sleeve width above cuff	7½	9	10¾	11¼
Upper-arm circumference (at armpit)	14	15	16	16¼–16½
Sleeve length (cuff bottom to 1 to 2 in. below armpit)	19	19	19	19

Normal shirt size: 16½ (or large)
Comments: Shoulders on size 16½ shirt are too wide. Very long-waisted (large size worn mostly for total body length). Likes loose sleeves.

Final plan for Stewart's sweater

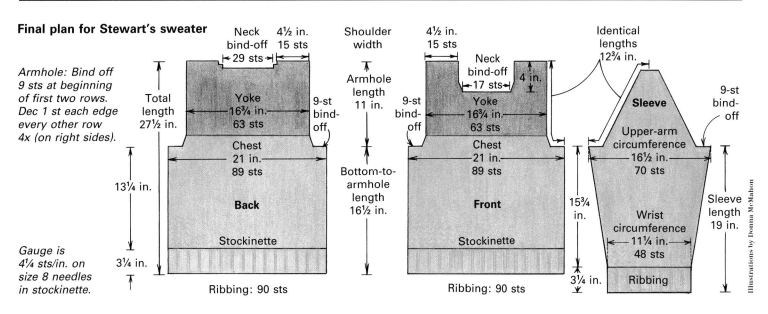

Armhole: Bind off 9 sts at beginning of first two rows. Dec 1 st each edge every other row 4x (on right sides).

Gauge is 4¼ sts/in. on size 8 needles in stockinette.

Neck bind-off 4½ in. 15 sts
29 sts
Total length 27½ in.
Yoke 16¾ in. 63 sts
9-st bind-off
Chest 21 in. 89 sts
Back
13¼ in.
3¼ in.
Stockinette
Ribbing: 90 sts

Shoulder width
Armhole length 11 in.
9-st bind-off
Bottom-to-armhole length 16½ in.
3¼ in.

4½ in. 15 sts
Neck bind-off 17 sts
4 in.
Yoke 16¾ in. 63 sts
9-st bind-off
Chest 21 in. 89 sts
Front
Stockinette
Ribbing: 90 sts

Identical lengths 12¾ in.
Sleeve
9-st bind-off
Upper-arm circumference 16½ in. 70 sts
15¾ in.
Sleeve length 19 in.
Wrist circumference 11¼ in. 48 sts
3¼ in.
Ribbing

Illustrations by Donna McMahon

Back-neck and shoulder treatments

Straight shoulders
(straight bind-off)

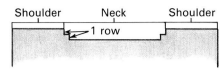

Moderately sloping shoulders
(two equal steps)

Severely sloping shoulders
(three equal steps)

All variations use 2 decreases at neck edge. Neck decrease is done on final shoulder bind-off row.

Details for Stewart's sleeve

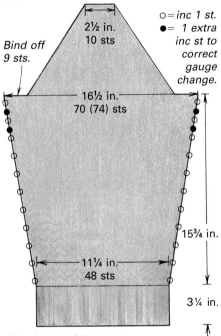

Calculation of increases
5¼ in. x 4¼ sts/in. = 22-st inc, 11 sts/side.

---

stretch. Second, since I decided to work the yoke and shoulders in a ribbing variation, I reduced the number of yoke stitches from 71 (for a stockinette stitch) to 63, and the shoulder stitches from 19 to 15 to compensate for the stretch and gauge of the alternative pattern. Remember to check your gauge for every pattern.

I used an odd number of body stitches to make it easy to decrease to the odd number of stitches in the yoke. For smooth side seams, I used an even number of stitches for the k1, p1 ribbing, maintaining one edge with k2 at the end of the row and p2 at beginning of the next row.

Knitting the sweater body—With the calculations complete, you have a general pattern to follow. For Stewart's sweater, I knit all ribbing on size 4 needles, then switched to size 8 for the body and yoke. At about one-third of the desired distance to the armhole, I rechecked the gauge. I also decided how to treat the armhole and how quickly I should bind off the stitches. I had to decrease the stitches by 26 (89-63), or to bind off a total of 13 sts on each edge. For most women's sweaters I bind off two-thirds of this number at the beginning of the first two rows of the armhole (8 sts in each row). Then I decrease 1 st each edge every other row. On men's patterns and on my own (I have broad shoulders), I normally bind off three-quarters of the total decreases for freedom of movement, then decrease 1 st each edge every other row.

Knitting the shoulders—With 63 sts I began the yoke pattern, continuing until the total length of the armhole was two rows fewer than I wanted. Most patterns shape the shoulders by doing successive step bind-offs, then bind off a final row at the neck. I find this method impractical, since it causes the neck ribbing to rise up to the hairline. Instead, I usually drop the neck by two rows below the shoulders, as shown in the top-left drawing. My method can be adapted to any shoulder slope and works remark-

ably well on crewnecks, turtlenecks, and cardigans. It gives a smooth curve to the back of the neck. The seam takes up the last row of each shoulder. Be careful to bind off the neck and shoulders loosely so the yoke width won't be reduced.

I worked the front of Stewart's sweater the same way I knit the back, but I dropped the center neckline and bound off the neck at about two-thirds of the total armhole length. You can make the distance slightly more or less, depending on the final look you want. You can achieve a smooth curve for the neckline by allowing for several sets of decreases at each neck edge. The greater the number of decreases, the rounder the final neck will be. I knit the neck by decreasing 1 st each edge every row until I had the same number of stitches for the front shoulders as there were on the back shoulders. I worked each shoulder section until the front and back armhole lengths were identical; then I bound off the shoulders loosely.

Knitting the neck ribbing—I sewed the shoulder seams together, taking care to maintain the specific yoke width, which the tightness of these seams controls. Next, I picked up the neck ribbing on a size 4 circular needle, going into every stitch as needed. Never plan to pick up a specific number of stitches, since the number varies with the front-neck depth. I start picking up stitches at a shoulder seam, continue around the entire neck, and then count the number of stitches on the needle. If the ribbing is to be k1, p1, the total number of stitches may be off by 1 st. If so, k2tog, and then continue p1, k1 across. The neck edge will be folded under and tacked down to the original neckline. I made the neck ribbing for Stewart's sweater twice the length desired, then bound off very loosely, leaving large, evenly made loops; the loops can be hidden when they are tacked down. If you can't control a loose bind-off, try using a needle several sizes larger. The double-length ribbing minimizes

Judging sleeve-cap length for fit

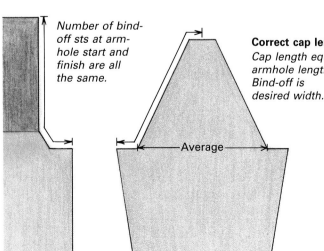

Number of bind-off sts at armhole start and finish are all the same.

Correct cap length
Cap length equals armhole length. Bind-off is desired width.

Cap too long
Cause: Too many sts in upper arm to take standard decreases.

Solution: Rip out. Dec 1 st each edge every row for one-third to one-half cap length; then dec 1 st each edge every other row.

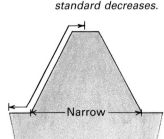

Cap too short
Cause: Too few sts in upper arm to take standard decreases.

Solution: Rip out. Dec 1 st each edge every 4th row for one-third to one-half cap length; then dec 1 st each edge every other row.

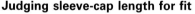

neck stretching and enhances the sweater's overall appearance.

Knitting the sleeves—Fitting the sleeves is generally the greatest design challenge. I drew a diagram (facing page, center) of the sleeve, using the gauge and the original measurements. The number of stitches to be cast on for the cuff is determined by the number required for the width above the cuff. I cast on 48 sts on size 4 needles to start the cuffs. The increases in the sleeve were spaced evenly along the length to the underarm, based on the distance to the armhole and the width desired at the widest point. After I'd knit about one-third the length to the underarm, I rechecked my gauge and found it had changed slightly. To get a final width of 16½ in., I added two sets of increases in the upper-sleeve section. Checking gauge and measurements every so often makes it easy to compensate for minor variations in knitting tension.

To make the sleeve cap, I started by binding off the same number of stitches that I'd used for the armhole bind-off on the sweater front and back (9 sts at the beginning of the next two rows). I needed 2½ in. for the bind-off at the top of the cap. I use a bind-off width from 2 to 3 in. for women's sizes 4 to 18 and from 2½ to 3½ in. for men's sizes 34 to 48. Then I finished the cap by decreasing 1 st each edge every other row.

The best way to get a cap that matches the armhole of the body is to check the cap as you work. When it's about half the length of the armhole, lay the sweater body flat next to the sleeve and look at how the decreases seem to be working (see bottom drawing, facing page). The standard decreases were perfect on Stewart's caps, and I bound off the last row for the top of the cap.

Finishing—To finish Stewart's sweater, I first sewed the caps into the armholes, then I closed the side seams. I like the person to try on the sweater at this point because any minor variations is size can be adjusted without too much difficulty by blocking.

I evaluate each sweater and make a sheet for my notebook, entering all pertinent information. I usually keep simple records, but for complicated patterns I include more details, and sometimes a close-up photo of the sweater.

Now that you've seen the process from beginning to end, try your own custom-designed sweater, perhaps with a pattern other than stockinette. Quick success is the greatest incentive, so I suggest that you first use yarn and needles that require no more than 4 sts/in. This way, you can easily complete the sweater in a few weeks. □

Mary Studeny is a handweaver and fiber artist in New Rochelle, NY, with 30 years experience in handknitting. She is also a research biochemist.

Surprise sweaters

If you don't have the luxury of being able to take direct measurements, you must rely on standard measurements, which are based on clothing size. Over the years, when faced with no way to get measurements, I collected dimensions to which I could refer. The chart below lists women's blouse and men's shirt sizes, along with the corresponding dimensions I use for those sizes when I don't have any other information. These measurements reflect sizes for a normal fit; that is, the classic fit of a traditional set-in-sleeve crewneck pullover, allowing only a minimum increase over body size in all dimensions for ease of motion. The chart is most helpful when you use it in conjunction with other information. For instance, two women may both wear size 12, but if one of them is 5 ft. tall and the other is 5 ft. 11 in. tall, they will require different sleeve lengths, different total lengths and, most probably, different armhole depths. I don't include children's sizes in my chart, because I've concluded that there's no rational sizing method for children.

When you're designing a sweater as a surprise, the best approach is to secretly obtain one of the person's shirts or blouses, get detailed sizing information from one of his or her friends or relatives, and use the guidelines in the chart below. I've used this technique repeatedly for my friends and family, as well as for customers who want a special surprise gift for someone. —M.S.

Sweater guidelines for women and men (in inches)

Women's blouse sizes	4	6	8	10	12	14	16	18
Actual bust	30	30½	31½	32½	34	36	38	40
Actual waist	22½	23	24	25	26½	28	30	32
Actual hip	32	32½	33½	34½	36	38	40	42
Sweater bust circumference	32	32½	33½	34½	36	38	40	42
Yoke-back width	13	13½	13¾	14	14½	15	15½	16
Shoulder width	3	3¼	3¼	3¼	3½	3½	4	4¼
Armhole length	7½	8	8½	8½	9	9½	9½	10
Total length	22	23	24	24½	25	26	26½	27
Bottom-to-armhole length	14½	15	15½	16	16	16½	17	17
Wrist circumference	6	6	6	6	6¼	6¼	6½	6½
Sleeve width above cuff	8¾	9	9¼	9¼	9½	10	10¼	10½
Upper-arm circumference	13	13¼	13½	13½	14	14½	14¾	15
Sleeve length	16½	16¾	16¾	17	17½	17¾	18	18¼
Men's shirt sizes	14	14½	15	15½	16	16½	17	17½
Actual chest	34	3C	38	40	42	44	46	48
Actual waist	28	30	32	34	36	38	40	42
Actual sleeve	32½	33	33½	34	34½	35	35½	36
Sweater chest circumference	36	38	40	42	44	46	48	50
Yoke-back width	15½	16	16½	17	17½	18	18½	19
Shoulder width	3½	4	4½	4½	5	5¼	5½	5¾
Armhole length	9¾	10	10¼	10½	11	11¼	11½	11¾
Total length	25¼	25½	25¾	26¼	27	27½	28	28¾
Bottom-to-armhole length	15½	15½	15½	15¾	16	16¼	16½	17
Wrist circumference	6½	6½	6½	6¾	6¾	7	7¼	7¼
Sleeve width above cuff	10	10¾	11¼	11¼	11½	11¾	12	12¼
Upper-arm circumference	15¾	16	16½	16½	16¾	17	17¼	17½
Sleeve length	18	18½	18¾	19	19½	20	20½	21

Fashion Doesn't Stop at 40 Inches

The key is fit, and the handknitter's secret is a fabric mock-up

by Deborah Newton

*a*s a handknit designer, I've had plenty of experience creating sweaters for the fashion model who graces the pages of knitting magazines and sweater pamphlets. Almost anything looks good on this willowy ideal, who is at least 5 ft. 8 in. and has bust and hip measurements of about 34 in. But to design successfully, I have to know that my sweaters will look good on a range of more realistic sizes, the ones that are usually included in handknit instructions. Some sweaters do look better on smaller figures, but sometimes I sense that a sweater design would flatter the fuller-figured woman as well, and I'm disappointed to see that the pattern excludes anyone whose bust exceeds 40 in.

Of course the heavier woman has always wanted to look good, to enjoy clothing that fits and that suits her personality. She wants choice in fabric and style and doesn't want to settle for polyester double knit. She yearns for a range of beautiful natural fibers and more attractive details and styling for her dimensions. With more fashion attention being given to the full-figured woman these days, I began wondering whether she really was finding it easier to clothe herself attractively. But even with plus sizes available in ready-to-wear styles and designer lines, what about the heavier handknitter?

The knitter who is heavier than average has few patterns from which to choose. She's often left considering men's patterns to find a chest measurement larger than the bust measurement offered in most women's patterns. It's not yet the norm for larger sizes to be included with the more average ones in handknitting instructions.

The knitting plight of the heavier woman intrigued me. But I had little experience with larger sizes and wondered whether the concerns were different. Obviously, the best way to find out was to become involved in a project. It didn't take long to find two enthusiastic, full-figured knitters who were eager to help me. I didn't want to create scaled-up versions of smaller sweaters. I wanted to design specifically for their figures, to flatter them and meet their needs, and I wanted to create a basic pattern that each of them could reuse.

The first knitter I chose, Holly Mendes, owns Ewe and Eye, a yarn shop in Davol Square in Providence, RI. Holly, stylish and attractive, had knit for herself, searching for sweater patterns that offered larger finished measurements and adapting others. She often helps the heavier customers and students in her knitting classes cope with the limited number of patterns available by suggesting a change in needle size to alter gauge or the addition of extra stitches to enlarge the pattern measurements.

Also eager to help was Gail Harrison, who had made sweaters for her family and friends, but never for herself. Gail was indeed an inspiration; I wanted to devise a pattern that would help her knit many sweaters in the future. A full-time nurse, very active with family and a multitude of interests, Gail longed for a straightfoward cardigan that she could wear in a variety of situations. We spoke about other design considerations. Like Holly, Gail loves wool, yet she wanted something cool enough to wear indoors. She also felt that a longer line was more flattering for her.

Both women had been discouraged in their attempts to find clothing for themselves. Despite the greater availability of larger sizes, finding garments that fit or flattered was still difficult. And price was a factor too. It was easier to find expensive garments that were attractive, but both felt there was little in the average price range.

The first step in my research was to look at ready-to-wear garments in the larger sizes. I visited specialty shops for large women, as well as major department stores, traveling with a tape measure and Holly's and Gail's measurements in mind. I found little on the racks that would flatter them and even fewer garments that would actually fit. The number of sloppy-looking dropped-shoulder sweaters with overly long sleeves and drooping, wide shoulders surprised me. In an affordable price range, I saw many plastic-looking synthetics that wouldn't appeal to Gail or Holly. And I was dumbfounded by the proliferation of horizontal stripes—I had thought that everyone knew this was a primary don't. The better-looking garments, which were generally more expensive, showed more thought in the crucial cross-shoulder measurement. A set-in sleeve seemed to provide a more refined fit around the armhole, while still accommodating width at the hip and waist.

Like any other sweaters I might design, I wanted those for Holly and Gail to flatter and to fit comfortably. The two knitters were built differently, so I needed to decide on the best measurements and shapes for each. I also needed to coordinate these elements with knit fabric, yarn, and color. It was exciting to design for two real people, rather than for some far-away model.

Looking at garments that fit—I often refer to other sweaters as well as to sewn garments to guide me toward an understanding of a certain style of fit. Woven-fabric garments don't stretch like knits do, but they provide a point of departure for planning a new project by supplying measurements that can be tested. I often test new proportions by borrowing measurements from another garment I like.

I began the design process with both knitters by referring to sweaters that they

Holly Mendes and Gail Harrison (right) wear sweaters designed to fit and flatter them. While helping author Deborah Newton, they learned to modify existing garments so they could continue to knit for themselves.

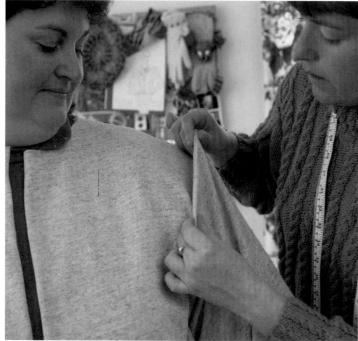

To adjust the droopy shoulder seam on Gail's mock sweater (above), Newton folds along the seamline of the sleeve cap and body and then pulls the seam further in toward Gail's actual shoulder line before beginning to pin it in place. After having decided on sleeve length, Newton pinned the wrist to simulate ribbing and to see whether there was enough length to allow the sleeve to drape slightly above the rib. Pinning the neck edges into a V at the depth Gail prefers (right) is the final step in fitting the mock-up.

owned. Holly had a black, medium-weight, machine-knit, hip-length pullover with a flattering jewel neckline. She liked the length and the narrow ribbing at the lower edge that was not as tight as some of her other sweaters. But she asked me about the dropped-shoulder styling because she found this type of sleeve uncomfortable. The simple squared-off construction of the dropped shoulder is popular among knitters because it is easier to make than the set-in sleeve that requires armhole and sleeve-cap shaping. But the dropped shoulder creates extra bulk under the arm that can be uncomfortable. In addition, the seam that joins the upper sleeve to the body can fall unflatteringly low on the upper arm, visually widening the upper torso, as it did in Holly's sweater.

Gail's only sweater was an Aran-style cardigan her father had bought for her on a trip to Ireland. She was disappointed that it didn't fit. We analyzed it together. The body of the sweater should have been a few inches larger than Gail's body measurements to provide the extra ease that a bulky fabric necessitates. In addition, the armhole depth was too shallow for comfort. Since this sweater didn't inspire us with any useful information, we turned to a favorite blouse and a comfortable lightweight jacket. Gail, like Holly, said that a set-in sleeve felt better—less bulk actually allowed her more freedom of movement. The jacket had a shallow sleeve cap that was just a bit more fitted than a dropped shoulder.

Charting the garments—To record the shapes of these garments, I plotted their measurements on graph paper, using one square to the inch, as shown by the black lines in the drawings on pp. 105 and 106. I measured the lengths and widths of Holly's simple sweater. The front and back were the same, except for neck depth. I plotted the sleeve width at the lower and upper arms, as well as the length. Graph paper is an essential tool that lets me visualize the individual pieces of a sweater in their proper proportion and in relation to each other.

For Gail, I had to create a graphed guideline from a composite of measurements from her two garments. Their widths were similar, so I averaged the two. I used the jacket's sleeve and armhole shapes and proportions. I measured the armhole depth and the width of the sleeve at the lower and upper arms. The sleeve cap required careful attention. I measured its height above the underarm; then I plotted its curve as accurately as possible, noting the width of the flat top. The blouse yielded a back-neck width and a comfortable length.

Plotting these basic shapes was the first step toward evolving the finished patterns for both sweaters. I decided to check the fit of the garment shapes before starting to knit the sweaters. Had I been sure of the fit, I could have duplicated the charted shapes exactly in knitting after swatching for gauge and calculating the number of stitches and rows necessary to obtain them. Instead, I took the extra time to make mock-up garments in knit fabric so that I could test the fit of the graphed shapes. That would enable me to refine the fit in such crucial areas as the cross-shoulder width and armhole shaping, which would ensure that the final knit garments were comfortable and flattering.

Fitting concerns—I thought about what I'd seen. The dropped-shoulder garment, which is straight from the lower edge to the shoulder, fits around the hips but often provides too much fabric in the upper torso. Gail's bust and hip measurements were similar, so this garment shape might suit her. But if Holly wore a dropped-shoulder sweater that fit her bust, the hip would be too tight; and if she accommodated her hip measurement, the extra fabric in the upper body would make her look bulkier than she is. I was sure that both sweaters would benefit from more armhole shaping.

Length was an important consideration. Since the sweater pieces were wider than average, they could tend to look boxy, particularly with the square effect produced by a dropped shoulder. I knew that the sleeve didn't need to be longer than for the average person, despite what I had seen when looking at ready-to-wear sweaters.

In any size, it is important to establish the correct amount of ease, or the necessary extra fabric beyond body measurements. Generally speaking, a lightweight fabric needs less ease to cover the body than a bulkier one. I wanted these sweaters

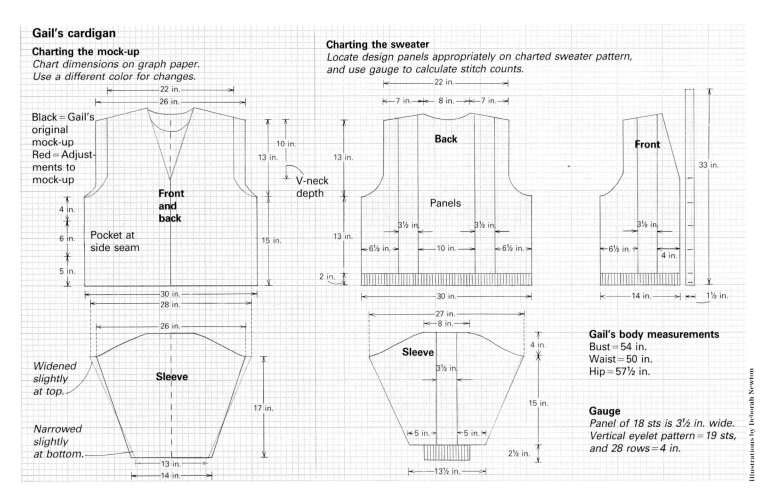

Gail's cardigan

Charting the mock-up
Chart dimensions on graph paper.
Use a different color for changes.

Black = Gail's original mock-up
Red = Adjustments to mock-up

22 in.
26 in.

Front and back

Pocket at side seam

4 in.
6 in.
5 in.

30 in.
28 in.
26 in.

Sleeve

Widened slightly at top.

Narrowed slightly at bottom.

17 in.
13 in.
14 in.

Charting the sweater
Locate design panels appropriately on charted sweater pattern,
and use gauge to calculate stitch counts.

22 in.
7 in. — 8 in. — 7 in.

Back

Panels

3½ in.   3½ in.
6½ in. — 10 in. — 6½ in.

10 in.
13 in.
13 in.
V-neck depth
15 in.
13 in.
2 in.

30 in.

Sleeve

27 in.
8 in.

3½ in.
4 in.
15 in.
2½ in.

5 in.   5 in.
13½ in.

Front

33 in.

3½ in.
6½ in.
4 in.

14 in.   1½ in.

Gail's body measurements
Bust = 54 in.
Waist = 50 in.
Hip = 57½ in.

Gauge
Panel of 18 sts is 3½ in. wide.
Vertical eyelet pattern = 19 sts,
and 28 rows = 4 in.

Illustrations by Deborah Newton

to skim the body, not cling. This would contribute comfort, as well as provide a flattering line. I took the body measurements of both women so that I could relate them to the garment measurements I had already plotted.

Making a fabric mock-up— I decided to test the measurements I had derived from Gail's clothes by making a mock-up cardigan. I bought some medium-weight knit fabric that felt like sweater fabric and would mimic the final sweater as much as possible. This mock-up would test the basic fit, not the more refined details, like button bands or ribbing.

Any knitter, regardless of size, can benefit from testing new ideas by creating a preliminary fabric "sweater." This process requires an investment in time and knit fabric. But by seeing what a sweater will do before you knit it, you'll avoid the discouragement of knitting a garment that just doesn't fit. Devising a mock-up is best as a two-person operation. But if you can't have someone help you with the alterations, stand in front of a large mirror. Remove the mock-up to adjust fit, and then keep trying it on until the fit looks right.

Try to find knit fabric that mimics the drape and thickness of the sweater fabric you hope to create. Knitting a swatch in the yarn you plan to use will help you make the comparison when you go to the fabric store. I've had great success using the fabric suggested for cuffs and ribbings

for sewn garments, but these are expensive. If you settle for a less expensive alternative, make sure your choice has some stretch. And, if it is lighter than your intended knit fabric, you may need an inch or so more of total body ease than the test garment reveals.

I translated the pieces from the graph paper onto the knit fabric, marking the lines with chalk. (I could have made a full-sized paper pattern, but I was able to eliminate this step with care.) The fold established the straight of the grain of the fabric, so I set the centerline of each piece along it. I drew only half of each piece, using the fold to cut a double layer. I cut the sleeve slightly longer so I could adjust the length. Since the mock-up would be sewn together on a machine, I added seam allowances to all the pieces. A loose zigzag stitch let the seams stretch slightly as they would in the finished sweater.

Fitting a mock sweater— When you try on a mock-up for the first time, it may be difficult to visualize how it could mimic the sweater you hope to design. Just remember that the mock-up is for testing fit and making adjustments before the knitting begins.

A test garment can't easily test the fit of ribbed areas at the lower edges of sleeves and body. If you're an experienced sewer, you might roll bands of a slightly narrower width and sew them on, but it's not really necessary, since the mock-up can't truly simulate knitting details, only fit. To hold

the fabric in place at the neckline, as a final ribbing would do, staystitch along the edges to keep an open or a lightweight fabric from stretching or raveling.

The body of Gail's mock-up cardigan fit fine. There was enough ease, so it didn't cling. The length was good, but there was still unnecessary fabric across the shoulders. I pinned the sleeve cap further in toward the body, eliminating some of the excess fabric across the front, while keeping the same curve in the new armhole, as shown in the left photo, facing page.

Gail removed the mock sweater, and I carefully marked the new seamline at the armholes. I removed the sleeves, added a seam allowance to the new armhole curve, and recut the line, making the shaping on the back and front armhole seams match exactly. I was able to fit the old sleeve into the revised armhole, but without much ease in the cap because the armhole was now slightly larger, due to the more pronounced curve. The mock-up fit fine, but I planned to widen the upper arm 1 in. or so to provide the extra ease the cap needed to fit nicely. An alternative approach would have been to shorten the armhole depth a bit, keeping the sleeve width the same, but Gail likes ease in the upper-arm area.

Now I could check sleeve length. I tried to allow enough so that the sleeve would "blouse" above a close-fitting ribbed cuff. I pinned the neck edges to form a V, as shown in the right photo, facing page. Gail had mentioned that she loved side pockets, so

Holly's pullover

Charting the mock-up
Begin with a garment that fits and chart its dimensions; make adjustments to improve fit.

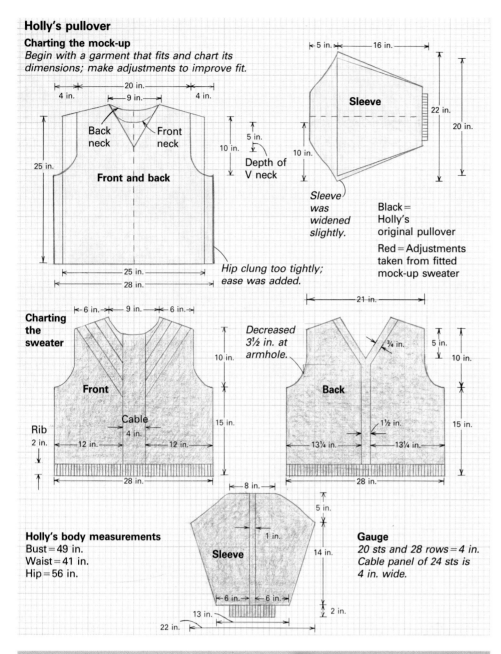

Back neck
Front neck

Front and back

20 in.
4 in.
9 in.
4 in.
25 in.
25 in.
28 in.

5 in.
Depth of V neck
10 in.
10 in.

Sleeve

5 in.
16 in.
22 in.
20 in.

Sleeve was widened slightly.

Hip clung too tightly; ease was added.

Black = Holly's original pullover
Red = Adjustments taken from fitted mock-up sweater

Charting the sweater

Front

6 in.
9 in.
6 in.
10 in.
15 in.
Cable
4 in.
Rib
2 in.
12 in.
12 in.
28 in.

Decreased 3½ in. at armhole.

21 in.

Back

¾ in.
5 in.
10 in.
15 in.
1½ in.
13¼ in.
13¼ in.
28 in.

Holly's body measurements
Bust = 49 in.
Waist = 41 in.
Hip = 56 in.

Sleeve

8 in.
5 in.
1 in.
14 in.
6 in.
6 in.
13 in.
22 in.
2 in.

Gauge
*20 sts and 28 rows = 4 in.
Cable panel of 24 sts is 4 in. wide.*

HOLLY'S PULLOVER

(cap sleeve) and set-in sleeve

decorative twist stitch panel at center front

Hip length

wide neckline

Twist stitch lines form yoke at upper body

Rose shade of "Mara"

tiny cable at center of sleeve

pretty rib

Deborah Newton

we marked where pocket openings would fall at the seams.

I returned to the original graphs, measured the altered pieces, and changed the graphs to reflect the new armhole and neck shapings, as shown by the red lines on the drawing on p. 105. I also added the extra width to the sleeve.

Changing a dropped shoulder to a set-in sleeve—I studied the graphs for Holly's dropped-shoulder sweater (top-left drawing). When I added the total number of inches of the front and back, I discovered that the sweater bottom was slightly smaller than Holly's hip measurement. Holly didn't need extra fabric in the upper body, so I added just enough to make the lower edge a bit looser.

To create a set-in sleeve would require shaping the armhole and forming a cap on the sleeve where there had been none. I wanted to make the mock-up first, incorporating these changes, and then check the fit on Holly.

I cut out the body pieces from a knit fabric, using the same measurements recorded on the graph, with seam allowances. First I joined the shoulders; then I joined the side seams to the underarm. I cut sleeves like the original version drawn on the graph, but I left more fabric at the top from which to cut the cap. I sewed the sleeve seam and marked the underarm line.

I measured Holly from shoulder to shoulder in her black pullover, trying to envision the best placement for the armhole seams of a set-in sleeve. I wanted the seams to fall where her arm joined her body, so I marked this line on the pullover with pins. Then I centered this measurement across the shoulders (left photo, facing page), and transferred the markings to the mock-up. To shape the armhole, I marked a gradual curve starting at the side seam and reaching the cross-shoulder line approximately halfway up the armhole. I measured along the length of this armhole curve, front and back. The cap would have to measure the same, plus a little ease. I cut the front and back the same, adding seam allowances.

The sleeve was already seamed to the underarm line, so the curve for the back and front could be cut at the same time. Beginning at the underarm marking, I laid my tape measure on its edge in a curve, attempting to obtain the same measurement as the armhole, plus ease (drawing, facing page). As with Gail's sleeve cap, I allowed approximately 8 in. across the top to remain unshaped. This curve created a cap height of about 5 in. I marked the line that my tape measure had set for me and added a seam allowance.

I cut away the extra fabric and assembled the mock-up. I hadn't added sufficient ease. The cap just fit into the new armhole. I felt that it was necessary to widen the upper arm slightly, as I had done with

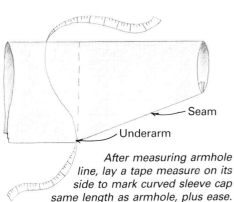

After measuring armhole line, lay a tape measure on its side to mark curved sleeve cap same length as armhole, plus ease.

Newton makes preliminary fitting adjustments with pins on Holly's black pullover. She marks a line much closer to Holly's shoulder than the original dropped shoulder seam and eases it back to the armhole at the side seam. Next, she measures the new cross-front width. A pin at center front allows her to make sure the armhole seams are equidistant from the center (left). Holly's mock-up with the new armhole shaping fits well. Newton pins in the back V-neck detail Holly wanted (center). Narrow cables down the center back of Holly's sweater emphasize the dressy neckline and echo the sweater's cabled front panel (right).

Gail's sleeve, in order to accommodate the larger armhole.

Holly tried on the mock-up, and we were pleased with the flattering fit. The sweater skimmed her hips; yet she had little bulk at the shoulders and bust.

Designing the knitting patterns—Gail likes open, eyelet-type patterns. Swatching yielded a graceful "lily" panel and a small eyelet pattern whose vertical lines would offset the width of the cardigan. I suggested a lovely wool, and Gail chose a warm gray. Finally, I sketched the cardigan to solidify my ideas.

It was time to get to the knitting. I measured my swatches to obtain gauge. Referring to my sketch and the graph, I plotted the panels for Gail's sweater to settle on their best placement, as shown in the three drawings at right on p. 105. I then calculated how many stitches of the vertical pattern were needed to bring the piece up to the graphed measurements. I planned the decreases for armhole shaping, neck width, and shoulder shaping by referring to my knit gauge. I multiplied sleeve length (above the ribbing) by row gauge to calculate the total number of rows. This would allow me to plot the regular increases needed to achieve the width of the upper sleeve. I referred to the row gauge again to plot the decreases for the cap and V-neck shaping. Now we could begin knitting Gail's sweater.

Since Holly's sweater was for the holidays, she asked if we could create a V-line at the back. It was easy to add this detail to

the mock-up (center photo). I plotted all these changes on the graphed pieces (red lines on facing page).

Holly's pullover would have some interesting details provided by pattern stitches. The allover fabric was to be a simple rib. Swatching in the same wool chosen for Gail (one of my favorite yarns, Maratona, from Lane Borgesesia), I worked a delicate twist-stitch cable. I sketched it at the center front. It visually elongated the sweater, which inspired me to extend the use of twist stitches to create a yoke framing Holly's face, as shown in the sketch on the facing page. A narrow pair of cables running down the center back from the V neck completed the neckline detailing (right photo). I transferred the details to the graph (center drawings, facing page).

We agreed that a pretty rose would highlight the pattern stitches beautifully. Referring to the graph, I figured out stitch counts for all the pieces. Now we could begin to knit Holly's sweater too.

To sum it all up—The three of us were rewarded by the extra time we spent in creating patterns from mock-ups. After the fitting sessions, I felt confident about the fit of both Holly's and Gail's sweaters. I provided Holly and Gail with the final instructions, as well as the all-important graphs for adapting their patterns. I hope Gail and Holly will knit other sweaters from this information, adapting yarns and patterns and perhaps changing length and details. They'll also be better equipped to choose and alter

commercial patterns by studying the measurements provided.

Above all, fit is crucial when you're planning a plus-size sweater or selecting a sweater pattern. Take your body measurements, and then be sure your sweater measurements meet or exceed them, depending on the weight of the fabric. Remember that a heavier fabric will require more ease.

If you're bulkier above the waist, a dropped-shoulder sweater may fit you well. But if you have larger hips, try to eliminate some of the fabric above the waist with a shaped armhole.

Visual tricks, such as using vertical patterns or darker colors are fine, but they serve only to enhance the essential good fit. If your sweater is shaped well, it can be any color or pattern you feel comfortable in. Consider your edges carefully. Tight ribbing at the wrist may be okay (Gail's and Holly's sleeve and neck ribbings were knit on needles two sizes smaller), but it's often a good idea to keep the lower edges looser by using the same size needle for the rib as for the patterns in the body.

Good fit for any garment in any size doesn't just happen. To design a sweater that fits you well, refer to one that already does fit well, or develop a pattern the way we did. By using a dependable prototype, you'll always know that your sweater will fit—before you begin to knit. □

Deborah Newton is a knitwear designer and frequent contributor to Threads. *Photos by Cathy Carver, except photo on facing page.*

Putting Knitted Pieces Together

Three stitches that go a long way toward finishing sweaters

by Susan Guagliumi

do you lose the zest for your knitting project when the front, back, and sleeves are ready to become a sweater? Are you paying your local yarn shop to finish it for you, or do the pieces end up sitting for weeks or even months until you've gathered your nerve to face the dreaded task? While poor finishing can ruin a perfectly knit sweater, finishing skills are not nearly as difficult to master as the techniques that you use to knit the pieces. It just takes practice, the right tools, and a bit of patience.

Planning ahead

Whether you knit by hand or machine, the finishing techniques are basically the same, and the results are identical. Everyone develops a favorite method for putting sweaters together, but you have to start somewhere. And the first step in finishing any sweater is to correctly gauge your yarn before you even start.

Care considerations—You don't want any surprises when the finished sweater is washed, and you won't have any if you test out your swatch before you measure it. Knit a gauge swatch large enough to accurately measure stitches and rows per inch. (And don't round off the measurement or stretch the swatch. If 20 sts measure 5.25 in., the gauge is 3.8 sts/in.)

Now, treat your swatch exactly as you plan to treat the sweater, as far as washing, blocking, and steaming are concerned. Read the directions on the skein label regarding heat or ironing. Many of the new synthetics are terrific, but they can't tolerate extreme heat from an iron, a steamer, or a dryer. Regardless of what the label says, check shrinkage with before-and-after measurements on the swatch. If you're using a synthetic or a cotton that you will wash and dry by machine, there is no reason to block. Throw the swatch into the washer and dryer before you measure it. For garments that will be dry-cleaned or hand-washed and dried flat—100% wool or wool-and-rayon blends—I often steam-block the swatch just as I steam-block the sweater pieces in order to make the edges lie flat before I assemble them.

If you plan to wash and block the sweater or the garment pieces, wash and block the swatch. Some wools are spun to "bloom," or fluff out, when washed, and cottons generally shrink temporarily. Most wools respond best to fairly warm wash and rinse water, but whatever you do, don't wash in hot and rinse in cold. Extreme changes in temperature felt wool fibers and shrink the knit fabric. You might have to knit looser or tighter than you thought to get a gauge that finishes to your satisfaction.

Shaping considerations—The types of increases, decreases, and bind-offs you use will determine which finishing methods are easiest or neatest, so plan ahead. Full-fashioned increasing and decreasing, in which the increase or decrease is made several stitches from the edge, produce smoother edges that are easier to seam, as the edge stitch remains constant. But, with some textured or patterned stitches, edge increasing or decreasing is easier to manage. Short-row shaping is good for eliminating stair-step edges and making smoother shoulder seams.

I prefer to construct shoulder seams (and any other seams I can) by working off "live" rather than bound-off stitches. This method eliminates the bulk—and the work—of the bound-off edge and makes a nice flat seam. Handknitters store live stitches on stitch

Finishing knits is easier than knitting—it needn't be a horrible chore. Mattress stitch is best for the even edges made by a full-fashioned decrease or increase. Susan Guagliumi mattress-stitches the second of four raglan shoulder seams on this machine-knit sweater. The "live" neck stitches are held temporarily on white waste yarn.

From *Threads* magazine (June 1987) 11:45-47

When seaming set-in sleeves, work consistently, one stitch from the edge. Guagliumi uses slipstitch crochet for a firm, but nonbulky seam. Contrasting color yarn is used for clarity of illustration.

holders, while machine knitters knit extra rows, called waste knitting or scrap knitting, that serve the same purpose.

Read through your pattern before you begin to knit, and decide how you want to handle the edges. For example, ribbing will be easiest to seam if you have a knit stitch on each edge; plan for this when you cast on. Most patterns provide some finishing suggestions. Between those given and my suggestions, you should be able to anticipate and solve your finishing problems. You'll need a blunt metal tapestry needle with an eye just large enough for the yarn to thread through, a crochet hook, long straight pins (those with colored plastic tips that quilters use), and a tape measure.

A basic assembly method

There are several methods for finishing a round-neck, set-in-sleeve sweater, but in what follows I'll guide you through a very basic approach. When possible, use the same yarn you knit your sweater with. If it's too textured to be manageable, choose a smoother yarn of the same fiber content.

Don't knot the beginning or ending yarn tails. If you left enough tail at the beginning of the knitting, use it to start the seam, and when it runs out, simply start another piece of yarn, leaving a tail at least 5 in. long to weave in later. It is better to run out and start a new yarn than to work with a long strand that must be pulled through each stitch. For crochet, simply work right off the ball or cone of yarn.

With right sides together, pin and complete one shoulder seam, using either slipstitch crochet or backstitch (see the drawings A and C on page 110). Either of these will produce a seam firm enough to support the sleeves without stretching. I prefer slipstitch crochet off live stitches held on waste knitting, but some handknitters find backstitch easier when working off a stitch holder. It's really a matter of personal preference, but don't use single crochet—it's too bulky.

For machine knitters and handknitters who prefer to work ribbing back and forth on straight needles, this is the time to knit the neckband. If front or back neckline stitches are on stitch holders or scrap knitting, replace them on the needles. You'll probably have to "make" some stitches along the vertical, selvage edges of the front neckline. To do this, pick up (or hang, on the machine) stitches in those areas so you end up with the required number of stitches for the neckband on the needles. If you bound off the neck stitches, pick up all the neck-edge stitches. Knit the neckband.

Complete the second shoulder seam the same way as the first. Work toward the neck, and join the ends of the neckband as well. Handknitters who prefer to knit the neckband on circular needles should do so after completing both shoulder seams and before adding the weight of sleeves.

Once the shoulder seams and neckband are complete, you can proceed in either of two ways. Some knitters prefer to complete the side seams first and then set in the sleeves. But it's easier for beginners to join the sleeve cap to the body and then complete the side seams. Pin the sleeve cap to the armhole, right sides together, and either backstitch or slipstitch-crochet the seam, always working one stitch from the edge, as shown in the photo above. Repeat for the second sleeve.

Construct the underarm and side seams, using slipstitch crochet, backstitch, or mattress stitch—also called weaving, invisible seaming, and vertical grafting (drawings B, D, and F). Mattress stitch is easiest to work on knit stitches with the right sides facing you. The other two methods are better for purl or texture stitches. Don't work a continuous seam. Rather, make one seam from hip to armhole, then a second seam from cuff to armhole so that any discrepancies can be eased in invisibly.

Raglans—Raglan finishing is basically the same as finishing for a set-in sleeve, except there are three raglan-shoulder seams to make before the neckband is knit. The mattress stitch (drawing E) is wonderful for the full-fashioned edges of raglan seams. Work it with the right sides facing. Leave one back seam open and complete it after knitting the neckband if you're working on straight needles or on the machine. Close all four seams if you knit a circular band.

Cardigans—For cardigans, complete all seams first. Then make the front bands. These can be crocheted, knit horizontally off the front edges, or knit as separate vertical bands, which are then backstitched, slipstitch-crocheted (fastest method), or mattress-stitched (neatest method) to the front edges. Most patterns recommend a method. If you make separate bands, knit them to the given center-front measurement of the finished sweater. Don't measure the front edges, because they usually will have stretched a bit. Knit or crochet buttonholes as you knit the band, or machine-stitch them later. Always try a swatch first. After you've completed the front bands, pick up the neckline stitches, making stitches as necessary, and knit the neckband.

At the end—Weave all yarn ends into the nearby seam. For ends shorter than 5 in., use a crochet hook. Tails that are not near seams (from pattern work) can be "duplicate-stitched" or worked with a needle into the back of the stitches.

Some synthetics and cottons don't have good return capabilities. The ribbing will be firmer if elastic is incorporated. You can thread a row of cotton-covered elastic thread (Rainbow is the brand I know) through the cast-on edge, or you can crochet a row or two of the elastic across the inside of the ribbing, catching only the knit stitches. Clear elastic thread can be knit along with the ribbing, but it tends to change the look of the yarn and may pop with repeated wearings. In any case, the elastic acts only as a reminder for the rib and shouldn't be used to correct loose ribbing.

Washing and blocking

There are two schools of thought about washing and blocking (or steaming). Some people always block pieces before assembling them; others assemble and then wash and block. Actually, the best method to use varies with the yarn and the garment style. As a machine knitter, I often assemble and block whole garments. It's easier to work off live stitches and to work in lots of tails before washing wools that will bloom or felt; and with cottons, shrinking or stretching of the pieces will be more predictable if they're assembled first. With some fibers, the edges of the pieces tend to curl up; in those cases I block the pieces first to make them more manageable. Handknitters may find themselves doing more corrective blocking of pieces before assembly because handknit fabric is less uniform than machine-knit fabric.

In either case, gently wash the sweater (or garment pieces) by hand in a mild detergent, and then pat it or block it out to the given finished measurements, pinning it in place to dry flat. Or pin it out to size and steam (not iron) it thoroughly. Do not lift dripping-wet sweaters, or they'll stretch. To speed drying and make the sweater more manageable for blocking out to size, put it into your washing machine with a few dry towels and set the machine to spin only. The centrifugal force will remove most of the water without harming the sweater. Lay the sweater out flat on dry towels to block, changing the towels as needed.

Instead of pinning every few inches to block pieces, which tends to flute their edges, use a set of wires, called Magic Wands, to thread through the edges of the knitting. The wires can be bent slightly to follow the desired contours of the pieces, and they need be pinned at the ends only. When the pieces dry, they'll have smooth edges.

Keep in mind that no single finishing method will be suitable or best for every situation. What worked beautifully on stockinette may be a disaster on garter stitch or lace knitting. Backstitch, slipstitch crochet, and mattress stitch can take you a long way, but the only way to be sure, as always, is to work up a swatch first and be ready to add to your repertoire of finishing skills.□

Susan Guagliumi is a knitting consultant for Singer and a contributing editor of Threads.

Resources

Elaine's Knitting Room
1677 Agnes Ave.
Neenah, WI 54956
Source for Magic Wands, $14.95 plus $1.75 shipping.

The Knitting Machine Studio Bookshelf
Box 746
Englewood, NJ 07631
(201) 568-3369
Sells Blocking for Machine Knitters, *by Pat Hampton, 1982, 67 pp., $11.95 plus $2.50 postage.*

Rainbow Elastic Plus
Box 12262
La Jolla, CA 92037
(619) 457-3950
Manufactures cotton-covered elastic thread in 47 colors. Write for nearest distributor.

Yarns+More
2249 S. Brentwood Blvd.
St. Louis, MO 63144
(314) 961-4377
Publishes Hand Finishing Techniques, *by Marjorie Ivey and Frances Slusher, 1986, 67 pp., $19.*

Six basic seams for knit sweaters

(A) Slipstitch crochet for shoulder seams

"Live" stitches are shown. Stitch holder is deleted for clarity. For a bound-off edge, the seam would be done in the row below the bind-off.

With right sides of fabric together and wrong side facing you, insert crochet hook through 1st st and pull loop of yarn through. With loop on hook, insert hook in 2nd st, and pull loop through stitch and through loop on hook so that one loop remains on hook. Continue.

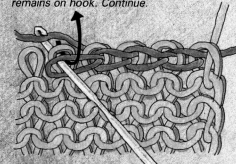

(B) Slipstitch crochet for side seams

With right sides together, work one full stitch from edge, into every other bar.

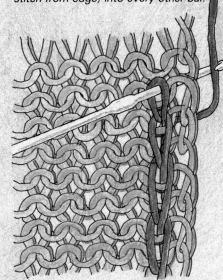

(C) Backstitch for shoulder seams

With right sides of fabric together and wrong side facing you, insert tapestry needle down into 1st st and up through 2nd st. Now go back down into 1st st, up through 3rd st, down into 2nd st, up through 4th st, down into 3rd st, up into 5th st. Continue. Live stitches are shown, with holder deleted for clarity.

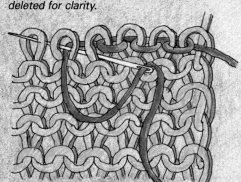

(D) Backstitch for side seams

With right sides together, work into every other space.

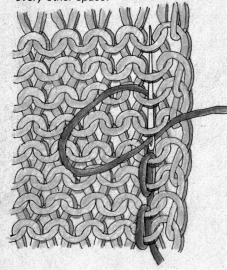

(E, F) Mattress stitch for raglan sleeves and side seams

Work with garment pieces side by side, right sides facing you. Work one full stitch from edge. Insert needle under two bars and back out on right-hand fabric, then under two bars and back out on left-hand fabric. Continue, the needle always entering a hole it previously exited. After every 6 sts, pull firmly on yarn to bring two edges together.

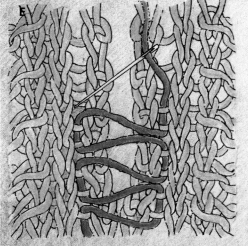

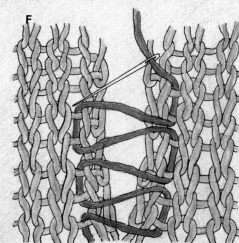

Crocheted Buttonholes

Decorative and functional closures that work for knitters and sewers as well

by Mary McGoveran

buttonholes are small, but they play an important part in both the look and usefulness of a garment. A buttonhole can be functional or decorative or even invisible. It can be angular, round, vertical, or horizontal. But it must fit the button and hold it securely. It should be positioned on the garment so the button's pull doesn't distort the fabric edge.

Buttonholes need to be firm enough to hold their shape against the stress of being buttoned. In a lacy fabric, buttonholes should be distinguishable by touch from the rest of the fabric. You can set them off by surrounding them with a block of solid stitching, by binding them with a round of slip stitches or single crochet, or by making them separately from the main fabric along the edge.

I know of three ways to make buttonholes: *Skip-and-chain* can be used to produce both horizontal buttonholes, where the holes are worked in a single row, and vertical buttonholes, where narrow slits are produced over several rows; *loops* can be added at the edge of the fabric; and *pattern stitches* isolate, enhance, or incorporate the open texture of a pattern stitch as a buttonhole. Depending on the background stitch of the fabric, the appearance of each type can vary enormously.

Yarn weight, button size, and garment design also help you choose the best buttonhole. You can plan and work the buttonholes as you crochet the garment fabric, or you can work them later—as an edging or a separate or worked-in placket. You can even crochet buttonhole and button-stand plackets along the front edges of a knit cardigan or simple woven jacket to produce a durable, decorative closure system.

Skip-and-chain buttonholes—Although single crochet works up too stiffly in a firm gauge for body fabric, it makes a good border or placket background for the most traditional buttonhole, the *horizontal skip and chain*. See p. 112 for all skip-and-chain buttonholes described below. When you reach the beginning of the buttonhole, place your button over the next stitches to see how many to skip. The height of the row adds to the size of the buttonhole, so, if your button is 4 sts across, skip only 3 sts, chaining instead.

Double crochet works up into an elegant, simple fabric that drapes well in a firm gauge. With the skip-and-chain method you can produce either round or vertical openings. A 1-st or 2-st skip makes what looks like a vertical or round buttonhole. This buttonhole doesn't hold a standard round button securely, but it works well with relatively large oval or toggle buttons. A larger skip makes a very large buttonhole because of the height of double crochet.

You can make the buttonhole smaller by working slip stitches or single crochet inside the perimeter for a *bound buttonhole*. Bind the hole right after you complete it, without cutting the yarn, so there are no loose ends. Don't bind around the entire bar of the double-crochet stitches on the edges. Insert the hook through only two threads at a time so the stitch won't be pulled away from its neighbor.

You can also use the 1-st skip and chain to make *invisible buttonholes on a mock-rib worked in double crochet.* Mock-rib is made with post stitches—double crochet worked around the bar of the double-crochet stitch in the previous row, rather than into the top of the stitch. Working a stitch around the bar makes it stick out on one side of the fabric. To make a front-bar double crochet (fbdc), insert the hook around the bar, starting on the fabric side that faces you. Make a rear-bar double crochet (rbdc) by inserting the hook from the other side. Alternate these two bar stitches to make a mock-rib fabric.

A variation on the horizontal skip and chain that makes a sensible double-crochet buttonhole is the *skip-and-foundation-stitch buttonhole,* where the chain stitches are replaced with foundation single-crochet stitches. Foundation single crochet is worked just like foundation double crochet, except that the extra loop is omitted.

This foundation stitch is smaller than the stitch of the fabric, so the buttonhole shows. If you use foundation double crochet to make the buttonhole, it will be taller than standard double crochet, and the base chain will cover the top of the stitches in the previous row, making the buttonhole hard to find in the finished garment.

Double crochet works well for conservative and neutral garment designs, but I prefer *sweater stitch* for a garment made in bright colors or for a more youthful design. Ch an even number of sts. Sc 1 in 2nd st from hook. *Ch 1, sk 1, sc 1* across, ending with sc 1 in last st. Ch 1, turn, not counting turn as an st. Sc 1 in last sc of previous row. Repeat from * for as many rows as needed. Worked loosely, this stitch drapes well in a cuff-to-cuff design.

Skip-and-chain buttonholes in sweater stitch work well, but if you want to produce a firmer edge, the easiest approach is to work plain single crochet below and above the buttonhole.

Vertical buttonholes are a bother to knit, but with crochet techniques they're easy to

Skip-and-chain buttonholes

Horizontal skip and chain
In single-crochet fabric, ch as many sts as you skip, and continue with row. Returning in next row, sc in ch sts as usual.

Bound skip and chain in double crochet
Complete first dc st ending hole. With right side facing, sc around inside perimeter, working 1 st into each st of long edges and 2 sts into bar of each dc. Combine each st on bar with adjacent st on long edge, like a decrease st, to prevent binding row from puckering. Complete round with sl st in top of last dc. Continue row.

Invisible skip and chain in mock-rib double crochet
With right side facing, ch 1 where you would normally work a rear bar st. Finish row. On return, work a standard dc in ch st (because there's no bar to insert hook around). Work bar sts on 3rd row; buttonhole retreats to back of fabric.

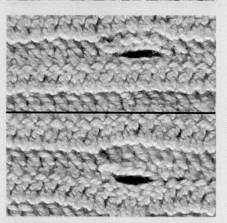

Skip-and-foundation single or double crochet
*Start foundation single crochet (fsc) by inserting hook through middle loop of last dc. Catch 2 loops. *Yo, pull through middle loop. Yo again, and pull through 1 loop on hook to make foundation st. Treat 2 remaining loops as a normal sc—yo and pull through both. To start next fsc, insert hook through foundation ch of previous st. Repeat from * as many sts as you skip. To finish buttonhole, continue with dc as follows: Insert hook in foundation ch of last st, yo, and pull through foundation ch only. Treat this loop as a yo for starting next dc.*

Skip and chain in sweater stitch
In row before buttonhole, sc where hole will be formed. Skip and ch in next row, as usual. In 3rd row, work sc along ch sts. Return to pattern st thereafter.

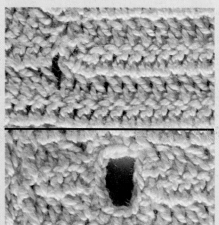

Vertical buttonhole
Pretend that start of buttonhole is end of row. Work back and forth on this side of hole an odd number of rows. If you plan to skip sts, ch or make foundation sts for width of hole. Then knot yarn and carry it loosely to beginning point on other side of hole. Enclose carried yarn in turning sts as you work same number of rows back and forth. Work next row across. When you get to knot, insert hook in last 2 loops of st as if you hadn't finished it before. This covers knot smoothly. A 3-st-skip vertical buttonhole (bottom) in dc is bound with sc. The binding sts keep the large hole from stretching or gapping.

make. I like to knot the yarn by passing the ball through the loop and carrying it across the hole to the next stitch. Enclosing the carried yarn in later stitches produces a smoother edge than the traditional method of working slip stitches along the edge to get from here to there. Since you work one side of the buttonhole at a time, it must be an odd number of rows tall so you'll end up at the hole edge to start the other side. If you want the buttonhole edges to be perfectly straight, count the turning chain as a stitch. If you want the perimeter of the hole to be more solid, don't count the turning chain as a stitch, as shown in the photo. You can control the height of a vertical buttonhole by working the joining stitch into the first side at the beginning, middle, or end of the stitch.

Loop buttonholes—Vertical and horizontal buttonholes are worked into the body fabric of the garment. But if you don't want to be bothered with buttonhole placement while you're making the garment, or if you want a more delicate arrangement, you can make loops.

Button loops are generally part of a finishing row worked along the edge of the garment. While you can always work only one row along the raw edge, the finishing will look nicer if you work at least two rows. Work a regular pattern along the raw edge for the first row to create a smooth outer edge. Sweater stitch is good because the row is short, and it doesn't call much attention to itself. Even better, since half the stitches are chains, there is little calculating, and it's a cinch to ease the two types of fabric with their different gauges together. Since half the stitches are single crochet, the edge looks firm.

Make your loops on the second row. They can end in the stitch they began in, in the next stitch, or a few stitches away—to look like the eyes of hooks and eyes—or they can be stretched all the way out to look like horizontal skip-and-chain buttonholes.

There are at least four ways to make loops (top photos, facing page). One handy way is to work what I call an *N-treble stitch*. This involves some trial and error, but it ends at the beginning of the loop, which is nice. Once the loop is made, you can continue to stitch in front of it or behind it, which will provide additional overlap between the two closed edges. The N-treble loop tends to twist once and curl back on itself when not in use.

A *twist loop* is also a matter of trial and error. You twist an elongated loop, double it back on itself, and secure its ends to the fabric edge. If you work a third row, catch the ends of the loop again to secure them more firmly.

The oldest loop technique is to make a series of chain stitches, but this loop isn't very attractive, and it can be weak. Working single-crochet stitches over the chain loop makes an elegant, stiff *covered loop* with a definite front and back.

The *enclosed loop* is a placket constructed around evenly spaced loops. It is very serviceable, and though it sounds complicated, it isn't. I developed the technique when I was about to make the buttonholes to finish a sweater that I'd been doodling with, and suddenly realized that I hadn't planned their placement. I worked a row of edging with a series of simple chain-loop buttonholes that started and ended in adjacent stitches. Since the spacing was worked out, it seemed silly to put in markers and take out the row in order to construct a conventional placket, so I just kept working over the loops.

Pattern-stitch buttonholes—The pattern-stitch buttonhole is not so much a different construction as it is a different perspective on buttoning (photos at bottom right). It allows a decorative element of the garment to function as well.

Shell stitch (5 dc in 1 st) is a common afghan pattern that has a nice drape when worked loosely. At a firm gauge, however, it doesn't drape, so I substitute *lite shell* (dc 1, ch 1, dc 1, ch 1, dc 1) in the same stitch. As with traditional shell stitch, 1 sc separates the shells. This makes a nice edging for a cardigan because it fits so well into the scalloped edge of a double-crochet fabric, where the turning chain is *not* counted as a stitch. After working one row to establish the pattern, work a second row of shells into the single-crochet stitches of the previous row. You form lite-shell buttonholes on this row, complete them on the next row, and another row or two of lite shells is optional.

The *V-stitch flower buttonhole* is a variation on the bound horizontal buttonhole. Often the pattern stitch for a top or light sweater is so open that any stitch could serve as a buttonhole, but it's nicer to designate buttonholes. I used V-stitch, but any lacy pattern stitch would do. After you work the flower around the hole in the pattern stitch, slip the hook back to the top of the last double-crochet stitch and continue. If you don't mind having to deal with loose ends, you can work the flower in a contrasting color.

An *eight-stitch cable pattern* worked over two rows is another pattern stitch that makes a nice edging. It is open enough for regular buttonholes, and it doesn't need additional stitching.

Once you have the idea of playing with pattern stitches to create buttonholes, the variations are endless. Just remember that the challenge is to retain structural integrity in the fabric without disrupting the overall flow of the stitch design. ☐

Mary McGoveran of Boulder Creek, CA, explores how crochet is just like knitting, only different.

Loop buttonholes

N-treble loop
Yo about 5 times or so. Insert hook in st where loop will end, yo and pull through st. Continue to yo and pull through 2 loops at a time until 1 loop remains on hook.

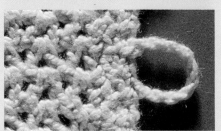

Twist loop
Elongate original loop to 2 or 3 times length of planned loop. With hook inserted, twist loop until it twists back on itself when folded in half. Then insert hook through base of twist at starting point and slip st to secure it to row. St to where you want to join twist to edge, insert hook through end of twist, and enclose it in next st.

Covered chain loop
Chain to desired length and join to start. Work sc sts over chain loop to improve its appearance and strengthen it.

Enclosed loop
To enclose loops in sweater-stitch placket, each time you reach a loop, dec in row, and work a layer of sl sts over loop. After 3 or 4 rows, edge will be even and loops will be covered. Work a few more rows to complete placket.

Pattern-stitch buttonholes
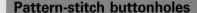

Lite-shell buttonhole
On 2nd row, work 5 fdc instead of a shell. To reconnect after fdc, insert hook through top of shell, then through chain at base of last fdc, yo, pull through 2; yo, pull through 2 loops for sc. On 3rd row of shells, work sc over center fdc.

V-stitch flower buttonhole
Form flower petals to delineate buttonhole by working (ch 5, sc 1) all around perimeter of hole in pattern stitch.

Eight-stitch cable buttonhole
Row 1 *(right-side facing): Fpdc 1 (1 front-post double crochet), dc 6, fpdc 1.*
Row 2 *(wrong-side facing): Bptr (back-post treble crochet) in 3rd and 4th sts from hook, dc in skipped sts. Dc in 3rd and 4th sts from hook, bptr in skipped sts.*

Knitting Notebook
Two Styles of Buttonholes

by Maggie Righetti

Finely and intricately knit sweaters can be ruined by badly made buttonholes. Unfortunately, most cardigan instructions give the same directions for baggy buttonholes. Many designers aren't aware that better buttonholes can be made, and most pattern printers refuse to devote the extra space required to explain them. Thus, many knitters won't knit cardigans because of the buttonholes. To encourage you to knit cardigans, here are two fine buttonholes. Try them with class C heavy (4-ply) smooth classic worsted yarn and No. 8 needles. Cast on 12 stitches, and knit a few rows in stockinette stitch (knit one row, purl the next) for a few rows, ending with a purl row.

Three-row buttonhole

The three-row buttonhole is a hand knitter's dream. It works in any pattern stitch, needs no final finishing, and is easy to remember and make. It is a vertical buttonhole that's three rows high. The size varies according to the yarn and needles used, but the button size appropriate for the yarn will usually fit the hole. Try it on your swatch.

First buttonhole row—On right side of work, work to desired location of buttonhole (knit five stitches on your swatch), yarn over twice, knit next two stitches together by knitting into back of two stitches, and continue across row (Fig. 1A, facing page).

Second buttonhole row—On wrong side of work, work to location of buttonhole, purl one (first yarn over), drop next stitch (second yarn over) off needle, and continue across row (Fig. 1B). I know it looks terrible, but have faith.

Third buttonhole row—On right side of work, work to buttonhole, knit into hole (below the next stitch), drop next ⟹

Tips from The Knitting Guild

by Mary Galpin

Tips and techniques for better knitting abound. The techniques themselves usually aren't hard; it's finding out about them that is. But when eight teachers and 100 avid knitters get together for three days, everyone is sure to go home with some new tricks.

The Knitting Guild of America's (TKGA) first seminar east of the Mississippi was held last July 26-28 in Baltimore. It offered eight classes; a "show-and-share" night, where all participants were invited to bring some of their work; and a retail market, where area shops displayed and sold their wares. The next national TKGA convention will be held in Milwaukee, WI, April 3-6.

The purpose of the Knitting Guild, which is almost two years old, is to "promote communication and education to those wishing to excel in workmanship and creativity in the knitting world of today." Besides organizing seminars, it sponsors local groups and publishes the magazine *Cast On*. Here's what I learned at the seminar:

Casting on—If you cast on using the two-needle method, your cast-on edge will be firmer if you knit between the last two stitches rather than into the last one, as in the drawing below. Don't pull the yarn too tight, or you'll have trouble getting the needle in. With this method, you would knit the next row if you are working in stockinette stitch.

Counting rows—If you have trouble counting rows, turn your work to the purl side, where the rows are more clearly defined. And don't be afraid to stretch your knitting. Pull it from top to bottom to separate the rows. Counting rows is more important than some people might think. If you've knit a ten-row pocket, for example, you should sew it row-for-row onto ten rows of your sweater front. And if you have two pockets that

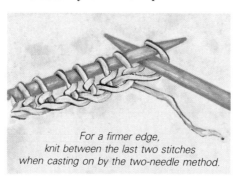

For a firmer edge, knit between the last two stitches when casting on by the two-needle method.

you want six rows up from the ribbing, count those rows so that the two pockets will be even.

Knitting a ribbing—If you're making a cardigan, you'll find it easier to knit the ribbing for the front edges while you knit the body of the sweater. You'll eliminate the need to sew the ribbing on later, and you'll also be assured of a row-for-row match. However, you must change to needles that are smaller than those you're using on the body so the ribbing won't sag. Use a pair of double-pointed needles one or two sizes smaller than those on which you are knitting the body. Knit the ribbing stitches with the smaller needles. Then continue across the row with the regular needles. Turn the work around, work across the row, and when you get to the ribbing, pick up the double-pointed needles to work the ribbing stitches. Your ribbing will be the perfect length. ☐

Mary Galpin is an assistant editor of Threads *magazine. For more information on TKGA, contact Corinne Hemmeter, TKGA, Box 1606, Knoxville, TN 37901; (615) 524-2401.*

stitch, and then continue across row (Fig. 1C at right).

Work another row or two in pattern stitch. Your buttonhole should look like the one in the photo at near right.

One-row buttonhole

The one-row buttonhole can be made any size you want. It is more complicated to knit and harder to remember, but it creates a nice horizontal opening. Try this one on the same swatch.

With right side of work facing you, work in pattern stitch to the desired location. (On your swatch, knit four stitches.) Slip the next stitch knitwise (as if to knit) onto the right needle. Bring the yarn between the tips of the needles to the front of the work and drop it (Fig. 2A at right).

Without knitting any stitches, bind off the number of stitches needed to make the size buttonhole you want. Binding off four stitches, for example, will give you a buttonhole that's four stitches wide. To bind off, slip the next stitch onto the right needle purlwise (as if to purl), and with the tip of the left-hand needle lift the first slipped stitch up and over the second and off the needle. Then slip the next stitch knitwise from the left needle to the right, and lift the previously slipped stitch up, over, and off. (Slipping the stitches first purlwise and then knitwise keeps the buttonhole's bottom edge from curling out.) Continue until the hole is as long as you want it. On your swatch, bind off three stitches.

Move the last stitch on the right needle to the left needle. Turn the work around so the wrong side is facing you. Bring the yarn that's now at the back of the work between the needles to the front and cast on purlwise one more stitch than you bound off, as follows: Insert the right needle into the front of the first stitch on the left needle, and make a purl stitch, but don't take the old stitch off the left needle. Move the new stitch to the left needle by inserting it in the front of the new stitch from right to left (Fig. 2C).

When the necessary stitches are cast on (four stitches cast on for your swatch), turn the work around again so that you are working in the original direction (right side of work facing you). Move the first stitch on the right needle to the left needle. Knit two together. Continue across the row. Then work another row or two to appreciate the good looks of the one-row buttonhole (see photo above, right).

Bind off your swatch, and keep it with a copy of these instructions for future reference. Now you can start dreaming about all those cardigans you can make. □

Maggie Righetti is a knitting designer and teacher in Atlanta, GA, and the author of Universal Yarn Finder.

The three-row buttonhole makes a nice vertical buttonhole and works in any pattern stitch.

Fig. 1. Three-row buttonhole

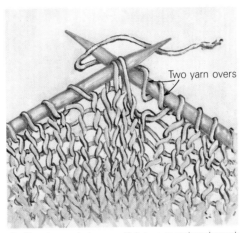

A. *First buttonhole row: Knit two together through the back of the stitches.*

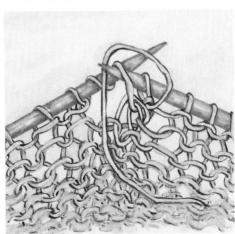

B. *Second buttonhole row: Purl first yarn over; then drop the second.*

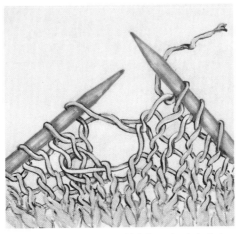

C. *Third buttonhole row: Knit into the hole below the next stitch.*

The horizontal one-row buttonhole can be made as wide as you need.

Fig. 2. One-row buttonhole

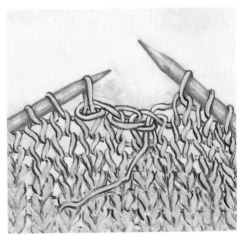

A. *Slip the next stitch knitwise; bring the yarn to the front of the work.*

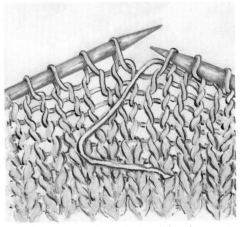

B. *Bind off the required number of stitches, and move the last slipped stitch to the left needle.*

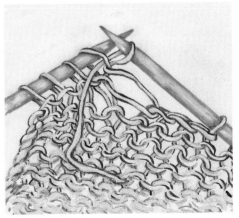

C. *To cast on purlwise, make a purl stitch, but don't take the stitch off the left needle. Then insert the left needle in front of the new stitch from right to left.*

Illustrations by Barbara Smolover

A Sampler of Knit Edgings and Applied Trims

Putting a professional and creative finish on handknit fabrics

by Deborah Newton

From *Threads* magazine (August 1987) 12:38-42

a few years ago, I designed a classically tailored knit blazer, worked in a simple but elegant seed stitch. The edges needed stabilizing, but I was reluctant to draw attention away from the garment by adding trim. I knew that I could add a crocheted edging, but why couldn't I find a narrow knit edging that would provide a discrete line of emphasis? After considerable testing on the edge of my first swatch, I tried picking up a row of stitches and binding them off. With these two basic knitting actions, I created a simple, perfect edging! I have since evolved a "vocabulary" of edgings and trims to suit the needs of any project.

Although as a handknit designer I place a great deal of importance on the fabric of a garment, I have found that an interesting edging or trim can solidify or specialize a design. I think more and more about the importance of the border line in my attempt to merge good technique with good design. Flat fabrics make durable, predictable borders; however, there is a tremendous challenge in experimenting with nontraditional edgings that curl, twist, or provide special effects.

In addition to being decorative, effective edgings and trims have a bearing on function and fit. For example, if the garment that is to be trimmed will receive hard wear, a traditional ribbing will provide an elastic border that holds its shape well. In the sampler garment at left, I challenged myself to create a sweater-jacket that included as many different trims as possible, most of them decorative. I also needed to consider garment shaping to accommodate all my choices, and the fiber, too. Wool is elastic, so it works well for all types of trims, but many beautiful synthetics, and some natural fibers like linen and cotton, lack stretch and resiliency.

Like all garmentmakers, we handknitters strive for a professional look. A firm, even edge on the fabric will help produce such a look. Edgings can be knit in at the beginning or end of the piece, picked up and bound off at an edge, or knit separately as trims and then attached to the completed garment.

To allow fewer rows in the band, bands at the front of garments can be successfully knit with the garment fabric if the body fabric is short-rowed or if the row gauge of the band fabric is tighter than that of the body fabric. It's best, however, to pick up bands at the front of garments later or to work them with a smaller needle and attach them.

Deborah Newton designed the sampler jacket at left to incorporate a variety of decorative knit edgings and applied trims. She combined many textural patterns in the blue lightweight-wool body of the garment and worked the trims in a contrasting color of the same wool for emphasis.

If the fabric edge is weak and flaccid, as with some novelty/synthetic yarns with little elasticity, picking up stitches with a needle several sizes smaller than the needle to be used for the trim will give a tighter join of the edging to the body fabric. A sewn-on edging will also provide stability.

When you are planning your edges, consider how you will work or attach them. Picking up stitches or knitting in an edging saves finishing time. For the most control and the neatest appearance, sew on applied trims from the right side. Crocheting is a quick method for attaching trim—a simple chain is easier to pull out than a line of handsewing—but it will produce a thicker wrong-side "seam."

Whether you are applying knit edgings or trims to a knit (or even a woven fabric), the best way to test their suitability is to work a swatch of the body fabric. The swatch provides a smaller, less intimidating testing ground for the final project. It should be large enough to incorporate any unique details planned for your garment, such as a pocket opening or curve. Testing all the edges on the swatch helps you anticipate the final look, especially if you are using a different yarn for the trim than for the garment body. If you are using a woven fabric, finish the edge of your swatch to prevent raveling. This may not be necessary if the edge is to be covered with a knit trim, although it will be less likely to unravel as you apply the trim. If the weave is loose enough to pick up stitches into, this swatch is crucial for you to determine how many stitches you need for a certain area. So as not to waste the time you invested in creating the swatch, try to utilize it in the final garment in some way—perhaps as a perfectly finished pocket lining or a unique shoulder pad.

A sampler of trims and edgings

Wool was my choice for the eclectic mix of edgings on my sampler jacket, as it responds well in all situations. But I also wanted a cool wool that was suited to a spring/summer transseasonal garment. After searching for a light yarn with a gauge that would work up quickly (to balance off the extra time that was needed for finishing), I chose Maratona from Lane Borgosesia, which is a lightweight and luxurious cabled merino wool. If you want to knit your own trim sampler, make sure you choose a yarn that has the stretch to accommodate the variety of trims.

Here are some reliable guidelines for picking up stitches along an edge:
• Generally 2 sts are picked up for every 3 rows, or 3 sts for every 4 rows, if the trim fabric draws in, as it does in ribbing.
• Curved edges require special attention: If the trim is wide, remember that the outer edge of a curve is longer than the inside curve. If you're using a flat, picked-up edge on a curve, increase or decrease stitches, depending on the direction of your knit-

ting. Ribbing, or folded-over ribbing, with its natural tendency to stretch when necessary, is very suitable for curved edges.
• One extra garter stitch that is worked along an edge to be trimmed will have a tighter row gauge than most patterns, and it will act as a selvage. After a row of trim stitches is picked up along the garter-stitched edge, the extra stitch will fold easily to the inside to make a firm and even seam allowance.

Knitting a sampler will help you gain some experience with trims, and I hope that this experience will encourage you to incorporate them into your own sweaters. If you decide to experiment more closely with edgings, you'll find that the following guidelines will help you work with other materials and techniques. While the edgings discussed are handknit, I hope they will provide inspiration for the machine knitter, as well as for the sewer who is looking for applied borders.

Ribbing—Ribbing is the most reliable and varied of edgings. It can be knit in, sewn on, or picked up. I did not include ribbing in my sampler, but instead of the flat trims at most of the jacket's outer edges, I could have substituted ribbing. Because I wanted an edge that would not draw in, if ribbing had been my choice, I would have taken care to pick up enough stitches to keep the same width as the body. For more on the versatility of ribbing, see Barbara Walker's *A Treasury of Knitting Patterns* (Charles Scribner's Sons, 1968).

To make firm, knit-in ribbed edges (such as on lower edges of pieces), use a smaller needle than you used for the body fabric and/or 10% fewer sts.

To pick up stitches on straight edges (such as button bands), use a smaller needle than you used for the body fabric and pick up 2 sts for every 3 rows, or pick up 3 sts for every 4 rows.

To make curved edges, you sometimes have to pick up more stitches than you would expect. If increases or decreases are necessary in order to keep the wide edges flat, work these decreases and increases in purl ribs on RS (right side) rows to make them disappear into the pattern.

To work narrow ribbed bands separately and then attach them (such as vertical bands for cardigan fronts or horizontal rib bands to be sewn along necklines), make them slightly shorter than the length they are to cover, and stretch them slightly as you apply them.

To make a double thickness of ribbing, suitable for necklines, curves, cuffs, etc., work the band to twice the desired length. Then fold it inside the body fabric and sew it in place. Folded ribbing provides a thicker edge, but a slight reduction in elasticity. For additional stretch at a tight edge, do not bind off; instead, sew the individual stitches down loosely to the ridge that is formed by the picked-up stitches. Wide

Sampler jacket of knit trims

Reverse stockinette stitch

Seed stitch for collar

Join two sides of shawl collar.

Back

Bias band (folded) around shawl collar

Fitted cap sleeve (shoulder pad too)

Garter stitch trim mitered at corners of back vent

Little flat cables

Textured sleeves

Picot folded edge

Pocket with knit lining

Row of stitches just picked up and bound off

"Idiot Cord" applied trim

Patch pocket

Flat garter stitch, with mitered corners

Buttonholes work well in garter stitch.

Flat pattern stitches (moss stitch, seed stitch)

Shoulder pad

Garter-stitch pad with picked-up and knit "Idiot Cord"

Deborah Newton

pieces of ribbing can be knit separately and sewn to edges.

To achieve color variation (horizontally or vertically): For a variegated horizontal stripe, change color at the beginning of the rib row of a new stripe (the purl stitches carry up the color from the row below); for a solid horizontal stripe, use a smaller needle than you used for the rest of the ribbing, and *knit* an RS row with a new color before resuming the rib pattern with the original needle. For vertical stripes in 1/1 or 2/2 rib (a Shetland technique), work two colors in each row—the knit stitches in one color, the purl stitches in another color. Carry the yarn that isn't in use loosely on WS (wrong side.)

Flat-fabric trims—The next most useful edgings are those that are formed by flat, non-curling fabrics. Even though it is more work to add these trims later at lower edges than it is to knit them in, you can sometimes achieve a firmer, more tailored look by picking up, working the trim, and binding off on assembled pieces. Buttonholes are best worked into flat, firm edges. This process is necessary when a mitered corner is desired.

The technique of mitering is used to join two adjacent edges of trim to form a corner. It is suitable for most ribbings, garter stitch, and some flat fabrics, and can be worked on inside and outside angles. To miter on inside edges, such as at a V neck, dec 1 st every RS row on each side of the corner, to either side of a center stitch, or work decs right next to each other, on each side of the corner. For the neatest appearance, use k2tog to slant to the right, and SSK (or sl1, k1, psso) for the dec that leans to the left; or use a double dec that creates a central stitch, like sl2tog k-wise, k1, p2sso. For those rare occasions when mitering in stockinette stitch, whose row gauge is not as dense as that of other patterns, you may have to work decs or incs more frequently. For example, *dec 2 sts at corner on next 2 rows, work 1 row even; rep from *. To miter on outside edges, do the opposite: Inc 1 st on each side of the corner or on either side of a central stitch.

Garter stitch (knit every row). Garter stitch is a classic, very flat trim. It is thicker than most plain fabrics knit in the same yarn. Buttonholes can also disappear neatly between the ridges of a garter-stitch trim (photo at top left, facing page).

When knit in or picked up, garter stitch has a tendency to gradually widen. Use a smaller needle than you used for the body fabric and/or 10% fewer sts.

When picked up on a garter-stitch body, garter-stitch trim works beautifully. For every 2 rows of garter stitch in the body fabric, 1 edge stitch is necessary. In the body, sl the 1st st of every row wyib (with yarn in back). Then pick up the edge stitches in the "bumps" along the body: 1 bump=2 rows=1 garter-stitch ridge.

For a striped ridge in solid colors, change color on RS rows; change on WS for variegated color.

Mosaic patterns, which combine slipped and garter stitches, are excellent at edges, whether picked up or knit in. They are especially dramatic when mitered at the corners, as shown in the photo at right on the facing page. For inspiration, see Barbara Walker's *Mosaic Knitting* (Charles Scribner's Sons, 1976).

Single-row bind-off edging. This trim, shown on the pocket edge in the photo on page 116, deserves a category of its own for its usefulness and simplicity. It works on many types of fabrics. To make this trim, pick up stitches along the edge and bind

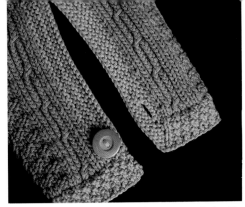

The buttonhole neatly disappears into the plain garter-stitch trim on this sleeve. The button is positioned on a striped garter-stitch trim that has been picked up along the edge. Moss stitch is used as a trim at the lower edge of the sleeve.

The large swatch shows a mosaic pattern with a mitered corner, an alternative to the trim used on the sampler jacket. Other flat-fabric trim swatches, edged in contrasting colors, are also shown as possible alternatives: double seed stitch (left), moss stitch (center), and seed stitch (right).

To add Elizabeth Zimmermann's Idiot Cord to a garter-stitch fabric with slip-stitch edges, such as these shoulder pads, Newton passed the smaller needle through the "bumps" of the slipped edge stitches and worked the trim into these stitches, one by one.

them off on the next row. Experiment with different needle sizes and choose the stitch count accordingly.

Knit/purl fabrics and their variations. Many flat knitting patterns make good edgings and fine body fabrics. These flat fabrics are good for textured and buttonhole bands (photo at bottom left, above). Use a small needle for a durable edge.

Seed stitch is simple, flat, and elegant. Over an even number of sts, for the 1st row: *K1, p1; rep from *. For the 2nd row: *P1, k1; rep from *. Rep rows 1 and 2.

Moss stitch is a slight variation on seed stitch. Over an even number of sts, for rows 1 and 2: *K1, p1; rep from *. For rows 3 and 4: *P1, k1; rep from *. Rep rows 1 through 4.

Double seed stitch is a bolder knit/purl check that should be used for wide edgings and worked firmly. In multiples of 4 sts, for rows 1 and 2: *K2, p2; rep from *. For rows 3 and 4: *P2, k2; rep from *. Rep rows 1 through 4.

Folded, stockinette-stitch bands. These flat-fabric trims are useful for button bands. They are also useful for smooth-line cardigan or kimono openings. In addition, a fold formed by a slipped stitch al-

lows them to be used as facings to cover openings if they are knit in as the garment progresses. To work these bands separately, cast on an odd # of sts to yield twice the desired width of the trim. Row 1 (RS): K to center stitch, sl1 wyib, k to end. Row 2 (WS): P all sts. Continue to the desired length. You must work buttonholes on both sides of the center slip stitch, which forms the fold line. Sew one edge of the band in place on RS (you may need to stretch it slightly around edge); then sew the other side to the inside of the garment. Align and join the buttonholes.

Elizabeth Zimmermann's Idiot Cord—This very useful, three-stitch tube creates a smooth, simple line that stabilizes edges. It can be knit separately and applied, picked up and knit along an edge, or knit in with the fabric, as shown above.

To pick up and knit the cord on garter-stitch fabric, prepare the fabric with slip-stitch edges as you would for garter-stitch trim. Pick up 1 st in each bump along the edge one at a time, or slip a fine needle through all the bumps on the edge. Cast on 3 sts with the same yarn at the end of this needle. *K2, sl 3rd st, k picked-up st, psso;

Sl3 back on the left-hand (LH) needle and rep from * along edge.

To knit-in the Idiot Cord on garter-stitch body fabric, *k to within 3 sts of the end of the row. Yf, sl3, as if to p, turn. K1 row. Rep from *.

To add the cord to other knit fabrics, pick up the # of sts along the edge (you can test for the # of sts on your swatch). Then rep the process in step 1. For additional firmness, *k2, k2tog-tbl; sl3 back to the LH needle and rep from *.

To use the Idiot Cord as applied trim, sew a length of cord as frogs or decorative trim onto the surfaces of woven or knit fabrics. To make a length of this cord, cast on 3 sts with a double-pointed needle. *K3 with another double-pointed needle. Then, without turning, sl sts back to the other end of the needle, pull the yarn firmly, repeat from *.

Curled edges—For a round edging, make use of a stockinette-stitch fabric's natural tendency to curl. Pick up sts along the edge, work in stockinette stitch (k RS rows), and bind off. The fabric will roll to RS.

A reverse-stockinette-stitch trim, which is a small edging formed by 3 or 4 rows of

The bind-off edge of this pocket has been folded and hemmed to the inside (top). The picot-point edging is worked on picked-up stitches, then folded to the inside of the pocket so the row of eyelets at the center of the trim forms a jagged, decorative edge (above).

As pictured below, bias bands can be pinned to curved edges, such as an armhole or a collar. The knitting on the needle shows that the stitches slant diagonally. The natural curl of the stockinette stitch helps the trim grab the edge as it is being sewn in place.

reverse stockinette stitch that rolls to WS, is very useful for edging flat body fabrics and is also suitable for other less stable areas. It provides a neat line without thickness and does not lose its shape easily. This trim is best in wool, but suitable for most other fibers with some elasticity.

To pick up a reverse-stockinette-stitch trim, pick up sts from RS, k 1 row, p 1 row, bind off in k on next row.

To knit in the trim, using a smaller needle than you used for the body, cast on about 10% fewer sts than for the body, and work 3 rows in reverse stitch (beg with k or p row depending on your method of casting on and the desired appearance). Follow these rows with a k row on RS, or a p row on WS: Inc necessary sts on this row.

To use the reverse-stockinette trim to give a decorative touch to a ribbing (an edge for an edge), use one needle size smaller and 10% to 15% fewer sts than you used for the ribbing. Knit in as explained above. Inc necessary sts on the plain row before you begin the ribbing. This trim works best with a stretchy yarn.

Hems and facings—For a knit-in stockinette-stitch hem, cast on loosely with a smaller needle and/or 10% fewer sts than for the body so the hem won't bulge after you sew it in place. To achieve the desired hem length, work a p row firmly on RS. Then inc the necessary # of sts on the next row in k. Change to a larger needle to knit the garment body, and sew the hem in place after you've completed the garment. If you use an invisible cast-on, you can sew the hem down stitch by stitch.

To add a hem to a cast-on edge after you've completed the garment, with RS facing and with a smaller needle than you used for the body, pick up 1 st in the back loop of each cast-on stitch; p next WS row, dec 10% sts if desired to reduce bulk, and work to desired length. Then sew the hem down stitch by stitch. You can also bind off loosely and sew the hem in place if elasticity is not essential.

To make a stockinette-stitch facing, pick up sts along the edge, k WS row (p this next round if you are working in the round) and work even in stockinette stitch for the desired length. Either bind off and sew, or tack down stitch by stitch. At a neckline, work gradual incs so that the facing lays flat to the inside.

To make a picot-point edging, a pretty folded edge with a sawtooth look, knit it in as a hem or work it on picked-up stitches, and then fold it to the inside and hem it in place. Over an odd number of sts, work the hem in stockinette stitch to the desired length (a few rows of stockinette is all that is necessary). End with WS. Next row (RS): K1, *yo, k2tog; rep from *. P next row. Continue in stockinette stitch to the hem length and bind off. Sew down stitch by stitch, or fold the bind-off edge to the inside and hem it in place.

Bias bands—Bias bands can be used to cover a curved edge, such as an armhole, a bolero-style front curve, or a neckline.

To make bias bands, cast on 1 st, and working in stockinette st, inc 1 st at the beg of every row until you have the desired # of sts for double the width of the folded band. Then work as follows: WS: P. RS: Inc 1 st at beg of row, k to last 2 sts, k2tog. Rep these 2 rows to the desired length. Then dec 1 st at the beg of every row until no sts remain. The nature of stockinette stitch helps this trim curl around an edge. Pin down and sew one edge in place from RS. Then tack it along WS.

To create striped bias bands, change colors after you've knit a band of the desired thickness. Because the fabric is knit on the diagonal, you'll get a barberpole effect.

Be creative!

One way to create an exciting design is to embellish an unexpected area of a garment. Small accessory pieces, such as pocket linings, shoulder pads, and belts, can also be enhanced by the creative use of edgings.

An interesting exercise is to design a garment with the emphasis on edging. Some of the most fashionable garments are deeply indebted to the strength of their trimmed edges—witness Chanel's ever-enduring jackets! By altering a successful pattern, the beginner can gain confidence, and an expert can experiment on foolproof ground. You might simply change the ribbing, first working a swatch to see if its gauge is interchangeable with the recommended ribbing, or you might alter a pullover pattern by dividing the front and binding the edges with bias bands. Often a change of border in a well-loved design offers a marvelous challenge, while keeping the familiar fit and structure. You can be creative without having to design an entire garment.

Try nontraditional flat patterns at garment edges, such as intriguing slip-stitch and twist-stitch patterns. (All have their peculiarities, so test each one.) Imagine a pattern stitch that you never conceived of as an edging—perhaps a textural pattern from one of your knitting dictionaries. Try to eliminate all your notions of what a traditional trim *should* do. Instead of lying flat, it could produce an interesting textural contrast or provide unexpected drama. Folding edges, trimming trims, edging unexpected areas, working edgings that vary in width, combining patterns along a single edge—all these variations test your ingenuity as a technician and designer.

These suggestions are ways I depend on to edge sweaters in traditional ways. Any knitter can master these techniques, but they should not be the final step. Learn to manipulate your trims, and don't be afraid to go beyond traditional uses.   □

Deborah Newton is a free-lance writer and knit designer in Providence, RI. Photos by Cathy Carver.

Knitted-Lace Edgings

Add an old-fashioned touch of elegance to household linens and garments

by Catherine Roberts

*l*ace knitting has been in and out of fashion ever since the 16th century, when faggot stitch was discovered, but knitted-lace edgings are a somewhat more recent development. The combination of faggot stitch and the well-known eyelet stitch (drawing, p. 123), coupled with the fact that wool, silk and linen yarns were being spun to a much finer degree than before, caused knitted lace to become popular. Queen Elizabeth I gave it her cachet when she wore a pair of silk knitted stockings patterned with an all-over diamond design.

In the 16th and early 17th centuries, lace knitting was used to produce fabric. No one considered making narrow knitted-lace edgings until all Europe fell in love with the new needle-made and bobbin laces that became the height of 17th-century fashion. Van Dyck immortalized these narrow laces in his society portraits and lent his name to them. Soon they became not only a status symbol but a political statement as well; the conservative reformers (Roundheads) opposed the extravagance of the Cavaliers, who spent fortunes on lace.

Sophisticated in technique as lace knitting was, it was still impossible to copy these amazing laces. But clever knitters quickly noticed and adapted the outstanding feature of these narrow trimmings, which were characterized by sharp, deep points or scallops along the bottom edges.

The key was to be able to knit a lacy strip that gradually widened and narrowed to imitate the sharp points of the needle-made laces. The knitter cast on a few stitches and

The delicate lace collar on Cornelia's party dress was knit by Betty Skewes of Cornwall, England. Since it is mounted to a facing, it can be worn on other things and won't be outgrown with this dress.

From *Threads* magazine (August 1988) 18:27-31

Even when you knit with #40 cotton and very thin steel needles, a lace collar grows rapidly. It will require nearly 60 pattern repeats to complete this version of the collar shown on p. 121 (pattern on p. 125), each one taking 15 to 20 minutes. (Photo by Michele Russell Slavinsky)

increased one or two stitches in each row (by making yarn overs without accompanying decreases, or by knitting into the front and back of one stitch). Decreases were then worked at the same rate as the extra increases over the same number of rows. Or they could be worked all at once as bind-offs to produce a sharp angle on the pointed edge of the lace strip. Careful blocking improved the sharpness of the points. The straight edge of the lace also imitated the needle laces. A few solid stitches were positioned on the extreme edge to provide a fabric for attaching the lace. A row of basic or feather faggoting often introduced the lacy portion of the strip.

Such edgings soon became stylish as trimmings for woven fabrics as well as knitted ones. Shawls were worn by all classes, and they made excellent showcases for hand-

some borders and edgings. In the late 18th century, Shetland shawls became fashionable. The early ones featured simple, garter-stitch centers and intricately patterned edgings and were knit of creamy-white natural yarn.

At about this time, exquisitely fine and sheer cotton fabrics began to arrive from India, and with them came delicate cotton threads. This gave enormous impetus to fine fancy ("white") knitting, which reached its peak during the Victorian period.

Naked edges of any kind weren't tolerated, and handknitted lace edgings were ideal as trimmings, being quick and easy to make and very inexpensive. They endowed everything they trimmed with elegance and charm. And they appeared on everything from bed and table linens, to sash curtains, doilies, clothing, and accessories, as well as

on innumerable gift items. Even when the exuberant Victorian love of trimming gave way to the more sedate Edwardian fashions, knitted-lace edgings continued to be used on everyday articles because they were pretty and economical.

Making these edgings was also a ladylike accomplishment. The work required little space and could be tucked into a fancy workbag to be carried on visits and trips. Another advantage was that it took only a few inches of knitting to determine a pattern's suitability and attractiveness, and changes could be made early in the project.

Many of the old patterns were passed from knitter to knitter, sometimes in written form but just as often by word of mouth. Even though many written patterns were lost, knitted examples survived that expert knitters could copy. Women's magazines also printed regular articles of instruction in what had become know as "thread laces." The wide distribution of instruction sheets and booklets produced by the manufacturers of silk and cotton threads stimulated continued interest in this rewarding handwork. My collection of knitted-lace-edging patterns comes from these sources.

How to make knitted-lace edgings–

Worked with fine threads, knitted-lace edgings add elegance to handmade gifts. The patterns are usually very short and require basic stitches that are easy to master. Eyelet stitch is used to form a round hole. The technique is very old, and it's simple, being merely a yarn over followed by a decrease (usually k2tog). The next row is worked plain. Eyelet stitch can be worked in an allover fabric, in a band, or to produce a pattern. Basic faggot stitch is more sophisticated, although it is almost as easy to make as eyelet stitch. The principal difference is that yarn overs and decreases are worked every row. The yarn over is made above the decrease of the previous row; then the decrease and yarn over are knitted together as the current row's decrease. This results in an open zigzag pattern that looks just like the faggot stitch that is used in embroidery. Feather faggot is a firmer version in which all the decreases are purled. Basic faggot and eyelet stitches, shown below, form the basis of almost all knitted-lace patterns.

Cotton knit/crochet threads, available in most variety stores are hard-twisted, so the patterns don't blur. Bedspread cotton, which is more loosely twisted, works up quickly on size 3 or 4 needles and makes an attractive edging for unbleached muslin curtains and summer coverlets. It might be difficult to find the right size needles. Good knitting shops carry size 1 or 0, which give an open, lacy effect with #20 thread. Try to get 8-in. double-pointeds; they're easier to work with, and the spare needle helps in picking back slipped stitches.

If and when you become madly involved in making fine knitted edgings, you'll have to get very thin needles (see supplies list, p. 124). Use a size 00 needle with #40 or #50 thread, and a 000 with tatting thread.

Tension is important. Since cotton threads have no elasticity, too tight a tension will make it impossible to work some of the decrease stitches, but a loose tension means that stitches might constantly slip off the needles. Make a practice piece—10 sts by 10 rows—to get a feel for the right snugness.

Before you start knitting, copy the instructions on a 4x6 index card. Double-check your copying against the printed master, and insert the card into the open core of the ball of thread when you're not knitting.

When you knit a lace edging, the first inch or two may seem agonizingly slow, even though very few rows are needed to complete a pattern (see patterns, p. 125). But as soon as the work is about 2 in. long, you can hold it between the second and third fingers of one hand as you knit. Pulling the edging down as you knit allows you to see each stitch more easily and helps keep them on the needle.

Check each row you knit against the instruction card before going on to the next. Don't stop in the middle of a row or pattern; but if you must, mark the place on the card so you'll know where to resume. Since there are few rows in most designs, you'll find it easy to remember them, but don't let this lull you into a false sense of security. Keep the instruction card handy.

All knitted laces require dressing to present them to their fullest advantage. This means washing and rinsing them and then dipping them into a light stiffening solution and blocking them to shape. In the old days, some people used a sugar solution, but today we have ready-made bottled starch. A dilute solution (half water) works well. Allow the edging to soak in it a moment; then squeeze out the excess. Pull the lace out gently to its fullest dimensions and press it dry without rubbing the iron

back and forth. To dress wool, dampen the lace, pull it into shape, and press lightly with a warm iron. Shape synthetic mixtures by hand and let them air-dry.

Using the edgings–Knitted-lace trimming is especially good on children's clothing since, despite its relative fineness, it is very sturdy. The same patterns can also be worked in knitting wools of various weights to dress up plain articles, like shawls and scarves and baby sacques and blankets.

To attach edgings to linens (photo, p. 124), examine the lace to determine the right side. You won't always be able to tell, but many edgings have a definite right side. Place the right side of the lace along the right side of the hemmed fabric, and whip the two edges together with fairly close stitches; don't pull them too tight. When opened out, the lace edging should lie flat without puckering or looking tight.

Victorian doilies and round tablecloths took lace edgings into another dimension. While some of the old edgings had a slight built-in curve, it was usually insufficient to make the edging fit well around a cloth. The introduction of short rows produced the right inner curve without distorting the design; and curved edgings were soon used as collars.

Lace collars are a lot easier to make than they look, and the edgings are dainty and elegant but wash well. It's a good idea to mount the collars on a dickey so you can wear them on different garments.

To make a dickey for a lace collar, finish all the edges, including the neckline. Then whipstitch the lace firmly but not tightly to the neckline of the dickey. Never machine-sew. If the dickey is deep enough, it won't need to be fastened inside the dress.

One of the best ways to attach a knitted-lace collar to the neckline of a dress is also the easiest. All knitted-lace collars have a heading (3 to 5 garter stitches) that you can baste inside the neckline. Make sure that when the collar is turned to the outside,

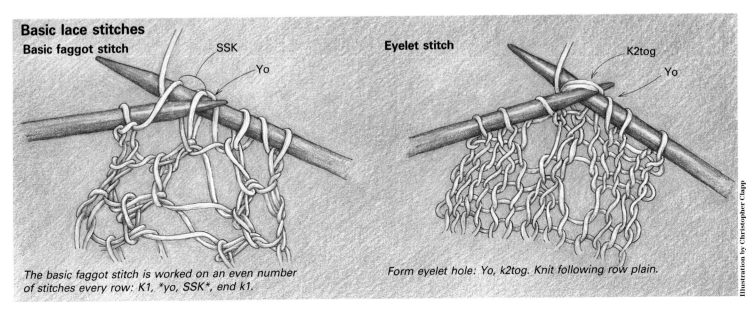

Basic lace stitches
Basic faggot stitch

SSK

Yo

*The basic faggot stitch is worked on an even number of stitches every row: K1, *yo, SSK*, end k1.*

Eyelet stitch

K2tog

Yo

Form eyelet hole: Yo, k2tog. Knit following row plain.

Illustration by Christopher Clapp

The edging on this fine linen towel, or bureau scarf, is a very old pattern dating back to about 1800. Similar borders with tiny tassels attached to each point were used on bedspreads in the mid-19th century. (Courtesy of Old Sturbridge Village; photo by Henry E. Peach)

the right side of the lace is uppermost. This method allows for easy removal when necessary. You can also attach the collar to a dickey this way, but sew it on securely.

Whipstitch lace-edgings to the hems of curtains, towels, and other household linens by hand. You needn't remove the lace to wash and dry them by machine. However, no-iron fabric with knitted-lace edgings attached will require an additional step because the heat of the dryer will have shrunk the lace. Spray the lace lightly with starch or water. Then pull it into shape and let it dry. A light touch-up with a medium-hot iron will speed up the drying.

Now that you're almost hooked, it's only fair to tell you that once you start experimenting with this charming lacemaking technique, you'll become addicted. □

Catherine Roberts, who lives in Brunswick, ME, learned to knit, crochet, sew, and embroider 78 years ago. She has been a fashion editor, a department-store buyer, a handcrafts lecturer, a teacher, and an author. She is currently working on a book about knitted-lace edgings.

Books

Hewitt, Furze, and Billie Daley. *Classic Knitted Cotton Edgings.* Kenthurst, Australia: Kangaroo Press, 1987. Available from Schoolhouse Press: 6899 Cary Bluff, Pittsville, WI 54466; (715) 884-2799; $19.95 plus $1.75 P&H.

Walker, Barbara G. *A Second Treasury of Knitting Patterns.* New York: Charles Scribner's Sons, 1985.

Supplies

Craft Gallery
P.O. Box 8319
Salem, MA 01971
(617) 744-6980

Lacis
2982 Adeline St.
Berkeley, CA 94703
(415) 843-7178

Mini-Magic
3675 Reed Rd.
Columbus, OH 43220
(614) 457-3687 (1-9 p.m. EST)

Patternworks
P.O. Box 1690
Poughkeepsie, NY 12601
(914) 454-5648

Easy eyelets

Aunt Nettie's petticoat lace

Triple loops

Mrs. Philpot's spider edging

Double faggot with picots

Old wagon wheel

Diamond point

Scallops with eyelets

Three eyelet points

Lace-edging patterns and a collar

Only a few simple techniques are required to make lace, but it helps to know the tricks. When you *yarn over two or more times* at once, on the return row knit the first yarn over and purl the next alternately until all the loops have been worked.

Cast-ons and bind-offs should be loose and stretchy. The *knitted cast-on* gives a soft, elastic edge that is especially good if you want to sew the two ends of lace together. Make a slip loop on the left needle. Knit 1 st into it and slip it back onto the left needle. Repeat, always knitting into the last-made stitch for the number of stitches required. It's also a good idea to knit across the cast-on stitches before knitting the first pattern row. In *binding off*, always slip the first stitch and start counting with the knitting of the second stitch.

Add a plain heading to any edging for short rows that will produce an inner curve. The swatches at left were worked with #20 crochet cotton and size 1 needles. Stitch abbreviations are identified in parentheses after their first appearance.

Easy eyelets—This curving edging combines two of the most important stitches in lace knitting: eyelet and faggot. This version of faggot stitch is called herringbone. The edging goes nicely around a curve.
Cast on 5 sts and knit across.
Row 1: S (slip one), k1, yo, k2tog, yo2, k1.
Row 2: S, k1, p1, k1, yo, k2tog, k1.
Row 3: S, k1, yo, k2tog, k3.
Row 4: Bind off 2, k1, yo, k2tog, k1.

Aunt Nettie's petticoat lace—This 1880's pattern is handsome on table linens and curtains and on petticoats and other garments.
Cast on 12 sts and knit across.
Row 1: S, k5, k2tog, yo, k1, k2tog, k1.
Row 2: K4, yo, k2tog, k2, yo, k2tog, k1.
Row 3: S, k3, k2tog, yo, k1, k2tog, k2.
Row 4: K7, yo, k2tog, k1.
Row 5: S, k4, yo, k2tog, k1, yo2, k2.
Row 6: K3, p1, k2, yo, k3, yo, k2tog, k1.
Row 7: S, k6, yo, k2tog, k4.
Row 8: Bind off 2, k2, yo, k5, yo, k2tog, k1.

Triple loops—This easy handkerchief edging became popular in the 1920s. Pay particular attention to keeping the faggot border even.
Cast on 8 sts and knit across.
Row 1: K3, yo, k2tog, yo2, k2tog, k1.
Row 2: K3, p1, k2, yo, k2tog, k1.
Row 3: K3, yo, k2tog, k1, yo2, k2tog, k1.
Row 4: K3, p1, k3, yo, k2tog, k1.
Row 5: K3, yo, k2tog, k2, yo2, k2tog, k1.
Row 6: K3, p1, k4, yo, k2tog, k1.
Row 7: K3, yo, k2tog, k6.
Row 8: Bind off 3, k4, yo, k2tog, k1.

Mrs. Philpot's spider edging—Spider stitch has been popular for almost 200 years as an allover fabric, an insertion, and an edging. Be particularly careful with the yo before the 2 slip sts on row 6. It tends to get lost.
Cast on 14 sts and knit across.
Row 1: K2, yo, k2tog, k3, yo, k1, yo, k6.
Row 2: K6, yo, k3, yo, k2tog, k2, yo, k2tog, k1.
Row 3: K2, yo, (k2tog)2, yo, k5, yo, k6.
Row 4: Bind off 4, k1, yo, k2tog, k3, k2tog, (yo, k2tog)2, k1.
Row 5: K2, yo, k2tog, k1, yo, k2tog, k1, k2tog, yo, k3.
Row 6: K3, yo, k1, yo, s2, k1, psso (pass the 2 slip sts over), yo, k3, yo, k2tog, k1.

Double faggot with picots—This attractive tailored edging looks good on linen collars and cuffs, but it also works well in wool on scarves and shawls. The picot technique might require a little practice to get it even.
Cast on 7 sts and knit across.
Row 1: S, k1, yo, k2tog, yo, k2tog, k1.
Row 2: Repeat row 1.
Row 3: Repeat row 1, but increase 2 in last st by knitting into front, back, and front of st to start picot.
Row 4: SKP (slip 1 st, knit the next st, pass the slipped st over), k1, pass first st over to complete picot, k1, yo, k2tog, yo, k2tog, k1.

Old wagon wheel—This edging was popular in the mid-19th century. You can make it wider or narrower by altering the lattice heading. Work the yo at the beginning of the odd-numbered rows snugly in order to keep the loops even.
Cast on 19 sts and knit across.
Row 1: Yo, k2tog, yo, k1, yo, SKP, k14.
Row 2: S, k1, (yo, SKP)4, p5, k5.
Row 3: Yo, k2tog, yo, k3, yo, SKP, k13.
Row 4: S, k2, (yo, SKP)3, p5, k7.
Row 5: Yo, k2tog, yo, k5, yo, SKP, k12.
Row 6: S, k1, (yo, SKP)3, p5, k1, SK2togP (slip 1 st, k2tog, pass the slipped st over), yo3, k2tog, k3.
Row 7: Yo, k2tog, yo, SKP, k1, p1, k1, k2tog, yo, k13.
Row 8: S, k2, (yo, SKP)3, p5, k3, k2tog, k1.
Row 9: Yo, k2tog, yo, SKP, k1, k2tog, yo, k14.
Row 10: S, k1, (yo, SKP)4, p5, k5, k2tog, k1.
Row 11: Yo, k2tog, yo, SK2togP, yo, k15.
Row 12: S, k2, (yo, SKP)4, p5, k1, k2tog, k1.

Diamond point—Dating from 1820, this edging has been in continuous use on linens, curtains, and fancy shawls. It looks best if you block it fully stretched out.
Cast on 11 sts and knit across.
Row 1: S, k1, yo, k1, (yo, SKP)3, k2.
Row 2 and all even rows: Purl.
Row 3: S, k1, yo, k3, (yo, SKP)3, k1.
Row 5: S, k1, yo, k5, (yo, SKP)2, k2.
Row 7: S, k1, yo, k7, (yo, SKP)2, k1.
Row 9: SKP, k1, yo, SKP, k3, k2tog, yo, k2tog, yo, k3.
Row 11: SKP, k1, yo, SKP, k1, k2tog, (yo, k2tog)2, yo, k2.

Row 13: SKP, k1, yo, SK2togP, (yo, k2tog)2, yo, k3.
Row 15: SKP, k2, k2tog, (yo, k2tog)2, yo, k2.
Row 16: Purl.

Scallops with eyelets—This versatile design works up well on almost any size thread and needle. It's very stretchy and would be good for knits.
Cast on 7 sts and knit across.
Row 1: K4, yo, k3.
Row 2: Yo, k2tog, k6.
Row 3: K5, yo, k2tog, k1.
Row 4: Yo, k2tog, k6.
Row 5: K1, k2tog, yo2, k2tog, k1, yo, k2.
Row 6: Yo, k2tog, k4, p1, k2.
Row 7: K4, k2tog, yo, k2tog, k1.
Row 8: Yo, k2tog, k6.
Row 9: K3, k2tog, yo, k2tog, k1.
Row 10: Yo, k2tog, k5.

Three eyelet points—One of the many variations on Van Dyke point, this pattern has enjoyed enduring popularity for trimming aprons and pinafores as well as muslin curtains and huck hand towels. The feather faggot heading is particularly good for items subjected to frequent laundering or hard wear.
Cast on 7 sts and knit across.
Row 1: K1, yo, p2tog, k2, yo2, k2.
Row 2: K3, p1, k2, yo, p2tog, k1.
Row 3: K1, yo, p2tog, k6.
Row 4: K6, yo, p2tog, k1.
Row 5: K1, yo, p2tog, k2, yo2, k2tog, yo2, k2.
Row 6: K3, p1, k2, p1, k2, yo, p2tog, k1.
Row 7: K1, yo, p2tog, k9.
Row 8: Bind off 5, k3, yo, p2tog, k1.

Ring-and-trellis collar (ca. 1887)—Directions for this collar, which is shown on p. 27, were supplied by Mary Wright of Cornwall, England. It was knit with #40 thread on size 00 needles, but it looks just as handsome when it is knit with #20 thread and size 1 needles.

Cast on 26 sts and knit across. Work short rows every fourth row to produce the desired inner curve.
Row 1: K15, (k2tog, yo)2, k3, yo2, k2tog, yo2, k2.
Row 2: K3, p1, k2, p1, k2, p15, turn (5 sts remain on left needle for all short rows).
Row 3: K9, (k2tog, yo)2, k11.
Row 4: K2, yo2, k2tog, k1, k2tog, yo2, k2tog, k1, p14, k5.
Row 5: K13, (k2tog, yo)2, k5, p1, k4, p1, k2.
Row 6: K12, p13, turn.
Row 7: P10, (yo, k2tog)2, k2, k2tog, yo2, SK2togP, yo2, (k2tog)2.
Row 8: K3, p1, k2, p1, k3, p4, k15.
Row 9: K5, p11, (yo, k2tog)2, k9.
Row 10: Bind off 3, k5, p4, k11, turn.
Row 11: P12, (yo, k2tog)2, k5.
Row 12: K5, p4, k17.
Repeat these 12 rows until the collar is long enough for the desired fit. Knit 1 row, and bind off on the next. —C.R.

Index

A

Abbott, deborah, on combining wovens and knits, 94-97
Afghans, knitted, 83
Ammon, Helen von, on knitting with furs and feathers, 62-65
Appliqué:
    on knitting, 89
    sequinned, source for, 52

B

Beading:
    in knitting, 56-61
    supplies for, 57, 61
Blankets, knitted, 83
Blocking, of knitting, 110
Brunner, Kathy with Sue M. Parker, on designing with cables, 86-89
Books, on knitting, 61
Borssuck, B.:
    on designer raglans, 42-46
    on finishing, 24-27
Buttonholes:
    for children, 38
    crocheted, 111-113
    knitted, 114-115

C

Cables, 86-89
Casting off, invisible, 27
Casting on, 26, 61, 114
Chanel, Coco, 16-17
Charting, 18-22, 99-100, 104-106
Children:
    hints for knitting for, 36-39
    tapestries by, 86
Circular knitting, 24-27, 30-35
Collars, knit-lace, 121-122, 125
Cotton:
    growing, 54
    knits, care of, 55
    knitting stitches for, 55
    qualities of, 53-54
    ribbing in, 53, 55, 109
    spinning, 54
    yarns of, 53
Crochet:
    of buttonholes, 111-113
    in knit finishing, 110
    slipstitch finish, 110
    with sequins, 52

D

Decreases
    in charting, 28
    in paired knitting, 46
Dickinson, Jean, on raglan sweaters, 40-41
Dyett, Linda:
    on cotton yarns, 53-55
    on hand-knit suits, 16-23

F

Fabric:
    sequinned, source for, 52
    sources for, 22
Feathers, yarn from, 64-65
Finishing, 24-27, 108-110
Fitting, 98-101, 102-107

G

Gaffey, Theresa:
    on selvages, 14-15
    on socks, 72-76
Gauge, in knitting, 108
Gloves, 66-71
Greer, Judith Eckhardt, on knitting for kids, 36-39
Guagliumi, Susan, on finishing, 108-111

H

Handbags, beaded, 56-61
Hats, knit, 49
Hems, knit, 120
Hoods, knitting, 37-38

I

Increases in paired knitting, 46
Interfacing, with knitting, 93

J

Jackets:
    blue-jeans, knit, 93
    knit, 16-23

K

Kelsey, Barbara Shomer, on sequins, 50-52
Knitting machines:
    publications on, 110
    sequins with, 52
    sewing-pattern pieces with, 92-93
Knitting, hand:
    garment sections, 49
    hexagonal shapes, 49
Knitting:
    combined with woven fabric, 94-97
    eyelet stitch in, 29
    fabric reinforcement for, 38
    from sewing patterns, 90-93
    in the round, 40-41, 77-80
Korach, Alice, on bead knitting, 56-61

L

Lace, 121-125
Linings, for knit fabrics, 22-23

M

Mats, striped knitted, 83
McGovern, Mary, on crocheted buttonholes, 111-113
McNulty. Shirley W., on the knitted yarn over, 28-29

Measurements, from store sizes, 101
Mittens, for children, 37-38
Mockups, knit fabric, 102-107
Morse, Pat, on knitting from sewing patterns, 90-93
Moss, Marilyn, on circular knitting, 30-32

N

Necklines, in knitting, 32, 42-45
Newton, Deborah:
    on edgings and trims, 116-120
    on fabric mock-ups, 102-107
    on gloves, 66-71

P

Patterns:
    ascot, 19
    houndstooth, 18-19
    (sewing), for knitting, 90-93
Pillows, knitted covers for, 83
Pockets, handwarmer, knit, 39

R

Ribbing:
    cable, 55
    casting off, 12-13
    casting on, 9-11
    for children, 37
    cloverleaf eyelet-rib, 76
    crossed-stitch, 55
    edges, 9
    firm, for cotton, 53-55
    for neck, 100-101
    planning, 107
    two noodlo tubo, 24 27
    types of, choosing, 8-9
Righetti, Maggie, on buttonholes, 114
Roberts, Catherine, lace edgings, 121-125
Rows, counting, 114
Rugs, striped knitted, 83
Runners, striped knitted, 83
Ruz, Otilia, handknit designer, 17-22

S

Seams, knit, 27, 110
Selvages, knitted, types of, 14-15
Sequins:
    crocheting with, 52
    knitting with, 50-52
Shoulders, knitting, 101
Short rows in, 80-81
Skewes, Betty, collar by, 121
Sleeves, knitting of, 142-46, 01
Socks:
    bobby-sock pattern for, 76
    calf of, knitting, 73-74
    designing, 72-73
    finishing, 75-76
    heel of, knitting, 74-75
    instep of knitting, 74-75
    knitting techniques for, 72

Spinning:
    of cotton, 54
    process of, 62-65
    supplies for, 65
Stanley, Montse, on ribbing, 8-13
Studeny, Mary, on knitting to fit, 98-101
Suits, knit, 18-23
Sweaters:
    circularly knit, 30-32
    drop-shoulder, 84-85
    in handspun, bulky, 64-65
    of hybrid yarns, 93
    from sewing patterns, 90-93
    raglan, 42-46
Sweaters:
    chevron-striped, 77-80
    for children, 36-39
    finishing, 108-110
    fitting, 98-101
    for large women, 102-107
    in the round, 33-35, 29, 77-80
    reversible, striped knitted, 83

T

Thread, elastic-covered, 110
Trim:
    cords for, 119
    design of, 117
    flat-fabric, 118
    knit, 117-119
    sequinned, source for, 52
Tubes, knit, 24-27
Tucks, in knitting, 38
Tudor, Ann, on chevron stripes, 77-81
Tunics, reversible, striped knitted, 83

W

Walker, Barbara G. on stripes, 82-83
Washing knits, 108-110
White, Jean baker, on no-sew set-in sleeves, 47-49

Y

Yarn:
    knitting, sources for, 65
    leftover, using, 77-80
    leftovers, using in knitting, 84-85
    spinning, 62-65
    wool-silk, sources for, 17
Yarn-over stitches, 28-29

Z

Zimmerman, Elizabeth, on seamless sweaters, 33-35